D0250491

THE LAYMAN'S COMMENTARY

ON THE HOLY SPIRIT

THE LAYMAN'S COMMENTARY ON THE HOLY SPIRIT

JOHN REA

Contributing Editors
Ray Corvin
David du Plessis
Howard M. Ervin
Fr. Joseph Orsini
Erwin Prange
J. Rodman Williams

Logos International
Plainfield, New Jersey

John Witherspoon College
Library

Unless otherwise identified all Scripture references are taken from the King James Version of the Holy Bible.

THE LAYMAN'S COMMENTARY ON THE HOLY SPIRIT
Revised edition © 1974
First edition © Copyright 1972
Logos International
Plainfield, New Jersey
All Rights Reserved
Printed in the United States of America
Library of Congress No. 72-92775
Paper ISBN 0-912106-38-7
Cloth ISBN 0-912106-22-0

JOHN REA, Th.D.

Bible teacher and religious editor; former Professor of Old Testament and Archaeology, Grace Theological Seminary, Winona Lake, Indiana; former member of the faculty, Moody Bible Institute, Chicago, Illinois; managing editor of the *Wycliffe Bible Encyclopedia*.

CONTRIBUTING EDITORS

RAY CORVIN, D.R.E., Ph.D.—Founder of Oklahoma City Southwestern College; Assistant General Superintendent of the Pentecostal Holiness Church.

DAVID DU PLESSIS, D.D.—Ambassador for the Society of Pentecostal Studies; Co-chairman of the Catholic-Pentecostal Dialogue.

HOWARD M. ERVIN, Th.D.—Professor of Biblical Literature and Chairman of the Department of Theology, Oral Roberts University, Tulsa, Oklahoma.

FR. JOSEPH ORSINI, Ed.D.—Associate Pastor of the Church of St. Edward, Pine Hill, New Jersey.

ERWIN PRANGE, S.T.M.—Pastor of St. Matthew Lutheran Church, Baltimore, Maryland.

J. RODMAN WILLIAMS, Ph. D.—President of the Melodyland School of Theology, Anaheim, California; former Professor of Systematic Theology and Philosophy of Religion, Austin Presbyterian Seminary, Austin, Texas.

CONTENTS

PREFACE

Why a commentary on the Holy Spirit? Why one written for laymen? During the current widespread interest in the person and work of the Holy Spirit, many have written very ably on the various aspects of this great doctrine. There is a value, however, in commenting in order on the major passages in the New Testament which are relevant to this present revival, often called the modern charismatic movement. Furthermore, there is a need to present the truths of Scripture and their application to the current scene in terms that the non-specialist can grasp. Wherever Greek words and phrases are given, it is hoped that the accompanying explanation will clarify the overall discussion without the necessity of consulting other references.

I wish to express my deep gratitude to Dan Malachuk of Logos International for his initial vision of such a commentary and for his confidence expressed in asking me to undertake the project. I count it a great honor to have had the help of the outstanding scholars listed on the previous page, whom Mr. Malachuk asked to edit the first draft. Their contributions and observations have been incorporated numerous times into the text of this edition; these have done much to strengthen and broaden the usefulness of the comments. The writings of many contemporary Bible commentators of non-Pentecostal persuasion, as well as men of former generations, have been consulted and quoted in seeking to establish the true interpretation and to lessen the objection of bias or one-sidedness. For their works, I am very grateful.

I especially wish to acknowledge the constant help of my wife Elaine, who read the entire manuscript in handwritten form and enabled me to clarify many points. In addition, I want to thank Mrs. Pat Brigide for the many hours of typing which she performed so capably.

It is a privilege to include as an appendix Dr. Ray Corvin's Chronology of the Work of the Holy Spirit in New Testament Times.

JOHN REA, Th.D.

Oak Park, Illinois

LIST OF ABBREVIATIONS

Bible Versions:

ASV	American Standard Version (1901)
Berkeley	The Berkeley Version of the New Testament (1945)
JPS	The Holy Scripture, Jewish Publication Society (1917)
KJV	King James Version (1611)
NASB	New American Standard Bible (1971)
NEB	New English Bible (1970)
Phillips	The New Testament in Modern English (1958)
RSV	Revised Standard Version (1952)
TAB	Amplified Bible (1965)
TCNT	Twentieth Century New Testament (1902)
TEV	Good News for Modern Man: The New Testament in Today's English Version (1966)
TLB	The Living Bible (1971)

Williams	The New Testament: A Translation in the Language of the People (1937)
Wuest	New Testament: An Expanded Translation (1961)

Bible Commentaries, Dictionaries, and Journals:

EGT	*Expositor's Greek Testament,* 5 vols. Grand Rapids: Eerdmans, 1951 (Reprint)
ICC	*International Critical Commentary*, many vols. Edinburgh: T. & T. Clark
JBL	*Journal of Biblical Literature*
JFB	Jamieson, Fausset, and Brown, *Commentary on the Whole Bible*, 1 vol. ed. Grand Rapids: Zondervan, 1962 (Reprint)
NBD	*New Bible Dictionary*. London: Inter-Varsity Fellowship, 1962
WBC	*Wycliffe Bible Commentary*. Chicago: Moody Press, 1962

Other:

cf.	compare
ed.	edition
f.	and following
Gr.	Greek
n.d.	no date
N. T.	New Testament

O. T.	Old Testament
p., pp.	page(s)
re	concerning
v., vv.	verse(s)
vol.	volume

THE LAYMAN'S COMMENTARY

ON THE HOLY SPIRIT

MATTHEW

MATT. 3:11-17 — THE BAPTISM OF JESUS.

The first important passage in our N.T. that mentions the Holy Spirit is the account of Jesus' baptism. This event, which introduced our Lord to His public ministry, is also described in the other Gospels (Mark 1:7-11; Luke 3:15-17,21,22; John 1:31-34).

John the Baptist was preaching that the people must repent and confess their sins in order to prepare the way for their long-awaited Messiah. The Lord was about to appear to set up His kingdom. It would be the kingdom of heaven or the kingdom of God (Mark 1:15), i.e., a kingdom with heavenly authority and governed according to principles originating in heaven (see John 18:36,37). Therefore, righteousness was to be the primary characteristic of the kingdom and the requirement of all those who would enter it and submit to its rule (Matt. 5:20).

So John commanded the people to stop their evil acts and begin doing honest work and showing kindness as the proof of their repentance (Matt. 3:7-10; Luke 3:7-14). Then he would baptize them in the Jordan River as the sign that their sins were forgiven and cleansed away in God's mercy. Many of the Pharisees refused to be baptized by John and thus rejected God's purpose for themselves, for they would not acknowledge their own self-righteousness and their need for God's righteous plan of salvation (Luke 7:29,30).

Mark and Luke say John preached "the baptism of repentance for the remission of sins" (Mark 1:4; Luke 3:3), meaning a baptism conditioned on prior repentance with reference to the forgiveness of sins. This baptism, then, was a ritual of purification which acted as a seal of the candidate's spiritual reformation begun when he confessed his sins. But how does John's baptism in water explain and prepare the way for Jesus' baptism in the Spirit?

John announced that there was One coming after him who was far greater than he was — he was not even fit to remove His sandals! That One would baptize people, not in or with water as John did, but in or with the Holy Spirit and fire (Matt. 3:11; Luke 3:16). They would be just as thoroughly immersed in or covered with the Spirit as John's candidates were with Jordan's waters. The significance of the accompanying fire is suggested in the next verse, a burning up of the chaff. Chaff symbolizes what is useless and unfruitful, as well as what is sinful and evil (Ps. 1:4). The Holy Spirit comes to take charge of the sanctifying and purifying process in the believer's life (Acts 15:8,9). Thus the fire stands for the sufferings and chastening which every true child of God must endure (Acts 9:16; Heb. 12:5-11; I Pet. 1:6,7; 4:12-14; for the work of the Holy Spirit in sanctification, see comments on I Cor. 6:11).

Jesus came from Galilee to be baptized by John. When the latter objected because he knew Jesus was no sinner, our Lord replied, "Permit it at this time; for in this way it is fitting for us to fulfill all righteousness" (v.15 NASB). As the righteous Son of God, who would provide righteousness for sinful humanity, He publicly identified Himself with those whom He came to redeem. While on earth, Jesus always performed the religious duties of a godly Jew, such as synagogue worship, payment of the temple tax, and attendance at the main feasts in Jerusalem.

As He came out of the water, the Holy Spirit descended upon Jesus in bodily form like a dove, and a voice from heaven said, "This is my beloved Son, in whom I am well pleased" (vv. 16,17). God in this way put His seal of approval (John 6:27) on His Son at the beginning of His ministry. The dove was the sign which assured John that Jesus was the one who would be the Baptizer in the Holy Spirit (John 1:32,33; see comments on John 1:29-34). As the Spirit came on judges and prophets in the O.T. to empower them to minister, so now He came without measure (John 3:34) upon Jesus to enable Him to do His messianic work. Because He voluntarily limited Himself to teach and preach and heal by the Spirit's power, Christ our Lord became a perfect example for us. (For further comments on baptism in the Spirit see Acts 1:4-8; 2:1-4; 10:44-48; I Cor. 12:13.)

MATT. 4:23-25 — THE MINISTRY OF JESUS AS THE PATTERN FOR ALL CHRISTIANS.

Basically, Christ's work consisted of teaching, proclaiming the Gospel, and healing every kind of disease and sickness (see also Matt. 9:35; 15:30,31). He never turned away any sick people who came to Him, no matter what their diseases or pains. The people brought to Him demon-possessed persons, epileptics, and paralytics; He healed every one of them. In explaining the Gospel to Cornelius, Peter summed up Jesus' ministry: "You know of Jesus of Nazareth, how God anointed Him with the Holy Spirit and with power, and how He went about doing good, and healing all who were oppressed by the devil; for God was with Him" (Acts 10:38 NASB).

The authority of Jesus' words astonished the Jews, for He did not rehash the old religious traditions, as their scribes and teachers of the Law of Moses were doing (Matt. 7:28,29; Luke 4:32). His authority and power also amazed the people whenever He commanded unclean spirits to come out of their victims and they obeyed (Luke 4:33-36). It must be remembered that Christ never spoke or acted on His own initiative, but spoke and did only what the Father told Him and showed Him (John 12:49,50; 14:10; 5:19,30; 8:28). He was full of the Holy Spirit, led by the Spirit, and ministered in the power of the Spirit (Luke 4:1,14). All of this divine enabling is available also to every child of God.

Compassion also motivated our Lord as He saw the crowds, "because they were harassed and helpless, like sheep without a shepherd" (Matt. 9:36 RSV; see also Matt. 14:14; Mark 6:34).

His miracles not only served as the credentials of His messiahship and deity — they were not simply signs — but they were also an essential part of His work of saving and helping the whole person.

Christ gave to His twelve apostles authority to conduct a similar ministry of preaching, teaching, and deliverance (Matt. 9:35-38; 10:1,5-8; Luke 9:1-6), and to seventy other disciples as well (Luke 10:1-9). After His resurrection, the Lord Jesus commissioned His followers on several occasions to go into all the world to preach the Gospel and promised that miraculous signs would be associated with those who believe (see comments on Matt. 28:18-20; Mark 16:9-20). Christ planned for the Spirit-filled (other authorities prefer the term "Spirit-anointed") believer to continue His ministry, for He said, "He that believeth on Me, the works that I do shall he do also; and greater works than these shall he do . . . And I will pray the Father, and He shall give you another Comforter . . . even the Spirit of Truth" (John 14:12,16,17). The record of the Book of Acts continues "all that Jesus began both to do and teach" (Acts 1:1), so that the Holy Spirit may be said to be carrying on the ministry of Christ even today. (See also comments on Luke 4:14-21; 10:17-20.)

MATT. 7:21-23 — A WARNING TO COUNTERFEIT CHARISMATICS.

Even if a person has prophesied in the name of Jesus and exorcised demons in His name and worked many miracles, this is no sure evidence he is a born-again Christian. The fruit of one's life is the proof. Doing the will of God is the true test (see comments on Gal. 5:22-23; Heb. 6:4-6). A case in point is that of some Jewish exorcists in Ephesus, including the seven sons of a priest named Sceva. These fellows invoked the name of Jesus over a demon-possessed man, who suddenly leaped on them and badly wounded them (Acts 19:13-16). Therefore, it is extremely important that one be wholly committed to Jesus Christ as Lord before he attempts to manifest any of the gifts of the Spirit. The devil deceives people in order to turn them away from Christ. He is able to give supernatural abilities to his followers so they can counterfeit the gifts and do great wonders (II Thess. 2:9,10).

On the other hand, the Spirit-filled believer must be charitable enough to recognize that sincere Christians in groups or denominations other than his own may have genuine power to cast out demons or perform miracles in Jesus' name (Mark 9:38-40; Luke 9:49,50).

MATT. 8:14-17 — JESUS CHRIST OUR HEALER.

The Lord Jesus Christ as a member of the Trinity may be compared to Jehovah (or, Yahweh), the God of the O.T. God clearly announced to Israel, "I am the LORD that healeth thee" (Exod. 15:26; "I, Jehovah, am your healer," original translation).

In this passage, Matthew relates a prophecy of Isaiah to the healing ministry of Jesus: "Himself took our infirmities and bare our sicknesses" (v.17). The KJV translation of the prophecy is as follows: "Surely he hath borne our griefs, and carried our sorrows" (Isa. 53:4). The Hebrew word for "griefs," however, usually means "sickness" (e.g., Deut. 7:15; II Chron. 21:15-19; Ps. 41:3; Isa. 38:9); and the word for "sorrows" can refer to physical pain and disease as well as mental and emotional suffering (Job 33:19; Exod. 3:7; II Chron. 6:29).

Note that Jesus healed people by divine power before His suffering and death, and that Matthew applies v.4 of Isa. 53 to Christ's ministry before Calvary. It is also evident from Isa. 53:5 that the benefits of His bodily suffering as our substitute extend to our physical as well as our spiritual needs: "With His stripes we are healed" (see comments on Matt. 12:15-21). The psalmist sang praise to the Lord, "Who forgiveth all thine iniquities; who healeth all thy diseases" (Ps. 103:3), revealing that God cares equally about our souls and our bodies.

The ultimate healing of the body of each believer is certainly in Christ's atonement, for He will change our weak mortal bodies to be like His glorious body (Rom. 8:18-23; Phil. 3:21) at the resurrection. Even now we may enjoy some initial or "first fruit" benefits in the healing of our mortal bodies by the power of the indwelling Holy Spirit (Rom. 8:11).

Why, then, are not all healed? Spiritual or divine healing is no more automatic than is salvation. Not everyone who makes a profession of faith is assuredly saved. Believing in Jesus Christ means understanding and believing who He really is, receiving Him personally and sincerely, and committing oneself unreservedly to Him as Sovereign and Lord for time and eternity. In like manner, while God is wonderfully gracious, He knows the motives of our hearts, the sincerity of the confession of our sins (I Cor. 11:28-30), and the genuineness of our faith when we come to Him for healing. Therefore, in effect, Jesus asks the same crucial question that He asked the sick man at the pool of Bethesda, "Do you want to get well again?" (John 5:6 Phillips). In healing two blind men, He touched their eyes, saying, "Be it done to you according to your faith" (Matt. 9:29 NASB).

MATT. 9:16,17 — NEW WINE IN FRESH WINESKINS.

The analogy is from biblical times when grape juice ("new wine") was stored in skin bottles made by skinning an animal whole and sewing up the leg and neck openings, etc. When the juice fermented, its vapor expanded the fresh elastic skin. But the skin would burst if it were old and stiff (see Luke 5:37,38). Jesus' lesson is that His new religion based on grace and the power of the Spirit could not be contained in the old forms of legalistic Judaism, but demanded a new and different expression of worship. The figure is apt, for the 120 filled with the Spirit at Pentecost seemed like men full of new wine to the onlookers (Acts 2:13).

MATT. 10:16-20 — A CHARISMATIC WORD OF WISDOM FOR THE PERSECUTED BELIEVER.

The Spirit-filled Christian need not fear what he will answer during times of trial and danger. Christ promises us that "it shall be given you in that same hour what ye shall speak" (v.19). This is an example of the charismatic manifestation of a word of wisdom (I Cor. 12:8), the Spirit of God speaking in you. The parallel passage in Luke's Gospel (12:12) reads, "For the Holy Spirit will teach you in that very hour what you ought to say" (NASB). Jesus also promises that when we are persecuted and brought before rulers for His name's sake, it will lead to an opportunity for a testimony. We should not prepare beforehand how to defend ourselves, "because I myself will give you power of utterance and a wisdom which no opponent will be able to resist or refute" (Luke 21:15 NEB).

Peter experienced this manifestation when he and John were on trial before the Jewish Sanhedrin (Acts 4:5-8). Overflowing with the Spirit, he preached Christ and salvation to the leaders and priests, and they could only marvel, and let Peter and John go (Acts 4:8-14,21). On another occasion, Jews were aroused by the miracles Stephen was performing among the people, and began arguing with him. But he was full of faith and of the Holy Spirit, and "they were unable to cope with the wisdom and the Spirit with which he was speaking" (Acts 6:10 NASB).

MATT. 12:15-21 — ISAIAH'S PROPHECY OF GOD'S SPIRIT-ANOINTED SERVANT.

In Matthew's Gospel, Isaiah's prophecies are quoted or referred to at least fifteen times. Isaiah is the evangelist-prophet of Israel, and his book is the one which tells the most about the Holy Spirit in the Old Testament. In the King James Version, there are fifteen verses in Isaiah that clearly mention the Holy Spirit, the Spirit of the Lord, or "My spirit." (The book refers to the Holy Spirit in Old Testament times [Isa. 30:1; 34:16;

40:13; 63:10,11,14], to the Spirit upon the coming Messiah [Isa. 11:2; 42:1; 48:16; 61:1], and to the outpouring in the messianic age [Isa. 32:15; 44:3; 59:21; and 59:19]).

In this passage, Matthew definitely shows that Jesus is the fulfillment of the wonderful prophecies about the Servant of the Lord in Isaiah (42:1-9; 49:1-7; 50:4-11; 52:13—53:12). God has put His Spirit upon Him, and He will bring forth justice to the Gentile nations as well as to the Jews. He shall be exalted and extolled, for He was wounded ("pierced," NASB) for our transgressions and bruised ("crushed," NASB) for our iniquities; the punishment which procured peace for us was upon Him, and by His stripes (His scourging with whiplashes, cf. Luke 23:16,22; Matt. 27:26), we are healed.

At this point in His ministry, Jesus did not want those whom He healed to advertise the fact and thereby reveal His identity as the Messiah. This could have easily led to an abortive uprising against Rome. According to Isaiah's prophecy, the Servant of the Lord was not to be a rabble-rouser or a fanatical, demagogic preacher (Isa. 42:2; Matt. 12:19). His purpose was not to lead a military revolution, but to achieve victory by tenderly caring for the unfortunate ("a bruised reed," "a smouldering wick," RSV). His "hour" — the time for His redemptive sacrifice, His supreme work on earth — had not yet come (John 2:4; 7:6,8; 8:20; 12:23,27; 13:1; 17:1). But now that He has been crucified and resurrected, His command no longer applies, and all Christians should bear witness concerning Him openly and fearlessly.

MATT. 12:22-37 — THE UNPARDONABLE SIN, BLASPHEMY AGAINST THE HOLY SPIRIT.

The context of Jesus' teaching about this subject is the critical, defiant attitude of the Pharisees regarding His work of exorcizing evil spirits. They kept accusing Christ of casting out demons by the power and authority of Beelzebub ("Beelzebul," RSV, NASB), the ruler of the demons. Beelzebub was the title and name of a Canaanite god adopted by the Philistines (II Kings 1:16), a name which the Jews applied to Satan.

Specifically, therefore, the Pharisees were blaspheming or slandering the Holy Spirit by giving the devil credit for Jesus' miracles of exorcism, when in reality these were wrought by the Spirit of God (v.28). But this false accusation was merely symptomatic of the underlying sin for which there is no forgiveness. In the parallel passage in Mark (3:29), Jesus says such a person is guilty of an eternal sin (RSV). In vv.33-37 the reason is clear — their evil, wrong ideas came from their corrupt hearts. Their words would condemn them, for these evidenced a fixed, unrepentant attitude of mind that persistently rejected the wooing and conviction of the Spirit.

The Holy Spirit is God's messenger to men, to convict them of sin and to convince them of divine truth (John 16:8-11). When a man deliberately resists the Spirit's messages to his conscience — whether through his seeing a miracle, hearing a sermon, or reading the Scriptures or a Christian book or tract — he is shutting out the only force that can lead him to repentance. He is making his heart callous against believing in the Son for forgiveness (John 3:36). Only God knows when that hardening process has become permanent. No one who is sorry that he has offended the holy God by his sin and who longs to be forgiven by Jesus the Savior need fear that he has committed the unpardonable sin. On the other hand, it is dangerous to begin a course of spiritual insensitivity by attributing to Satan true manifestations of the Spirit such as the charismatic gifts of I Cor. 12 (see comments on I Cor. 12:4-11). On the dangers of falling away and openly rejecting Christ, see comments on Heb. 6:4-6.

MATT. 25:1-13 — THE PARABLE OF THE TEN VIRGINS.
Many Christians find an allusion to the Holy Spirit in this passage, because oil is one of the symbols of the Spirit in the Bible. While this is a difficult parable to interpret correctly,

Jesus' main teaching is clear enough. He ends the story by
telling His disciples to watch, to be on the alert, since they do
not know the day nor the hour of His return (v.13). It is a
continuation of His instruction to be ready when He comes
back (Matt. 24:44; cf. 24:36-51).

All ten virgins seem to represent believers in the Lord (cf. II
Cor. 11:2; Rev. 14:4). They are pictured as invited guests or
attendants of the bride (Song of Sol. 1:3; Ps. 45:14), expecting
to participate in the wedding feast (KJV "marriage," v.10).
Five were "wise," sensible, prudent, and resourceful; five were
"foolish," careless, or unconcerned.

The words "wise" and "foolish" describe two basic heart
attitudes: one is a godly fear and love of the Lord evidenced in
obedience and faithfulness; the other is a love of self that makes
him unheeding and disobedient and spiritually blind. The
contrast between the wise and the foolish is strikingly portrayed
in Jesus' illustration of the two men who built their houses, one
upon the rock and the other upon the sand (Matt. 7:24-27).
The wise man is the one who hears Christ's words and acts upon
them; the foolish man does not heed and obey them. The wise
servant in charge of his master's household, who properly
performed his duties, is also called *faithful* (Matt. 24:45; Luke
12:42). By diligently seeking godly wisdom, the wise person also
becomes prudent and shrewd ("wise as a serpent," the fabled
symbol of wisdom, Matt. 10:16) and resourceful like the
steward commended in Luke 16:8. John the Baptist was sent in
the spirit and power of Elijah (i.e., filled with the Holy Spirit) to
turn the disobedient to the wisdom or prudent attitude of the
righteous, and thus to make ready a people prepared for the
Lord (Luke 1:15,17).

The fool, on the other hand, is like the Pharisees, blind and
hypocritical (Matt. 23:17). In current English usage, *foolish*
means stupid, silly, thoughtless, easily deceived, or even embar-
rassed. In the Bible, however, the fool is not merely stupid or
ignorant, but one who knowingly rejects God, who says in his

heart, "There is no God" (Ps. 14:1), who, like Job's wife, would even curse God (Job 2:9,10). Like King Saul, he does not pay attention to the word of God's prophet (I Sam. 13:13). He may be harsh, unfeeling, and callous like Nabal, whose very name means *fool* (I Sam. 25:3,25). At heart, he is perverse, with a moral spot, a spiritual defect, and thus is called foolish and unwise (Deut. 32:5,6), unwilling to consider his latter end (32:28,29). He is foolish: he does not really know God (Jer. 4:22) or fear Him, because he has a stubborn or rebellious heart (Jer. 5:21-24), because like King Asa his heart is not perfect toward God (i.e., not completely His, II Chron. 16:9).

Because the Bridegroom excludes the five foolish virgins and says, "I know you not," we may conclude that they represent professing believers who actually are not really born again. They took no oil, so that we may say they were not filled with the Spirit themselves. But they were not rejected for that reason; that was only a symptom or result of their foolish indifference. They did not know the Lord personally (contrast Paul in Phil. 3:10) and did not have the Spirit of Christ at all (Rom. 8:9). They did not really "love His appearing" (II Tim. 4:8) enough to prepare themselves by getting their hearts cleansed and totally committed to their Lord. So they were ashamed before Him at His coming (I John 2:28; 3:2,3). Like the professing Laodicean Christians, they were lukewarm and needed to be zealous and repent (Rev. 3:15-19).

Whatever light their lamps gave forth for a while, whatever testimony the foolish virgins may have had, was the result of a "borrowed" religious experience. They expected to get more oil from their associates. Many professing Christians today depend entirely for their "oil" on church services and meetings, or on imitating the experience of others, instead of seeking the Lord directly through His Word in times of personal devotion, meditation, and prayer. Disobeying the command in Eph. 5:18, "Be filled with the Spirit," they reveal a basic lack of love for the Lord Jesus Christ.

MATT. 28:18-20 — THE GREAT COMMISSION.

Each of the four Gospels (here; Mark 16:15-18; Luke 24:46-49; John 20:21) and the Book of Acts (1:8) contains a missionary charge by the Lord Jesus, spoken to His disciples after His resurrection. Every Christian has been given the responsibility to be a witness of Christ. Note the four "alls" in this passage: Jesus has received *all* power or authority to make this command, based on His personal triumph over Satan in the wilderness and His defeat of the forces of darkness at the cross. We are to go and make disciples of (RSV, NASB) *all* nations, sealing them in their new faith by baptizing them in (Gr. *eis*, unto, with reference to) the name (singular) of the triune God — of the Father, and the Son, and of the Holy Spirit. Water baptism, therefore, is not optional, but is clearly commanded by the risen Christ, and this is His "formula " (see comments on Acts 2:38-40). We are to teach the converts to observe, to be continually practicing *all* things that Jesus taught and commanded us. And He has promised to be with us by His Spirit *always* (literally, *all* the days) even to the end of the world, i.e., of this age, when He will then return in person (see comments on Mark 16:9-20; Luke 24:44-53; John 20:21-23; Acts 1:4-8).

MARK

MARK 5:25-34 — TOUCHING JESUS.

This story vividly illustrates the value of the human touch as a point of contact for faith, i.e., as an aid to believing. The experience of the woman who suffered with a chronic hemorrhage also provides several other keys for the one seeking healing. First, she heard about Jesus and thought of Him as the One to help her in her desperate need. Then she actually came to Him, overcoming her embarrassment and fear of the crowd.

Third, she kept affirming her faith by saying to herself (the tense of verb "said" in v.28 implies repeated action), "If I touch even his garments, I shall be made well" (v.28 RSV). Finally, she reached out and touched the Lord's garment, thereby releasing her faith (exercising full-fledged trust without any doubt). And she was miraculously healed!

Other passages mention this normal reaction of wanting to touch the One who could give healing (Mark 3:10 and Luke 6:19; Mark 6:56 and Matt. 14:36). After Christ ascended and was no longer physically present, people naturally sought to come in contact with the apostles through whom the healing power of God was channeled (Acts 5:15; 19:12).

There is no essential difference, as far as the flow of Christ's healing virtue or power (Gr. *dynamis*, Mark 5:30) is concerned, between individuals touching Him and His touching them (Luke 4:40). In one case, Jesus saw a woman who had been sick for eighteen years and was bent double. When our Lord laid His hands upon her, immediately she was made erect and began glorifying God (Luke 13:11-13). In like manner, Christians may lay hands on the sick in the name of Jesus to enable them to believe more easily (Mark 16:18; Acts 28:8). Peter took the hand of the cripple at the temple gate and lifted him up and the man was healed (Acts 3:7). For anointing the sick with oil and the prayer of faith, see comments on James 5:13-20.

Just as Elijah and Elisha had raised persons from the dead centuries earlier (I Kings 17:21; II Kings 4:34), Paul lay upon Eutychus and embraced him, and the young fellow was restored to life (Acts 20:9,10). Thus physical contact seems to aid the faith of the Lord's servant as well.

The laying on of hands for healing is a serious and sacred ministry that should be conducted only by those whose own lives are pure and holy. These servants of God should not be harboring any known sins or resentments in their own hearts, lest they be unclean channels that would block the flow of God's power. For the ministry of the laying on of hands see comments on Acts 6:6.

MARK 16:9-20 — CONFIRMING THE WORD WITH SIGNS FOLLOWING.

This is one of the few passages in the N.T. about which scholars still have a doubt as to the original Greek text. In the two most trustworthy Greek manuscripts of the N.T. (the Vaticanus and the Sinaiticus, both copied around A.D. 350) the Gospel of Mark ends with 16:8. The other important early codices (A,C,D,W,Θ), however, all contain this ending, as well as by far the greater number of later manuscripts. All the ancient versions (Old Latin, Syriac, and the various Egyptian translations) have these verses, with the exception of some copies of these versions. Several Greek manuscripts and copies of versions do offer shorter substitutes in the place of vv.9-20. Also, the style of this passage seems to differ from the usually concrete and pictorial style of Mark. Eusebius and Jerome in the fourth century were the chief authorities who doubted the passage. The present ending, however, was quoted by Tatian and Irenaeus in the second century, so it must have been written very early and accepted as canonical.

If Mark wrote his Gospel in codex form (a book with pages) instead of on a scroll, the last page of his original work may have been torn off and lost before additional copies could be made. In such a case, apparently some other recognized Christian prophet who was acquainted with the post-resurrection ministry of Jesus was inspired by the Spirit to supply this substitute ending. The N.T. scholar Henry B. Swete called it "an authentic relic of the first Christian generation." As Morton T. Kelsey explains, "This passage certainly represents the experience and expectation of the early church. . . . (It) becomes a primary indication that the practice of tongues (and other charismatic gifts) was not confined to the first days of the church" (*Tongue Speaking* [Garden City: Doubleday, 1964], p. 25).

By accepting these verses as the inspired word of God, we have the only passage in the four Gospels where Jesus mentions speaking in tongues ("They shall speak with new tongues," Mark 16:17). In vv.17,18, the risen Lord clearly promises that signs will accompany those who believe as a result of Christians down through the centuries going into all the world and preaching the Gospel to all creation (vv.15,16). Therefore, these attesting miracles cannot be limited to the apostolic age, but were meant to confirm the ministries of the servants of Christ in every generation.

These "signs following" are the credentials of the ambassador of Christ and characteristic marks of God's people under the New Covenant. Jesus had already delegated to His disciples the authority to cast out demons and to heal the sick (Mark 6:12,13; Luke 9:1; 10:17,19), and in Acts we read that this ministry of exorcism continued (5:16; 8:7; 16:18; 19:12). The "new tongues," new to the speakers because they have never learned them previously, are also the one new sign peculiar to this church age. They were first manifested on the Day of Pentecost (see comments on Acts 2:1-4). "They shall take up serpents," not in religious ceremonies, but to get rid of them without being harmed in the process (see Paul's experience on Malta, Acts 28:3-6). The verb "take up" (Gr. *airo*) can also mean *remove, take away, cast away* (Matt. 14:12; Luke 11:52; I Cor. 5:2; Eph. 4:31). Missionaries entering heathen territory have experienced the miraculous protection of the Lord when they have survived with no ill effects after being served poisoned food or drink. And finally, many wonderful healings are recorded in Acts and in the writings of the church fathers or leaders during the next several centuries. All of these signs have occurred repeatedly in this century (see other comments on Matt. 4:23-25; 28:18-20).

LUKE

Luke 1:13-17 — THE PROPHECY OF THE SPIRITUAL EMPOWERING OF JOHN THE BAPTIST.

Luke gives much prominence to the work of the Holy Spirit. In this, his first passage mentioning the Spirit, Luke is narrating how the angel announced to the childless old priest Zacharias that his wife Elizabeth would bear him a son even though she was getting on in years. The boy was to be named John, and he would be filled with the Holy Spirit while yet in his mother's womb (v.15). Zacharias would understand this, as in the cases of Samson and Jeremiah (Judg. 13:3-7; Jer. 1:5), that the Spirit of God was sanctifying or setting John apart to special service for the Lord from the moment of conception. Then the angel concluded by saying that John would go as a forerunner before the Lord "in the spirit and power of Elijah" (v.17).

John the Baptist belonged to the dispensation of the Law and the prophets, to the period of the Old Covenant given at Mount Sinai through Moses. John was a prophet (Luke 1:76; 20:6), but even more than a prophet, for he was the predicted special messenger to prepare Messiah's way before Him (Mal. 3:1; Matt. 11:7-10; Luke 7:24-27). As such, there was no one greater in the O.T. period (Matt. 11:11). He was like the outstanding prophet Elijah in many ways, a stern preacher of moral righteousness who lived apart from society and wore a garment of camel's hair with a leather belt instead of a cloth sash (Matt. 3:4; II Kings 1:8 RSV). Most important, both were empowered by the Spirit of God.

In the O.T., the Spirit had not been poured out on all of God's people. That empowering would not become available for all until Joel's prophecy began to be fulfilled at Pentecost (see comments on Acts 2:14-21). Therefore, the younger prophet Elisha specifically requested that he might become heir to

Elijah's spirit: "Let a double portion of thy spirit be upon me" (II Kings 2:9; cf. v.15). The "double portion" signified the rights of the firstborn son or chief heir (Deut. 21:17); thus Elisha was asking for the right to be Elijah's main successor, not to do twice as many miracles as his master. More than the prophet's own human spirit is in view here, for in those days people expected the Spirit of the Lord to enable men to prophesy (I Kings 22:24) and even to transport a prophet or man of God miraculously to another place (I Kings 18:12; II Kings 2:16). This would correspond to Philip's experience after witnessing to the Ethiopian eunuch (Acts 8:39). Some believe that the Spirit lifted Ezekiel up and took him, for example, from Babylonia to Jerusalem, although he clearly says these trans-portings were in visions (Ezek. 3:12-14; 8:3; 11:1,24; 43:3-5). Certainly Elijah's and Elisha's many miracles of healing, raising from the dead, providing food, etc., demonstrate that they were empowered by the Holy Spirit. No one is recorded in the Bible to have performed more miracles than Elisha, except Jesus Himself.

Other O.T. persons who are said to have been filled with the Spirit are Moses (Num. 11:17), Bezaleel and other craftsmen for the tabernacle (Exod. 28:3; 31:3; 35:31), Joshua (Deut. 34:9; Num. 27:18), and the prophet Micah (Mic. 3:8). Also, the pharaoh recognized that the Spirit of God was in Joseph (Gen. 41:38), even as the rulers of Babylon knew that Daniel was possessed of the Spirit of God (Dan. 4:8; 5:11; 6:3). The Spirit of the Lord came temporarily upon many of the judges and kings to give them leadership ability and to enable them to perform superhuman feats of strength (Judg. 3:10; 6:34; 11:29; 13:25; 14:6,19; 15:14; I Sam. 11:6; 16:13). The Spirit also came upon various men and caused them to prophesy, such as the seventy elders and Eldad and Medad in Moses' time (Num. 11:25-27). When he was newly anointed to be king, Saul prophesied (I Sam. 10:6,10), as well as Azariah (II Chron. 15:1), Jahaziel (II Chron. 20:14), and Zechariah the son of

Jehoiada the priest (II Chron. 24:20). Some even prophesied against their will, such as King Saul and his messengers (I Sam. 19:20-24), and the false prophet Balaam (Num. 23:26; 24:1,2).

David and the other O.T. writers were inspired by the Spirit as they wrote down the words of God for His people (II Sam. 23:2; Zech. 7:12; see comments on II Pet. 1:19-21). The great rallying message for the poverty-stricken returned refugees from Babylon was "Not by might, nor by power, but by my spirit, saith the Lord of hosts" (Zech. 4:6). But Moses' wish expressed to Joshua — "Would God that all the Lord's people were prophets, and that the Lord would put his spirit upon them!" (Num. 11:29) — would have to wait for the universal outpouring of the Spirit (Isa. 32:15; 44:3; Joel 2:28) at the coming of Messiah.

LUKE 1:35 — THE CONCEPTION OF JESUS BY THE HOLY SPIRIT.

The virgin birth of Jesus Christ, the unique God-man, is clearly taught in the Scriptures, especially in this passage (Luke 1:26-38) and in Matt. 1:18-25. From John 1:14 (RSV), "And the Word became flesh and dwelt among us," theologians have derived the term *incarnation* (from Latin *incarnare*, to make flesh). By this is meant that God took on human form in the body of Jesus. Christ had no earthly father — Joseph served only as a foster-father to give Him legal parentage and His royal ancestry in the house of David. Jesus' conception cannot be explained scientifically. It was a creative miracle wrought by the Holy Spirit in the virgin womb of Mary. There is no suggestion of the Spirit assuming human form and having physical intercourse with Mary, as in the ancient pagan legends concerning the reputed offspring of gods and humans. The angel said the power (*dynamis*) of the Most High would overshadow her, using familiar terminology from the Old Testament with reference to the cloud over the camp of Israel. The pillar of cloud symbolized the immediate presence of God (Exod. 13:21; Num. 9:15-23; 10:34).

In His birth, as in His entire life, Christ is the pattern and example for believers (I Pet. 2:21). The true Christian has experienced a supernatural rebirth or regeneration by the Holy Spirit (Titus 3:5). He has been born again spiritually (see comments on John 3:1-8). Even as Jesus was baptized later on and empowered for His ministry when the Spirit came upon Him, so the believer in Christ should experience the baptism in the Holy Spirit after this new birth (see comments on Matt. 3:11-17).

LUKE 4:14-21 — JESUS AND THE PROPHECY OF ISAIAH.

Some scholars have claimed that Jesus grew in "His messianic self-consciousness," the awareness that He was actually the predicted Messiah of Israel. But this passage reveals rather clearly that from the start Jesus knew His identity. When handed the Book of Isaiah to read in the synagogue of His hometown of Nazareth, Jesus deliberately unrolled the long scroll almost to the inner end and found the place where it was written:

> "The Spirit of the Lord is upon Me,
>> Because He anointed Me to preach the gospel to the poor.
>> He has sent Me to proclaim release to the captives,
>> And recovery of sight to the blind,
>> To set free those who are downtrodden,
>> To proclaim the favorable year of the Lord."
> (vv.18,19 NASB)

By comparing these words with the original passage in Isa. 61:1,2, one can notice several differences. Some of these may result from Luke's having quoted the passage from the Septuagint version, the Greek translation made by Jewish scholars in Egypt 200 years before Christ. But the fifth line of Luke's quotation seems to be an original comment on Isaiah's text added by Jesus Himself. He obviously knew the passage well and had meditated much on it. He suddenly stopped reading after the first line of Isa. 61:2, rolled up the scroll, gave it back to the attendant, and announced, "Today this scripture has been fulfilled in your hearing" (v.21 NASB). The next phrase in Isaiah reads, "to proclaim . . . the day of vengeance of our God." Undoubtedly Jesus stopped purposely, since the "day of vengeance" still awaits His second coming. The "favorable year of the Lord," i.e., the era of the Lord's favor and grace, describes His first coming and this present age.

From His baptism on, Jesus was full of the Holy Spirit and was led by the Spirit (Luke 4:1). After His temptation in the wilderness, He returned in the power of the Spirit into Galilee (v.14). He *knew* that He cast out demons by the Spirit of God (Matt. 12:28; see comments on Matt. 12:22-37). Although He had always existed as the Son of God with all the powers and privileges of deity, Jesus Christ did not regard His equality with God a thing to be selfishly exploited. He "made Himself of no reputation" by voluntarily depriving Himself of the use of His divine attributes and powers, and took the form of a servant (Phil. 2:5-7). In this position of humility, He depended completely upon the Father and the Spirit (John 5:19,30).

As a Spirit-anointed *Man*, Jesus is a perfect example for the Christian. Each believer should *know* he is a son of God (see I John) and that he has the Spirit of Christ (Rom. 8:9). After his baptism in the Spirit, he should *know* that he can count on the Spirit to work supernaturally in and through him. Anointed with the same Spirit that descended upon the Lord Jesus, the Christian should expect to do the works of healing and deliverance that Isaiah prophesied for the Messiah to perform (see also comments on Matt. 4:23-25).

LUKE 9:23-26 — SELF-DENIAL AND CROSS-BEARING.

It is noteworthy that our Lord spoke these words to the twelve apostles after He had given them power and authority over all the demons and to heal diseases (Luke 9:1). They had already conducted successful preaching and healing missions (Luke 9:6).

Therefore, the Spirit-baptized Christian who has had various charismatic gifts manifested through him should give ear to Jesus' exhortation. He, too, as much as any other follower of Christ, must deny himself and take up his cross every day (v.23). He must be willing to suffer persecution and to lose his possessions, his position and power, and even his personal rights. He must accept these deathblows to his pride in a spirit of meekness without becoming angry at man or God. The crucified life means yielding one's will moment by moment to the control of the Spirit and staying fully surrendered to Christ the Son and God the Father. Each new day he should consider himself dead to his old sinful tendencies and alive to God in Christ Jesus (Rom. 6:4-11).

Paul wrote to the Corinthian believers, who were not lacking in any charismatic gift (I Cor. 1:7), that they should no longer live for themselves, but only for Him who died and rose again on their behalf (II Cor. 5:15). In saying farewell to the Ephesian elders, Paul testified he did not count his life dear unto himself, in order that he might finish his course and the ministry Christ had given him (Acts 20:24). He gloried only in the cross, through which the world had been crucified to him, put to death as far as he was concerned, and he to the world (Gal. 6:14; cf. 2:20).

In this same ninth chapter of Luke, Jesus warns a would-be follower, "No one who sets his hand to the plow and then keeps looking back is fit for the kingdom of God" (v.62 NEB). Later He urges disciples to count the cost and says literally, "Whoever does not carry his own cross and come after Me cannot be My disciple" (Luke 14:27 NASB).

LUKE 10:17-20 — THE SUBJECTION OF DEMONS TO CHRISTIAN DISCIPLES.

The Lord Jesus had appointed seventy other disciples in addition to the twelve apostles and had sent them on ahead of Him, two by two, to prepare hearts where He Himself was going to come (Luke 10:1). Christ's principle of His laborers in the harvest working two or three together is basic and extremely important to follow, to strengthen their witness and to give each other the wisdom and encouragement that one might lack from time to time. When two are agreed on earth about anything that they may ask of the Lord, He has said that it shall be done for them by His Father in heaven; this promise includes binding evil powers and loosing people from their grip (Matt. 18:18,19). Two persons teamed together more than double the effectiveness of the individual. In Deut. 32:30 the Lord suggests that if one can chase a thousand, two can put ten thousand to flight. Lev. 26:8 is another verse showing how the cooperation of a few more individuals multiplies their power over the enemy. Note other passages dealing with the two-by-two principle (Deut. 17:6; 19:15; Eccl. 4:9-12; Amos 3:3; Matt. 18:16; Mark 6:7; 14:13; Luke 7:19; John 1:35-41; 8:17; Acts 9:38; 10:7; 13:2-7,13; 15:36-41; 17:4,14-16; 18:5; 19:22; 20:4-6; II Cor. 13:1; I Tim. 5:19; Heb. 10:28; Rev. 11:3-6,10-12). Paul suffered severe discouragement when he remained alone in Ephesus and in the Roman province of Asia (Acts 19:22), until at last Titus rejoined him in Macedonia (II Cor. 1:8-11; 2:12,13; 7:5-7).

The seventy returned with joy because they found that even the demons were subject to them when they used Jesus' name (v.17). The name of someone signifies all that that person represents — his character and reputation, his authority and titles, his very power and influence. The Lord then explained to them why they had such success over Satan's forces. To bring out the meaning of His words in v.18, we translate: "I was watching Satan in the act of falling from heaven like lightning."

Jesus saw in His own exorcisms (Matt. 12:25-29) and in the success of His disciples the beginning of the downfall of Satan's kingdom. "Like lightning" suggests that the devil's power would be broken worldwide, "as the lightning comes from the east, and flashes even to the west" (Matt. 24:27 NASB; cf. Luke 17:24). The great dragon Satan will ultimately be cast down from heaven, and he will no longer be able to accuse our Christian brethren before God (Rev. 12:7-10; cf. Job 1:11; 2:5; Zech. 3:1; Luke 22:31).

The actual reason for Christians having dominion at present over evil spirits is that Jesus Christ has given or delegated to us His divine power (authority) "to tread on serpents and scorpions, and over all the power (*dunamis*) of the enemy" (v.19). "Serpents and scorpions" are symbolic terms for crafty and dangerous enemies and cruel oppressions (cf. for serpents, Ps. 58:4; 140:3; Jer. 8:16,17; Mic. 7:17; Matt. 23:33; Rev. 12:9; 20:2; for scorpions, 1 Kings 12:11,14; Ezek. 2:6). Paul promises that the God of peace will soon crush Satan under our feet (Rom. 16:20). This figure harks back to Ps. 91:13 and to Gen. 3:15; in the Genesis verse the serpent who deceived Eve is told that the "seed" of the woman (the virgin-born Messiah) will "bruise" his head. Of course, this crushing will be completed by our Lord Jesus Christ at His return (Rev. 20:2,3,10); but Paul's words "under *your* feet" suggest that even now *we* may experience signal victories over the devil. We *now* are seated or enthroned with Christ in the heavenlies, in the supernatural sphere where the spiritual warfare is constantly being waged, and thus we fight from His position of supreme authority.

Jesus was thrilled — "He rejoiced greatly in the Holy Spirit" (NASB) — that God the Father had revealed "these things" about how to achieve victory over demons to "babes," to His disciples who were uneducated in the wisdom and knowledge of this world (Luke 10:21-24). But He told them not to rejoice in their momentary triumph over evil spirits but in the fact that their names are recorded in heaven for eternity (v.20). He warned them not to get so delighted in His delegated authority that their ego would become puffed up. Lucifer lost his place in heaven because of pride in himself and in the authority given him (Isa. 14:12-15; see comments on Matt. 4:23-25).

LUKE 11:5-13 — PERSISTENT ASKING FOR THE HOLY SPIRIT.

In His Sermon on the Mount, Jesus had given almost identical instruction on the certainty of answer to prayer (Matt. 7:7-11). On this separate occasion, the Lord adds an interesting parable that places prayer on the basis of personal friendship with God (vv.5-8). He climaxes His teaching by encouraging the child of God to keep on asking for the Holy Spirit, whereas in Matt. 7:11 the corresponding object of prayer is "good things." In the Greek text in vv.9, 10, the verbs *ask, seek,* and *knock,* as well as the verb *ask* in v.13, are in the present tense; this suggests that we are to keep on asking, to be as persistent as the man was who went to his friend's home at midnight to get bread. We may also conclude that just as we ask in the Lord's Prayer for God to give us each day our daily bread (v.3), so our Heavenly Father will keep on giving us the Holy Spirit day by day. Therefore, this passage is helpful instruction not only for the Christian seeking the baptism in the Holy Spirit, but also for the Spirit-baptized child of God to keep on walking in the fullness of the Spirit each day (see comments on Eph. 5:15-21).

LUKE 12:49-53 — THE BAPTISM OF SUFFERING.

In v.50 Jesus states that He has a baptism to be baptized with. Obviously He does not mean His baptism previously performed by John in the River Jordan. He had not yet undergone this baptism, for He adds, "and how distressed I am until it is accomplished" (NASB). This was to be His "baptism" of suffering; in a figurative sense, He would become completely immersed in the pain and agony leading to His death.

Christ realized that His ministry was going to disturb many

and cause fires of division to burn even within families (vv.51-53). Nevertheless, He wished that His death on the cross were already finished, so that the fire He came to cast on the earth were already kindled (v.49 NASB). What does He mean? We know that Jesus came to destroy Satan and sin. John the Baptist said that the One coming after him would baptize in the Holy Spirit *and fire* (see comments on Matt. 3:11-17). Here the Savior is longing for the time when His work of salvation will be completed so that He might fully kindle that fire. It will have a twofold effect, to destroy evil and to purify and refine His faithful followers. This process of judgment had already begun in the hearts of men with the commencement of Jesus' ministry, but only after His death and resurrection and the pouring out of the Holy Spirit would it burn and purify in full measure.

When James and John the sons of Zebedee came asking Him for positions of honor in His kingdom, Jesus asked them if they were able and willing to drink the cup that He was going to drink and to be baptized with the baptism He would soon experience (Mark 10:38). In Gethsemane He spoke of His approaching crucifixion as a "cup" (Mark 14:36). Very likely this figure came from the O.T. prophets through whom God spoke of the cup of the wine of His wrath against sin (Isa. 51:17,22; Jer. 25:15,17; Ezek. 23:31-34; Hab. 2:16). Our Savior, as our substitute, drank this cup meant for us; are we willing to suffer for His sake?

LUKE 24:44-53 — THE PROMISE OF THE FATHER.

The appearance of the risen Lord Jesus described in vv.44-49 comes shortly before His ascension back to heaven. It must have occurred after He had met His disciples in Galilee (Matt. 28:7,10,16-20; John 21:1-23), because here He commands them to stay in the city of Jerusalem until they are endued with power from on high (v.49). This is one of the occasions when Jesus commissioned His followers to be witnesses (see comments on Matt. 28:18-20). Here He stresses the doctrine of repentance leading to the forgiveness of sins that they should preach in His name (v.47). "In his name" literally is "upon his name," on the basis of His name which stands for His deity and authority and finished work of redemption through His death and resurrection.

In v.49 Jesus says, literally, "And behold, I Myself am going to send forth the promise of My Father upon you." As a result, they would be clothed with power (*dynamis*) from on high, i.e., with supernatural power. For the figure of being clothed with a virtue or power, see Job 29:14; Ps. 93:1; and Judg. 6:34. In the last passage, the Hebrew literally says, "The Spirit of the Lord clothed Gideon."

The promise of the Father refers to God's promised gift of the Holy Spirit. The outpouring of the Spirit was first promised through the prophets (Isa. 32:15; 44:3; Joel 2:28; Ezek. 39:29). In the Upper Room, Christ told His disciples that His Father would send the Holy Spirit "in My name" (John 14:26; cf. 14:16; 15:26; 16:7). Just before He ascended to heaven, He specifically related the promise to the baptism in the Holy Spirit (see comments on Acts 1:4-8). On the Day of Pentecost, Peter explained the startling words of praise to God in other languages that the crowds in the temple area had just heard, by saying about Jesus: "Therefore having been exalted to the right hand of God, and having received from the Father the promise of the Holy Spirit, He has poured forth this which you both see and hear" (Acts 2:33 NASB). When many Jews were convicted, Peter told them to repent and be baptized and that they too could receive the gift of the Holy Spirit, "for the promise is for you and your children . . ." (Acts 2:39 NASB). Paul agreed that all of the Christian life should be lived in faith because we receive the promise of the Spirit through faith (Gal. 3:14). Also, he taught that we are sealed with the promised Holy Spirit (literally, "the holy Spirit of the promise," Eph. 1:13).

According to vv.50-53, after the Ascension, the disciples awaited the fulfillment of this promise with great joy. They were continually in the temple, praising God, as well as devoting themselves to prayer (Acts 1:14). The earnest child of God today seeking the baptism in the Spirit may well imitate their attitude of expectancy, joyous praise, and prayerfulness.

JOHN

John 1:29-34 — JESUS, LAMB OF GOD AND BAPTIZER IN THE HOLY SPIRIT.

John the Baptist was divinely commissioned to bear witness of the Light, Jesus Christ. His two greatest statements about Jesus and His work are recorded in this passage. John points Him out as (1) "the Lamb of God which taketh away the sin of the world" (v.29), and (2) "he which baptizeth with the Holy Ghost" (v.33). Jesus is the perfect, infinite sacrifice who, like a sheep brought as a sin offering to the tabernacle, dies in the place of the sinner (Lev. 4, 5). As the blood of the Passover lamb was put on the Israelite's doorway (Exod. 12:6,7,13), so Jesus' blood was shed for the remission or forgiveness of our sins (Heb. 9:12-14,22,26) and to save us from eternal death (cf. I Cor. 5:7). As the scapegoat carried away the sins of the people into oblivion in the wilderness on the annual Day of Atonement (Lev. 16:20-22), so Jesus our Savior removes completely and permanently the sins of people all over the world who trust in Him.

Equally important to His atoning work through pouring out His lifeblood is His work of pouring out the Spirit. God's words to John in v.33 may be translated literally, "This is the Baptizer in the Holy Spirit." Just as surely as Jesus came to earth to seek and to save the lost (Luke 19:10), He returned to heaven to send the promised gift of the Holy Spirit to the Church (see comments on Luke 24:44-53). John 1:33 clearly teaches that

Jesus Christ is the Baptizer in the Spirit. It is not a minister of the Gospel or some other Christian who does the baptizing, as in the case of water baptism. Therefore, the one seeking the baptism in the Holy Spirit should ask the Father with confidence (see comments on Luke 11:5-13) and expect to receive the gift from Christ Himself (see comments on Matt. 3:11-17).

JOHN 3:1-8 — BORN OF THE SPIRIT.

In talking to the Jewish teacher, Nicodemus, our Lord Jesus spoke of salvation as a new birth: "Ye must be born again." When Nicodemus questioned how an adult could be born a second time, Jesus explained, "Except a man be born of water and the Spirit, he cannot enter into the kingdom of God. That which is born of the flesh is flesh; and that which is born of the Spirit is spirit" (vv.5,6).

The theme of the Gospel of John is life — eternal life (cf. John 20:30,31). Because the aim of Christ's conversation was to tell Nicodemus how to have eternal life (John 3:15,16), He means that to be born again is the only way to have this new kind of life. Jesus was not talking about another physical birth, about being "born of the flesh." The natural human birth produces only another weak, sinful human being with a mortal body controlled by a selfish inner nature or soul. "No," Jesus said in effect, "you have to be born of the Spirit. Only the one who is born of the Spirit has a true spiritual nature."

In the beginning, God created man in His image (Gen. 1:27), and pronounced what He had made to be "very good" (Gen. 1:31). Man's character reflects the rational and moral qualities of the nature of God, who is spirit (John 4:24). Man is basically a compound of matter ("dust," "flesh") and spirit. In his original state, Adam was commanded to exercise dominion over the earth through the instrument of his body. Before the fall, he was able to know God and respond to Him. "This function or aspect of personality is known as "spirit." Adam was also fully

able to react to his environment and to understand himself —
the function known as "soul." As a separate individual, Adam
was a free moral agent. That is, his will was free to choose
anything he wanted, even to obey God or to rebel against His
commandments and suffer the consequences.

Why, then, does man need a new birth? Very soon after their
creation, Adam and Eve disobeyed God and thus broke their
contact with Him. When they did, they died spiritually — what
we call the fall of man. Through human reproduction, they
passed on that spiritual death to all their descendants. Therefore, the Bible says human beings are "dead in trespasses and
sins" (Eph. 2:1), spiritually cut off from the life of God (Eph.
4:18). Without the control and guidance of God's Spirit, they
live *soulishly*, operating only from their soul and body. That is
why Paul wrote, "We all once lived in the passions of our flesh,
following the desires of body and mind, and so we were by
nature children of wrath, like the rest of mankind" (Eph. 2:3
RSV).

The human spirit of the lost sinner is guilty, defiled, and
unresponsive to God, "dead" or asleep as far as He is
concerned; but it is not nonexistent. A medium, for instance,
makes contact in his spirit with evil spirits from the demonic
realm. Because of its wretched condition, one's spirit must be
forgiven, cleansed, and made alive to God. This is essentially
what happens when a person repents of his sins, receives Christ,
and is converted or saved. On the basis of Christ's dying in our
stead, God forgives us and reckons His perfect righteousness to
our account — this is what Paul means by justification (Rom.
3:21—5:21). God also sets us apart unto Himself, accounts us
holy as He sees us in His dear Son, and works to purify us —
this is sanctification (I Cor. 1:30; Eph. 5:26; Heb. 9:13,14;
13:12). Thus the image of God, which was terribly marred by
the fall of Adam as well as by our own sin, is restored through
the redemption which is in Christ Jesus.

In v.5 it is mainly our need of cleansing and a new life that

are in view. In saying we must be "born of water," Jesus
signifies the cleansing work of regeneration, and by His
expression, "born of the Spirit," He refers to the renewing work
of the Holy Spirit (see comments on Titus 3:4-7).

Jesus expected Nicodemus, an important Bible teacher in
Israel at that time, to understand these things (John 3:10). He
was not advancing some novel idea, for Ezekiel had long before
prophesied about the new birth: "Then I will sprinkle clean
water on you, and you will be clean; I will cleanse you from all
your filthiness. . . . Moreover, I will give you a new heart and
put a new spirit within you; and I will remove the heart of stone
from your flesh and give you a heart of flesh [i.e., a soft,
spiritually responsive heart]. And I will put My Spirit within
you and cause you to walk in My statutes" (Ezek. 36:25-27
NASB; John 4:10-14). These promises were to be part of the
New Covenant (Ezek. 37:24-26; Jer. 31:31-34; 32:40), and now
Messiah had come to initiate that Covenant.

But what is the water that cleanses? Nicodemus was well
aware of what John the Baptist was preaching — the necessity
of repentance. So water symbolizes the cleansing action of God's
word when we respond to God by turning away from our sins.
Paul wrote that Christ died to sanctify the Church, having
cleansed her by "the washing of water with the word" (Eph.
5:26). Later on, Jesus said to His disciples that they were
already clean because of the word which He had spoken to
them (John 15:3). And Peter declared that we have been born
again through the living and abiding word of God (I Pet.
1:3,23; cf. also Jas. 1:18). The inner cleansing that results when
we are convicted by hearing God's word and then confess our
sins, is to be sealed as soon as possible by our submission to
water baptism (see comments on Acts 22:16).

Forgiveness and cleansing are not all the sinner needs,
however. He must be "quickened" or made alive to God in his
spirit. He must be tuned in to the frequency of heaven in order
to hear and understand God's further teaching. Only the Holy

Spirit can produce this regeneration or new birth. "It is the Spirit that quickeneth" (John 6:63), i.e., the Spirit is the lifegiver (II Cor. 3:6). He is the One who plants the incorruptible seed of God's word in the human heart (I Pet. 1:23). The Holy Spirit enters the human spirit and brings it from spiritual death to eternal life. Thus the one who gives himself unreservedly to Christ becomes spiritually one with the Lord (I Cor. 6:17) and shares in the divine nature (II Pet. 1:4). By being born "again" (the Greek word can also mean "from above," John 3:31; 19:11; James 1:17; 3:15,17), the individual becomes a new creature (II Cor. 5:17, cf. Eph. 2:10). This means he is now a member of the new creation which began with the resurrection of Christ and His defeat of sin, death, and Satan. The new, divine nature supernaturally imparted to us is the indwelling Christ, "Christ in you, the hope of glory" (Col. 1:27). Because Jesus in His glorified resurrection body is now in heaven at the Father's right hand, it must be His Spirit that is in us. Therefore, Paul clearly states that if anyone does not have the Spirit of Christ, he does not belong to Him at all (Rom. 8:9). Lost sinners are described as "having not the Spirit" (Jude 19). So we may confidently say that every truly born-again believer has the Holy Spirit indwelling him (see comments on John 20:21-23).

How, then, can a person be born again? In the prologue of this Gospel, John declared that as many as received Jesus Christ the Word of God, to them He gave the right to become children of God, even to those who believe in His name. Such persons experience a birth that is not one of blood (i.e., physical descent), nor of the will of the flesh (i.e., sexual impulse), nor of the will of man (the desire of a husband for descendants), but of God alone (John 1:12,13). Thus one must believe with biblical faith in Jesus Christ as God's dear Son who gave Himself to die in the sinner's place and who rose again bodily in proof that He had accomplished our redemption (John 3:16; Rom. 10:9,10; I Cor. 15:1-4). According to the Bible, believing in Christ

includes mentally assenting to the facts about Christ and the
Gospel message (John 12:11,42), personally accepting Jesus as
one's Savior (John 9:35-38), and daily trusting and depending
on Him, confessing Him (Rom. 10:9,10), and committing one's
entire life and destiny to His care and guidance (II Tim. 1:12).

JOHN 3:34 — THE SPIRIT WITHOUT MEASURE.

In times of the mighty outpouring of the Holy Spirit, it is well
to remember that only to His Son Jesus Christ has God given
the Spirit without limit. In this verse, "he whom God hath sent"
refers to the Son of God. While John the Baptist and others
were God's messengers and prophets, Jesus was uniquely both
the message of eternal life and the predicted messenger of the
New Covenant (Mal. 3:16). He spoke the words of truth
because He was and is the Truth. Christ is God's ultimate and
perfect Spokesman because God did not give the Spirit to Him
by measure (see comments on Matt. 3:11-17; 4:23-25; Luke
4:14-21).

As His disciple, the Spirit-baptized Christian should humbly
recognize that in Jesus alone is the work of the Spirit seen in
fullest measure. In Him alone all the fullness of deity dwells in
bodily form (Col. 2:9). Jesus did promise the believer that he
could perform the same works that He did and even greater
works (see comments on John 14:12-14). But we must remember that God has allotted to each Christian a *measure* of faith
(Rom. 12:3). Therefore the one through whom the Spirit
operates in an unusual way should recognize his charismatic
ministry is from God and not think of himself more highly than
he ought to think.

Jesus Christ is God's perfect revelation to mankind (Heb.
1:1-3). He is the Head of the body; we are but members. No
Christian will ever surpass Jesus in beauty of character and
fruits of the Spirit, and no miracle or vision or utterance given
through one of us by the Spirit will ever transcend the glory and
perfection of Jesus' works.

JOHN 4:21-24 — TRUE WORSHIP.

In this hour, under the New Covenant, God is no longer requiring His worshipers to go to Jerusalem. Jesus came to usher in a new era of worship as its High Priest. At the moment of His death on the cross, the veil of the temple was torn in two from top to bottom, and the necessity of worship at the one temple ceased to exist. Christ states simply but profoundly, "God is spirit; and those who worship Him must worship in spirit and truth" (v.24 NASB).

God is spirit, i.e., completely spiritual in His essence. Therefore, if worship is to be effective, it must be spiritual in nature. It is primarily a matter of inner devotion and whole-hearted sincerity, not of outward ritual and ceremony. This is not to say that the latter have no proper function, for as Howard Ervin notes, even spiritual worship has certain liturgical forms to express its meaning. But it is true that the help of the Holy Spirit is needed to make worship genuine. Paul said that Christians worship by the Spirit of God (Phil. 3:3 ASV). The Spirit gives us a sense of the reality and presence of God as He takes the things of Christ and the Father and shows them unto us (John 16:14,15; cf. Matt. 11:27).

Genuine worship that pleases God operates in the realm of *truth* — the true knowledge of God. Our Lord has made possible a more intelligent worship of God by revealing in His teaching and through His perfect life and deeds on earth what God is really like. Even the Pharisees admitted that Jesus taught the way of God in truth (Matt. 22:16). The Spirit of truth directs the heart into prayer and praise that is in full harmony with the truth about God as revealed in His Word. God is holy; we should worship Him in the beauty of holiness (Ps. 29:2; 96:9). God is righteous and just; thus obedience is better than sacrifice (I Sam. 15:22), and the practice of righteousness should characterize our lives (Matt. 5:20; 6:33; I John 2:29; 3:7,10). God is love; therefore we are to love Him with all our heart and soul and mind and strength, and our neighbor as ourselves (Luke 10:27).

The Lord is near to all who call upon Him in truth (Ps. 145:18). In the O.T., "truth" may also mean "faithfulness." True worship and service entails turning from every other god (any person, thing, or ambition that is granted first place in one's heart) and yielding absolute loyalty to the one true and living God. Thus Joshua exhorted Israel to fear the Lord and serve Him in sincerity and in truth and to put away the idols which their ancestors had worshiped in Mesopotamia and in Egypt (Josh. 24:14; cf. Jer. 4:1,2). As the incarnate Son of God and Lamb that was slain, Jesus Himself is worthy to receive the same adoration and loyalty that belongs to the Father (Rev. 5:8-14; 4:8-11).

JOHN 6:27 — GOD'S SEAL ON CHRIST.

To prove to the assembled crowd in Capernaum that He was truly their expected Messiah, Jesus declared that God the Father had set His seal on Him (see RSV). This divine certification refers to the Holy Spirit who came upon our Lord at His baptism and to the accompanying voice from heaven, "This is my beloved Son, in whom I am well pleased" (Matt. 3:16,17; see comments on Matt. 3:11-17). In like manner, the believer is sealed with the promised Holy Spirit when he experiences the new birth (see comments on Eph. 1:13,14). In each case, the character and the works that the Spirit produces (the fruit and the supernatural gifts) are the evidence for all to see that the individual belongs to God.

JOHN 7:37-39 — RIVERS OF LIVING WATER.

Tradition says that on the last day of the week-long Feast of Tabernacles, a procession of Jewish priests would draw water from the pool of Siloam and pour it out in the temple court. By that ceremony the people were reminded how God had provided water for their thirsty ancestors in the wilderness. On this occasion, six months before His death, Jesus publicly promised to quench the spiritual thirst of everyone who will come to Him and drink (v.37).

Previously Jesus had offered "living water" to the woman of Samaria instead of the physical water from the deep well outside her village (John 4:10). Then He said, "Whoever drinks the water that I shall give him will never suffer thirst any more. The water that I shall give him will be an inner spring always welling up for eternal life" (John 4:14 NEB). Undoubtedly our Lord had in mind such passages as Isa. 12:3: "With joy shall ye draw water out of the wells of salvation," and Jer. 2:13: "They have forsaken me the fountain of living waters." In these verses, water is symbolic of salvation and everlasting life which alone can satisfy the universal desire for rest and peace and security both now and in the life to come. So to the crowd of worshipers in the temple, Jesus promised that the person who continually comes to Him will have a constant supply of life and the indwelling Spirit. But our Lord added another great promise: "He who believes in Me, as the Scripture said, 'From his innermost being shall flow rivers of living water' " (v.38 NASB). This verse describes something more than receiving salvation as in the previous verse. Here the believer becomes a source of living water to supply others. Guided by the Holy Spirit, the apostle John explains what Jesus meant: "He was speaking of the Spirit which believers in him would receive later; for the Spirit had not yet been given, because Jesus had not yet been glorified" (v.39 NEB). This passage is the clearest reference in the Gospel of John to the promise of the Holy Spirit fulfilled in the baptism beginning on the Day of Pentecost. On how to receive the baptism in the Holy Spirit, see comments on Acts 2:38-40.

No particular passage of Old Testament Scripture is quoted in v.38. But Isa. 58:11 describes a godly believer in similar fashion: "Thou shalt be like a watered garden, and like a spring of water, whose waters fail not." Jeremiah 31:12 employs this same expression. Perhaps both prophets found inspiration in the bridegroom's description of his bride, "a garden fountain, a well of living water, and flowing streams from Lebanon" (Song of Sol. 4:15 RSV). Also, the child of God is exhorted in Proverbs to watch over his heart, "for from it flow the springs of life" (Prov. 4:23 NASB). Jesus' figure of speech may also have been suggested by Ezekiel's vision of the lifegiving river flowing from the future temple in Jerusalem during the millennial kingdom (Ezek. 47:1-12; cf. Ps. 46:4; Joel 3:18; Zech. 14:8; Rev. 22:1,2). In this age, each individual Christian is a temple of the Holy Spirit (I Cor. 3:16; 6:19), out of which the Spirit may flow in blessing and healing power. The O.T. connects the pouring forth of refreshing streams with the coming of the Spirit (Isa. 32:15; 44:3). Therefore, taking all these passages together, the clause in v.38, "as the scripture hath said," is entirely justified.

This beautiful word picture teaches us much about the overflowing life of the Spirit-filled Christian. First of all, his own needs are met. His own deep spiritual thirst is already being quenched through the regenerating work of the Spirit of God living in his spirit (John 3:5; 7:37). Then when Jesus baptizes him in the Holy Spirit, the Lord causes the Spirit to rise and overflow from where He is dwelling inside the believer, to inundate his soul and body as well.

In many cases, this experience brings about a needed release of the whole person, as if a dam were opened and the pent-up waters rushed forth. To use Dennis Bennett's illustration of an irrigation ditch, before the canal is filled, it is dry and so are the fields around. Then the gate of the reservoir is opened. First, the canal itself is washed clean of dust and debris, and grass and flowers begin to spring up along its banks. But the water doesn't stop there; all along the way farmers open sluices, and the life-giving water streams out into the fields to make "the desert rejoice and blossom as the rose" (Isa. 35:1).

"So with you and me. The reservoir, the well, is in us when we become Christians. Then, when we allow the indwelling living water of the Spirit to flow out into our souls and bodies, *we* are refreshed first. Our minds come alive in a new way to God's reality. We begin to think of Him, even dream of Him, with a new frequency and joy. Our emotions respond, and we begin to be happy in Him. Our will responds, and we begin to do what He wants. Our bodies respond, not only by feelings of well-being, but by actual renewed strength and health and youth. Then the living water begins to pour out on others, and they see the power and love of Jesus in His people. He is now able to use us to refresh the world around us" (Dennis & Rita Bennett, *The Holy Spirit and You* [Plainfield: Logos, 1971], p. 21).   A second point to notice in Jesus' word picture is that the waters flow out from the belly and not the brain. The Greek word for "belly" or innermost being is *koilia*, the abdomen or body cavity containing the entire digestive tract including the stomach (Matt. 15:17; Luke 15:16; I Cor. 6:13; Rev. 10:9,10). It also means the womb (Luke 1:15,41,42; John 3:4). Here, following the usage of the corresponding Hebrew word, it denotes the hidden, innermost recesses of one's being (Job 15:35; Ps. 31:9; Prov. 18:8; 20:27,30; Hab. 3:16). The O.T. does not associate the spirit with the head or brain or mental capacity but with the heart (Ps. 51:10,17; Prov. 15:13; 17:22; Isa. 57:15; Ezek. 11:19; 18:31; 36:26). Paul also distinguishes his spirit from his mind, for by means of tongues he can pray with the spirit, and he can pray with the understanding also (I Cor. 14:14,15).

It is God's intention for the Holy Spirit to "flow forth" from the Christian's innermost being and control his entire person. Actually this is a great blessing to the believer. As David du Plessis says, he no longer has to pump up the water and pour it forth himself; the rivers *flow* out of him. God does not expect the Spirit-filled Christian to reach out to others by means of ingenuity or superior intelligence. Rather, he waits for the Spirit to direct and empower him.

Third, Jesus makes His promise to the one who continually

believes in and relies on Him. This is the force of the Greek present tense in the word "believeth" in v.38. An uninterrupted flow — continuous fruitbearing, regular witness, and faithful service — results from depending on the Lord moment by moment and being continually filled with the Spirit (see comments on Eph. 5:15-21). In the new Jerusalem, the river of the water of life will enable the tree of life to bear twelve kinds of fruit, yielding its fruit every month (Rev. 22:1,2). Let each believer be such a tree now (cf. Ps. 1:3; Jer. 17:8).

Fourth, the word "rivers" in v.38 suggests a copious flow of blessing. The person abiding in Christ bears "much fruit" (John 15:5). The believer is empowered to do the works of Christ, yes, even greater works (John 14:12). He experiences the abundant life (John 10:10), always abounding in the work of the Lord (I Cor. 15:58). The virtues of the Christian life abound in him so that he is assured of a glorious entrance into the eternal kingdom of our Lord and Savior Jesus Christ (II Pet. 1:5-11). He pleases the Lord in all respects and is always increasing in the knowledge of God, strengthened with all might according to His glorious power (Col. 1:10,11). God enables him to fulfill every good resolve and work of faith by His power (II Thess. 1:11 RSV).

A verse in Proverbs suggests one of the main channels through which the "rivers of living water" may flow out of the believer's life to others. "The words of a man's mouth are as deep waters, a flowing brook, a fountain of wisdom" (Prov. 18:4 JPS). Similar is Prov. 10:11, "The mouth of the righteous is a fountain of life" (NASB). In the N.T., James compared the mouth from which blessing comes with a fountain that sends forth "sweet" (fresh, pure) water (James 3:10,11; see comments on James 3:1-12). The Holy Spirit brings forth prophecies that edify and exhort and comfort (I Cor. 14:3). Spirit-overflowing Christians are those who talk with each other much about the Lord (cf. Mal. 3:16), love to sing psalms and hymns and charismatic songs, and are always giving thanks for everything to God (Eph. 5:18-20).

JOHN 14:12-14 — GREATER WORKS THAN THESE.

The promise that the Lord Jesus makes here regarding prayer is almost breathtaking. Preparing to place His ministry in the hands of His disciples, He says to them in the Upper Room and to us today, "He who believes in Me, the works that I do shall he do also; and greater works than these shall he do; because I go to the Father" (v.12 NASB). Greater works through the Church, His new body.

Most Bible commentators believe that the "greater works" are greater in quantity or are miracles of conversion in the spiritual realm. Jesus had scores of converts; the apostles numbered theirs in the thousands. Jesus ministered only to the Jews in Palestine; Peter opened the door for Gentiles to be saved at Cornelius' house, and the early Christians soon reached the known world.

Finis J. Dake, however, points out in his annotated Bible that by the term "works," Jesus is referring to His miracles, healings, signs, and mighty acts of power (Matt. 11:2; cf. 11:5; John 5:20,36; 9:3,4; 10:25,32; 14:10-12; 15:24). His works included healing every kind of disease, casting out demons, raising the dead. He controlled the wind and the waves, walked on water, multiplied food, and turned water into wine. The promise here is that each believer can receive the Holy Spirit and be endued with power so that potentially he can do all the works of Christ.

Dake continues: "To make this a promise of spiritual works only, when He did (both) material and spiritual works, is a poor excuse for unbelief. . . . The greater works are not those of reaching more people by means of radio, television, and the printed page, for these are natural means and can be used by unsaved men who do not have the Holy Spirit power to do the works of Christ. No man can receive greater power than Christ,

for He received the Spirit without measure (John 3:34; Isa.
11:2; 61:1,2). Therefore, the greater works could not consist of
doing greater things than Christ could have done had He had
the occasion to do them. The thought is that each believer can
have equal power with Christ to do what He did as well as
greater things if and when the occasion requires it" (*Dake's
Annotated Reference Bible* [Grand Rapids: Zondervan, 1961],
p.112a of the New Testament; see also p.121 for twenty-one
reasons why greater works are now possible). See comments on
John 3:34.

JOHN 14:15-18,26 — ANOTHER COMFORTER.

Some of the most important passages in the Bible about the
Holy Spirit occur in the Upper Room teachings of Christ (John
13-16). Only on that night before He was betrayed did Jesus
ever refer to the Spirit as Comforter. In response to the love and
obedience of His disciples, He promised to request the Father to
give them "another Comforter" (v.16).

Much can be learned about the Holy Spirit from this
expression. The Greek term for Comforter, *parakletos,* is difficult
to translate by a single English word. Thus newer English
versions have Helper (NASB), Counselor (RSV), or Advocate
(NEB). In I John 2:1, the same Greek word is used of Christ
and is translated in nearly all English versions as "Advocate."
In v.16, *The Amplified Bible* also suggests Intercessor, Strengthen-
er, and Standby. To cover all these meanings, an English
word, Paraclete, has been coined from the Greek term.
Basically it means one who is called alongside to help, to
counsel, or to intercede in behalf of someone else. A Paraclete is
like an intimate friend who acts as a personal adviser, such as
an aide-de-camp or special consultant or a private assistant to
an emperor or a president.

The Holy Spirit is our "Comforter" because He pleads,
convinces, and convicts when necessary; because He both
strengthens and defends us in time of formidable attacks. Now

we have two divine Paracletes. Christ has gone to heaven to be the Advocate who pleads the believer's case with the Father against the accuser Satan. The Holy Spirit has come to earth to be the Advocate who helps the believer take a stand against the world (John 15:18-27; 16:8-11). He also "comforts" churches by the exhortation and encouragement which He supplies through His gifts (Acts 9:31; I Cor. 14:3-5).

The phrase, "another Comforter," distinctly marks the personality of the Holy Spirit and His true deity. The Greek word *allos*, for "another," indicates simply a distinction of individuals, not a difference in kind. Therefore the Spirit is another Paraclete of the same kind as Jesus; and our Lord is both a person and God. The Holy Spirit is of the same divine essence or nature as God the Son. Thus He is also called the Spirit of Christ (Rom. 8:9; Phil. 1:19; I Pet. 1:11), the Spirit of Jesus (Acts 16:7 NASB, cf. 16:6), and the Spirit of God's Son (Gal. 4:6).

Christ promises not to leave His disciples "comfortless" (v.18). The Greek word is *orphanous*, "orphans." Disciples of a teacher were often called his children (Gal. 4:19; I John 2:1; 3:18); and when he died they considered themselves as orphans, as in the case of Socrates' friends. Jesus has just called His disciples, "children" (John 13:33), and now assures them that they will not be orphans, because He is going to come back to them in the sending forth of the Spirit at Pentecost. The coming of the Holy Spirit does not exclude Christ but makes real to us His continual presence and fellowship (John 14:21-23).

Jesus identifies this other Comforter as the Spirit of truth in John 14:17,26; 16:13. John also uses this description of the Spirit in his epistle (I John 4:6; 5:6). Literally, the expression is "the Spirit of the truth," the truth about God and Christ and salvation. He is the Spirit of the truth because He guides men to the very fullness of the truth ("into all the truth," John 16:13 NASB). As the *Jerusalem Bible* points out (p.179, note r), He teaches us to understand the mystery of Christ (Eph. 3:4; Col.

4:3), such as Jesus' fulfillment of the Scriptures that bear witness of Him (John 5:39; 12:14-16) and the meaning of His enigmatic words (John 2:19-22), actions (John 13:6,7,12-17), and signs (Matt. 12:38-40; 16:1-4).

In v.26 Christ gives the Comforter His full title, "The Holy Spirit." We need always to be reminded as He guides our lives that the moral character of the Spirit of God is *holy*. While He has come to glorify Christ and not Himself (John 16:14), we should always speak reverently of the Holy Spirit and honor Him as we honor the Father and the Son. It is very possible to grieve the Holy Spirit of God by unwholesome words and bitterness and malice (see comments on Eph. 4:30).

Jesus' Upper Room discourses reveal several specific reasons for sending the Comforter. First, the Holy Spirit came to teach Christians "all things" (v.26a), everything that is necessary for their salvation and fellowship with God and for the work of witnessing (cf. Matt. 10:20; I John 2:27). Included are various truths which Jesus had not specifically taught during His time on earth (John 16:12,13,25). Part of this promise covers bringing to remembrance the very words Christ spoke (v.26b), thus explaining how Matthew, Mark, Luke, and John could write down the actual teachings of Jesus years after His ascension (see comments on II Pet. 1:19-21). The Spirit of truth will also disclose to us what is to come (John 16:13), i.e., announce future events. Often this revelation will be given by a prophecy, such as Agabus' warning of a coming famine (Acts 11:28).

Second, the Spirit came to bear witness concerning Christ (John 15:26). He interprets and applies the message of redemption to the Church and through the Church to the world. By effecting miracles, the Holy Spirit, together with Christians, produces an irrefutable testimony to the fact that Jesus Christ has risen and is Lord (I Cor. 12:3). As a result of the Pentecostal empowering (Acts 1:8), the Holy Spirit and believers in Christ bear a joint witness (Acts 15:28 — "It seemed good to the Holy Ghost, and to us"; Rev. 22:17 — "The Spirit and the bride say, Come").

Third, the Paraclete serves as the Christian's defense attorney when he is persecuted by the world. He not only instructs the believer what he ought to say (see comments on Matt. 10:16-20), but also takes the position of prosecutor against the hostile world by convicting it of the sin of unbelief and warning it of future judgment (John 16:7-11). He reproves the world of sin, which is defined basically as the refusal to accept Jesus and His message (John 16:9). He convinces the world of righteousness, which was supremely demonstrated in Jesus Christ, and vindicated when He rose victorious over sin and death and ascended to the Father. Now the Holy Spirit convicts the sinner of his need of righteousness as he hears the Word of righteousness or as he sees it exemplified in the life of a godly Christian. The Spirit convicts the world of judgment; for the same ministry, death, and resurrection of Jesus whereby God condemned Satan, the present evil ruler of this world system, will be God's basis for judging the unrepentant sinner (Acts 17:30,31).

After studying the verses about the Comforter, one may ask, Who sent the Holy Spirit, and when did He come? Verses 16 and 26 teach that *the Father* gives or sends the Spirit, whereas in John 15:26 and 16:7, Jesus said, "I will send Him to you." There is no contradiction, for the Father and the Son always exist in closest intimacy. John 15:26 is the most important of these verses, in which Christ says that He will send the Comforter to His disciples from (Greek *para*, from alongside) the Father, "even the Spirit of truth, who proceeds from (*para*) the Father." The verb "proceeds" is in the present tense, suggesting that the Spirit as a person continuously comes forth from the presence of the Father.

On the basis of this verse, the Eastern Orthodox churches have always claimed that the Spirit eternally proceeds from the Father *through* the Son. They eventually split with the Roman

Catholic churches which believed that the Spirit proceeds from the Father *and* the Son. In keeping with His being called the Spirit of Christ and with the equality of the Father, the Son, and the Holy Spirit, the latter, or Western position, seems to be more scriptural (see also Acts 2:33).

By these promises about the Comforter, did Christ signify the giving of the Spirit in regeneration after His resurrection (see comments on John 20:21-23), or the Pentecostal outpouring of the Spirit on the church? In v.16 Jesus says, "I will pray the Father . . . ," indicating a future time when He will make a formal request of the Father to give the Spirit. In John 16:7, He states that His ascension is a necessary precondition of the coming of the Spirit: "It is to your advantage that I go away; for if I do not go away, the Helper shall not come to you; but if I go, I will send Him to you" (NASB). It is in His *absence* that the Lord Jesus will *send* the Comforter to them. Therefore He clearly points to the Day of Pentecost and not to the night of His resurrection when He personally imparted the Spirit of life to His followers. Peter's testimony in Acts 2:33 confirms this view: "Therefore having been exalted to the right hand of God, and having received from the Father the promise of the Holy Spirit, He has poured forth this which you both see and hear" (NASB).

Our Lord further promises that when the Father gives another Comforter, the Spirit will be with us *forever* (v.16). In this age, since Pentecost, the Holy Spirit does not come on men temporarily merely to perform some task, as He did in O.T. times. The pattern for the life and ministry of each believer in this age is to be found in Jesus Christ, and it is to be noted that at His baptism the Spirit descended *and remained* upon Him (John 1:33). The continual abiding of the Spirit is an integral promise of the New Covenant: " 'This is My covenant with them,' says the Lord: 'My Spirit which is upon you, and My words which I have put in your mouth, shall not depart from your mouth, nor from the mouth of your offspring . . .' " says the Lord, " 'from now and forever' " (Isa. 59:21 NASB). The Holy Spirit is not to be taken away from the world at the Rapture, as some men have taught (see comments on II Thess. 2:6,7), but will be present during the Tribulation, to aid believers (Mark 13:11; see comments on Matt. 4:23-25; Luke 4:14-21; Acts 2:14-21).

Speaking of the Holy Spirit, in the latter part of v.17 Jesus says, "But ye know him; for he dwelleth with you, and shall be in you." Actually all three Greek verbs were probably in the present tense in the original manuscript of John. Jesus is simply anticipating the future period when the gift of the Comforter will be a reality. We may paraphrase: "The world will not be able to receive the Spirit of truth when He is given, because it will neither see Him nor know Him. But once the Spirit has arrived, you will know Him, because He will both dwell at your side and be within you."

It is by the Holy Spirit, then, that Jesus Christ, the glorified Son of God and our great Shepherd and High Priest, now pours His love into our hearts and manifests Himself to each believer (John 14:21).

John 20:21-23 — RECEIVE YE THE HOLY GHOST.

The setting of this command was the Upper Room at evening time on the first day of the week, several nights after the crucifixion. The disciples had locked the doors for fear of the Jewish leaders. Suddenly Jesus was standing there among them! Yes, the reports were true; He had risen from the dead! He showed them the wounds in His hands and His side, and they were convinced. "How wonderful was their joy as they saw their Lord!" (John 20:20 TLB).

After greeting them Jesus breathed on them and said, "Receive the Holy Spirit" (v.22 RSV). How should we relate this giving of the Holy Spirit to the outpouring of the Spirit at Pentecost? Luke recorded a subsequent appearance of Christ after His resurrection, and at that time He ordered His disciples to wait in Jerusalem until they would be endued with power from on high (Luke 24:49). So they did not receive supernatural power when the Lord breathed on them. Rather, they received the new resurrection life of Christ who had just risen from the dead. This was the first occasion when He could actually impart to them eternal life in its fullest sense. This is the climax of the Gospel of John, the Gospel of life in the Son of God. It is the beginning of the new creation. The disciples enter the New Covenant through the new birth.

The Greek verb for "breathed," *emphusao,* occurs only here in the N.T. But it is used in Gen. 2:7 in the Septuagint (the Greek translation of the O.T.) in the account of man's original creation: "And the Lord God formed man *of* the dust of the ground, and breathed into his nostrils the breath of life; and man became a living soul." The verb is also found in Ezekiel's vision of the dry bones, depicting the national and spiritual rebirth of Israel: "Then He said to me, 'Prophesy to the breath . . . "Thus says the Lord God, 'Come from the four winds, O breath, and breathe on these slain, that they come to life' " ' " (Ezek. 37:9 NASB). The new birth is pictured here because God says in Ezek. 37:14, "I will put My Spirit within you, and you will come to life" (NASB). The Hebrew word *ruach,* like the Greek word *pneuma,* means either "wind," "breath," or "spirit," according to the context. Thus wind or breath is an especially fitting symbol of the Spirit of God in His invisible operation (see John 3:8).

When God breathes, a creative act takes place. This was true of Adam in the Garden of Eden. Job's friend Elihu recognized that the breath of the Almighty gave him life (Job 33:4). The psalmist says that all the hosts of heaven were made by the breath of God's mouth (Ps. 33:6). "All scripture is given by inspiration of God" (II Tim. 3:16); literally, "all Scripture is God-breathed" (Greek *theopneustos*). The Holy Spirit has inspired every word of the original manuscripts of the Bible so that it is truly God's creation (see comments on II Pet. 1:19-21). Therefore, when Jesus blew upon His disciples, His act had symbolic significance. He was imparting the Holy Spirit to convey regeneration to His followers and make them new creatures (II Cor. 5:17). At that moment they were born of God.

Along with the life of Jesus which they received was the responsibility and authority to minister His new life to others. In order for lost sinners to be born again, their sins must be forgiven. Thus Christ commissioned His disciples to act as prophets in pronouncing either God's grace or His judgment: "If you forgive the sins of any, their sins have been forgiven them; if you retain the sins of any, they have been retained" (v.23 NASB). Bishop B. F. Westcott explained that this promise "gives a living and abiding power to declare the fact and the conditions of forgiveness. . . . The exercise of the power must be placed in the closest connexion with the faculty of spiritual discernment consequent upon the gift of the Holy Spirit. Cf. I John 2:18 ff." (*Gospel of St. John* [London: John Murray, 1898], p.295). It is God alone who can forgive sins (Mark 2:7); the Christian worker can only declare that which God has already done. What the Lord commits to us is the privilege of giving assurance of the remission of sins by God as we correctly announce the terms of forgiveness to be found in the Word of God.

ACTS

ACTS 1:4-8 — YE SHALL RECEIVE POWER.

The Holy Spirit is a favorite theme of Luke, who wrote both the third Gospel and the Book of Acts. He was inspired to select the source material (cf. Luke 1:1-4) and to narrate the incidents which emphasize the activity and power of the Spirit (e.g., Luke

1:35; 4:14; 10:19-21; 24:49; Acts 4:31,33; 10:38). Therefore
this book has appropriately been called "The Acts of the Holy
Spirit."

The words of the risen Lord Jesus in Acts 1:4,5 prove beyond
the shadow of a doubt that the baptism in the Holy Spirit, and
not the new birth, is the fulfillment of God the Father's
"promise" (see comments on Luke 24:44-53). Taken in connection with Acts 1:8 and 2:1-4, these words also show that the
outpouring of the Spirit on the Day of Pentecost was the first
historical occurrence of the baptism in the Spirit. This was to be
the baptism which Christ Himself performs, as John the Baptist
had originally announced (see comments on Matt. 3:11-17).
After Pentecost, the Holy Spirit fell upon Cornelius and his
household so that they spoke in tongues just as the first
Christians did. That reminded the apostle Peter of these very
words of Jesus in Acts 1:5: "And I remembered the word of the
Lord, how he said, John indeed baptized with water; but ye
shall be baptized in the Holy Spirit" (Acts 11:16 ASV).

While giving His final instructions to the apostles concerning
the kingdom of God, Jesus warned them about going forth
excitedly but unprepared. He commanded them to wait in
Jerusalem for the coming of the Holy Spirit before they began
their service for Him. But they seemed more interested to find
out when He as Messiah would restore political freedom to
Israel. He did not correct the disciples regarding their expectation of a future literal kingdom, but said it was not for them to
know those dates. Much more relevant was the immediate task
ahead of them.

"But you shall receive power when the Holy Spirit has come
upon you; and you shall be My witnesses . . . even to the
remotest part of the earth" (v.8 NASB; see comments on Matt.
28:18-20; Mark 16:9-20; Luke 24:44-53; and John 20:21-23).
Here He clearly stated the effect and purpose of the baptism in
the Spirit. It is power — power to be His witnesses.

The Greek word for "power" in Acts 1:8 is *dynamis*. It is not

exousia, the power or right to become a child of God as in John
1:12, which speaks about the new birth. *Dynamis* means
inherent strength (II Cor. 1:8) or ability to perform effectively
(Matt. 25:15; II Cor. 8:3). The power of the Holy Spirit is not
an external possession that one can purchase or sell (cf. Acts
8:18-20), but is a living and abiding presence in the Christian.
Those who have received the Spirit-Baptism have a new
potential. The more the Spirit overflows and uses them, the
more powerful and skillful are their words and deeds.

The power to be Christ's witness (Acts 4:33) can be both
miraculous (Acts 6:8) and moral (II Cor. 6:6,7; Eph. 3:16; Col.
1:11). Christians are empowered to perform signs and wonders
in order to bring men into obedience to Christ (Rom. 15:18,19)
and give them full assurance of the gospel message (I Thess. 1:5;
Heb. 2:4; I Cor. 2:4,5). In the N.T., believers were given power
to heal and to cast out demons (Luke 9:1; Acts 8:6,7,13;
19:11,12). But also the power of Christ enables one to endure
and be strong in times of weakness and suffering (II Cor.
12:9,10). This, too, is a witness.

Witnesses (*martyres*) are those who "testify" (from *martyreo*) by
act or word their "testimony" (*martyrion*) to the truth. A
distinctly legal term, as it still is, in Christian usage "testimony"
came to mean the witness given to Christ and His saving and
delivering power. Such witnessing often meant arrest and
scourging (Matt. 10:17,18; Acts 16:16-24), exile (Rev. 1:9), or
even death (Acts 22:20; Rev. 2:13; 17:6); hence the English
word "martyr" came to mean one who dies rather than give up
his faith.

Witnessing is at the heart of all evangelistic and missionary
activity. Several principles emerge from a study of the N.T., as
the article on "Witness" by Fred L. Fisher in *Baker's Dictionary of
Theology* (Grand Rapids: Baker Book House, 1960 [pp.555f.])
points out. (1) Witnessing is the universal obligation of every
Christian (Luke 24:48; Acts 1:8). Not only the apostles but all
120 believers bore witness to Jesus' resurrection on the Day of

Pentecost (Acts 2:4,32). We are to entrust the message to others who will continue the witness (II Tim. 2:2). (2) Our testimony is to concentrate on the facts and meaning of Christ's earthly ministry, death, and bodily resurrection (Acts 4:33; 10:38-41) and on His salvation from sin (Acts 10:42,43; I Cor. 15:1-4). (3) Christians are to confess Jesus Christ before men regardless of the opposition and their own personal safety or comfort (Matt. 10:32-42). (4) Christian witnessing will be attended by the ministry of the Holy Spirit and the manifestation of His power (Mark 16:15-20; Rom. 15:18,19; Heb. 2:3,4).

Acts 2:1-4 — PENTECOST!

The long-anticipated day had finally come! A new era in God's gracious dealings with mankind was dawning. God the Father would keep His promise! Jesus Christ the Son would pour forth the Spirit! Joel's prophecy was about to be fulfilled!

Unaware of the momentous significance of this day, multiplied thousands of Jews had congregated in Jerusalem for the Feast of Weeks. At the great Jewish feasts as many as 180,000 came to worship, and 120,000-150,000 might be pilgrims from other countries speaking other languages as their native tongue (see Joachim Jeremias, *Jerusalem in the Time of Jesus* [Philadelphia: Fortress Press, 1969], pp. 58-84).

The Feast of Weeks was the second of the three principal harvest festivals requiring the attendance of the godly Jew at the temple (Exod. 23:14-17; 34:18-23). The first was the Feast of Unleavened Bread, and the third the Feast of Booths or Tabernacles (Deut. 16:16). It was called the Feast of Weeks because it came a week of weeks (seven weeks) after the Feast of Firstfruits when a sheaf of newlycut barley was waved before the Lord (Lev. 23:10-16; Deut. 16:9,10). Firstfruits closely followed the Passover. The Passover sacrifice began the weeklong Feast of Unleavened Bread, and Firstfruits was the second day of that feast, the first day being observed as a sabbath. On the fiftieth day after Firstfruits, every Hebrew male was to return to the Lord's house to present a new grain offering, the firstfruits from his wheat harvest (Exod. 34:22; Lev. 23:15-21; Num. 28:26; Deut. 16:9-12; see comments on Rom. 8:23-27). According to early Jewish writings (Tob. 2:1; II Macc. 12:31,32), the feast was already called Pentecost before the birth of Christ. The term simply means "fiftieth" in Greek.

The average Jew in O.T. times had no conception that the Day of Pentecost had any typical significance. Much later, according to the Talmud, they began to observe it as the day commemorating the giving of the Law on Mount Sinai. This was without scriptural warrant, but because they calculated that God had appeared to Moses on the mountain top on the fiftieth day after Passover. But the meaning of Pentecost to the Christian is far richer than that! Passover, of course, is a type of Christ, our Passover, sacrificed for us at Calvary (I Cor. 5:7), and illustrates our redemption from death. The Feast of Unleavened Bread, which lasted for seven days, typifies the lifelong walk of the child of God separated from the leaven of sin and evil. The Feast of Firstfruits perhaps can be said to be a type of the resurrection of Christ, "the first fruits of those who are asleep" (I Cor. 15:20, 23 NASB); cf. John 12:24; Rev. 1:5). The crossing of the Red Sea a few days after the first Passover historically set Israel free from Egyptian slavery. Therefore its account often is used to depict our liberation from bondage — the bondage of sin — through our resurrection with Christ. And finally, Pentecost, coming as it does at the end of the grain harvest, pictures for us the great harvest of souls in this age which began that very day and resulted in the first Christian church. As the followers of Moses were united at Mount Sinai under the Old Covenant and were given the Law to prepare them to go forth to possess the Promised Land, so at Pentecost the disciples of Jesus were empowered by the Spirit under the New Covenant to go forth to give the Gospel to the farthest corners of the earth.

Luke records that when the Day of Pentecost had come, or

"was in process of being fulfilled" (Wuest), the 120 disciples (Acts 1:15) were all together in one place (2:1). While many have supposed this place was the Upper Room because Luke uses the word "house" in 2:2, several factors point to their being at the temple: (1) no roof-top room (Acts 1:13) of an ordinary Jewish home in crowded Jerusalem was large enough to handle 120 persons; (2) Luke specifically says that after Jesus' ascension His followers "were continually in the temple, praising God" (Luke 24:53 NASB); (3) the disciples were devout Jews and were expected to be present in the temple area for the ceremonies of the Feast of Weeks; (4) on several other occasions Luke refers to the temple by the term "house" (Greek *oikos;* see Luke 11:51; 19:46; Acts 7:47,49; cf. also Matt. 21:13; Mark 11:17; John 2:16; and often in both O.T. and N.T., it is called the house of God or the Lord's house); and (5) the multitude gathered around the disciples right away upon hearing the sound of their voices praising God in many new tongues (v.6). Note that Luke indicates the crowd came to the Christians, not that the latter left their house to come to the temple. From a practical standpoint, this could happen only if the Christians were already in the broad open area of the temple court, for the streets of the city were like narrow, winding alleys. Also, the traditional house of the Upper Room (cf. Acts 1:13) is far removed from the site of the temple, on the opposite side of the city.

All the more wonderful, then, that the Holy Spirit should fall (cf. Acts 11:15) on the disciples of Jesus in plain view of the vast crowd of Jews present at the temple that morning. God sovereignly displayed His power on that occasion. There were unique signs for that initial outpouring of His Spirit that seldom, if ever, have combined on subsequent occasions when men have received the Holy Spirit. Symbolizing the Spirit as wind or breath, "suddenly there came an echoing sound out of heaven as of a wind borne along violently" (Wuest), and it filled the whole temple where the disciples were quietly sitting. And symbolizing the individual, inward, purifying work of the Holy Spirit coming to indwell God's people, there appeared *to them* — therefore evidently not to any onlookers — tongues as of fire. These distributed themselves so that a flame rested on each one of the believers. John the Baptist had foretold this phenomenon when he announced that the One coming after him would baptize with the Holy Spirit and fire (Matt. 3:11,12; see comments on Matt. 3:11-17). Maynard James calls the "cloven tongues like as of fire" the emblem of dynamic purification. He points out that Jesus had no need of purification from sin, for He had no taint of depravity. Hence the Holy Spirit who came "without measure" to the spotless Son of God appeared as a dove (*I Believe in the Holy Ghost* [Minneapolis: Bethany, 1963], p.48).

Also there was another sign given for the first time that day but which has continued. In the early Church it became the normal accompaniment of receiving the Baptism in the Holy Spirit. Jesus had told His disciples that certain signs would accompany those who believe, and speaking with new tongues was one of those signs (Mark 16:17). When the disciples were inundated with the Holy Spirit, they "began to speak with other tongues, as the Spirit was giving them utterance" (v.4 NASB). This is the phenomenon often called glossolalia, coined from the two Greek words *glossa,* meaning "tongue," and *laleo,* meaning "to speak."

Without going into a long proof (for such proof see Henry Alford, *The Greek Testament,* 4th ed. [1861], II, 15-17), it is certain that the "tongues" which the Christians spoke were not gibberish, but real languages. However, these were "other" than their native language or any other language which they had ever learned. "The miracle was in the giving of the ability to speak these languages, not in sensitizing in some way the ears of the hearers" (C. C. Ryrie, *The Acts of the Apostles* [Chicago: Moody Press, 1961], p.19). This sign was meant especially for the unconverted Jews present at the festival, just as Paul later wrote that tongues are for a sign, not to those who believe, but to unbelievers (I Cor. 14:22). Certainly the result on the Day of Pentecost agrees with this stated purpose, because the Jews were amazed and marveled when each one heard his own particular language or dialect spoken by one of the Christians. What they heard was not incoherent, unintelligible utterance, but men and women praising the Lord in languages which communicated "the wonderful works of God" (Acts 2:11). Most of them could account for it only by recognizing it as something miraculous and supernatural, although a few mockingly said the disciples must be drunk. It is evident from the experience of the Day of Pentecost, however, that speaking in tongues is not only a rational discourse in an unknown language but may be accompanied by a holy joy, a kind of divine inebriation.

Luke states that the 120 brethren were "all filled with the Holy Spirit" (v.4 NASB). This was the baptism in the Holy Spirit for which Jesus had prepared them just before His ascension (Acts 1:5). This was their reception of the gift of the Holy Spirit promised by the Father (see comments on Luke 24:44-53). It is important to remember that the Holy Spirit was already dwelling in them, for the Lord Jesus had conferred on them new life in the Spirit on the night after His resurrection (see comments on John 20:21-23). That new life was the Holy Spirit joined to their spirits. From that moment on, they were spiritually united to Christ (I Cor. 6:17; Rom. 8:9).

Now on the Feast of Pentecost, the Father poured out the Holy Spirit upon the waiting disciples. As Dennis Bennett explains it, the Spirit of God "overwhelmed them — this is what the Scripture means when it says He 'fell upon them,' or 'came upon them' — baptizing their souls and bodies in the power and the glory that was already dwelling in their spirits. . . . He overflowed from them out into the world around, inspiring them to praise and glorify God, not only in their own tongues, but in new languages, and in so doing, tamed their tongues to His use, freed their spirits, renewed their minds, refreshed their bodies, and brought power to witness" (*The Holy Spirit and You*, pp. 28,29). For additional discussion on being filled with the Spirit, see comments on Acts 4:8; on controlling the tongue, see comments on James 3:1-12; on other instances of speaking in tongues, see comments on Acts 8:5-25; 9:1-22; 10:44-48; 19:1-7; I Cor. 14:1-33.

Acts 2:14-21 — JOEL'S PROPHECY.

Dr. A. J. Gordon of Boston once called Joel's prophecy of the outpouring of the Spirit the Magna Charta of the Christian Church. Truly it is God's great charter of spiritual power and liberty for every true believer in Jesus Christ.

Joel was one of the earliest of the writing prophets of the O.T., prophesying about 830 B.C. to warn the people of Jerusalem concerning the judgment of the Day of the Lord. But he also gave the clearest prophecy in the Jewish Scriptures of the mighty revival to be brought by the Holy Spirit (Joel 2:28-32). This was the passage which the apostle Peter used in order to explain the amazing events of the Day of Pentecost.

One may well ask, What was new or different about the coming of the Spirit on that day? Was not the Holy Spirit active throughout the O.T. and during the life and ministry of Christ? Yes, certainly. But Pentecost marked a new beginning of the work of the Spirit in two ways: His coming was universal, and it was permanent.

The miracle of Pentecost was that the Holy Spirit was poured out upon *all* believers (Acts 2:1,4,17,18). In O.T. times, the Holy Spirit was given only to the few — chiefly to priests, kings, judges, and prophets — whereas now He may be received by every child of God. Joel foretold the Spirit's being poured out "upon all flesh," upon every significant division of mankind. The Spirit's coming is universal in the four basic categories of human beings. (1) As to race, He is poured out upon both Jew and Gentile, "upon *all* flesh" (cf. I Cor. 12:13); (2) as to sex, upon both male and female, "your sons and your daughters" (cf. Gal. 3:28); (3) as to age, upon both young and old, "your young men . . . and your old men"; and (4) as to social rank, upon both slave and free, "even upon My bondslaves, both men and women" (Acts 2:18 NASB; cf. I Cor. 12:13). This universal aspect is new and unique to this age. Moses had lamented in his day, "Would God that all the Lord's people were prophets, and that the Lord would put his spirit upon them" (Num. 11:29). Joel's prophecy concerning the Spirit is as extensive as his promise that everyone who calls on the name of the Lord shall be saved (Acts 2:21). Therefore Peter boldly declared that the promised gift of the Holy Spirit was for the Jews and their descendants and for all who are "afar off" — i.e., Gentiles — even as many as the Lord will call to Himself (Acts 2:39).

The other unprecedented feature of the outpouring of the Spirit at Pentecost is that He came to *abide* in those who receive Him. His power is now available to each and every believer constantly, for the needs and emergencies of every day. He no longer comes upon a certain man only occasionally and fleetingly, as He did on Othniel (Judg. 3:10) or Gideon (Judg. 6:34) or Jephthah (Judg. 11:29) or Samson (Judg. 14:6; 15:14; cf. 16:20). As the Spirit descended upon Jesus at His baptism to remain upon Him (John 1:33), so the Lord promised that the Comforter would remain with His followers forever (John 14:16). In this factor lies the import of God's prophecy to Isaiah in 59:21: " 'And as for Me, this is My covenant with them,' says the Lord: 'My Spirit which is upon you, and My words which I have put in your mouth, shall not depart from your mouth, nor from the mouth of your offspring,' says the Lord, 'from now and forever' " (NASB). Likewise John the Apostle wrote that the anointing which Christians receive from the Lord *abides* (permanently) in them (I John 2:27 TAB; see comments on I John 2:20,27). It is this constant supply of divine power which distinguishes the Pentecostal ministry of the apostles from their evangelistic tours during the lifetime of Jesus. Then He had to delegate His power and authority for each mission (Luke 9:1,2), and sometimes they were unable to minister deliverance in particularly difficult cases (Mark 9:14-18,28,29).

Joel's prophecy also clearly states that the outpouring of the Holy Spirit was not to be fulfilled all in one day. Thus the scholar cannot limit the supernatural signs of Pentecost to that day alone. Verse 17 states, "And it shall come to pass in the last *days*" — plural — "saith God, I will pour out of my Spirit upon all flesh"; and v.18 repeats the idea by saying "in those days." The power of Pentecost was meant for the entire Church Age. Prominent leaders of the Church such as Irenaeus, Justin, and Origen testify that the miracles and gifts of the Spirit continued to be much in evidence well on into the second and third centuries, long after the close of the apostolic period. The power described in Acts began to wane, not according to God's directive will, but because apathy and worldliness crept in to quench the fire of the Spirit. Now in the twentieth century God is sending a revival of Pentecostal power to prepare the Church for the coming of her Bridegroom. The outpouring is to continue to the very time that the wonders in the heavens above and the terrible signs on the earth beneath that Joel speaks of (vv.19,20) occur, just before the great and notable Day of the Lord comes.

Someone may ask what connection Peter saw between the speaking in tongues which he and his associates experienced, and the prophesying which Joel predicted (vv.17,18). Since this is the part of Joel's prophecy that deals with speech, Peter quite obviously was implying that the telling of the mighty works of God in the various native languages of the Jewish pilgrims to the feast was a fulfillment of Joel's words.

The term for "utterance" in Acts 2:4 also suggests that the newly empowered Christians were speaking forth the praises of God with a prophetic ring in their voices. According to Arndt and Gingrich (*Greek-English Lexicon*, p. 101), the Greek word *apophthengesthai* means to speak forth boldly as a prophet or other inspired person, and occurs several times in the Septuagint (the Greek translation of the O.T.) in a prophetic context (Ezek. 13:9,19; Mic. 5:12; Zech. 10:2; and I Chron. 25:1, the clearest O.T. example). Luke himself uses the Greek word again in v.14, where he writes that Peter raised his voice and "declared" (NASB) to the great crowd the message that follows. Also in Acts 26:25 Paul says to Festus, "I am not mad . . . but speak forth the words of truth and soberness." In these instances, both Peter and Paul were speaking under an anointing as prophets. Therefore, we may conclude that the Holy Spirit gave the 120 the ability to speak as boldly and clearly as prophets, in this case in foreign languages that were readily understood by people from those countries. They did not, however, preach the Gospel in the "other tongues." This was done by the apostle Peter in Greek or Aramaic, in a language known by every Jew who would come to Jerusalem in that day. The speaking with tongues served the purpose of gathering a large crowd around the disciples.

It is worthwhile noting that the disciples opened their mouths to speak and used their own lips and tongues and vocal cords to form the sounds. The Holy Spirit did not have to overcome their reluctance, but in the joy of the moment they voluntarily began to speak. Yet it was the Spirit who formed the words, so that each one uttered a language that was intelligible to one who knew it. In like manner today, many when they are baptized in the Holy Ghost speak in a language which they themselves do not know (see comments on I Cor. 14:1-33).

ACTS 2:38-40 — RECEIVING THE GIFT OF THE HOLY SPIRIT.

On the Day of Pentecost, the Jewish worshipers asked two questions. When they heard the 120 Christians speaking in tongues and asked, "What meaneth this?" (Acts 2:12), Peter took his stand with the other apostles and delivered his great sermon (2:14-36). This wrought conviction in their hearts and evoked their second question, "Men and brethren, what shall we do?" (Acts 2:37).

In his message, Peter had explained that this was the beginning of a new age — the days foretold by the prophets — to be lived in the power of the Spirit. Thus their second question was really two in one: "What shall we do to escape our share of guilt in the crucifixion of Jesus the Messiah?" and "What shall we do to experience the outpouring of the Holy Spirit which was promised us in Joel's prophecy?" In his reply, Peter answered both questions at the same time. "Repent and let each one of you be baptized upon the authority of Jesus the Messiah with respect to the forgiveness of your sins, and you shall then take the step of receiving the gift of the Holy Spirit. For the promise is for you and your children and for all who are afar off, as many as the Lord our God shall call unto Himself" (vv.38,39 *original translation*). "And with many other words he solemnly testified and kept on exhorting them, saying, 'Be saved from this perverse generation!' " (v.40 NASB).

First, let us consider who may receive the promised Spirit, and then we shall discuss how to receive the gift. Peter interpreted Joel's prophecy to refer to this whole Gospel era by changing "afterward" (Joel 2:28) to "in the last days" (Acts 2:17), a recognized term for this dispensation. Thus it is certain that the power of the Holy Spirit is meant for every born-again Christian, for every one who is saved throughout the entire period between the first and second comings of Christ.

Michael Harper makes this very clear in his book *Walk in the Spirit* ([Plainfield: Logos, 1968], p. 13): "The whole of the NT substantiates these two facts: first, that the only entry into the benefits of the New Covenant is by repentance and baptism. And secondly, that the benefits of the New Covenant include the gift of the Holy Spirit as well as the forgiveness of sins. From Pentecost onwards the Church faithfully proclaimed that Christ forgives *and* baptises in the Holy Spirit. They taught that all who repent and believe are justified by faith, and that all who are justified by faith may receive the Holy Spirit by faith. The one should normally lead to the other."

The offer of the gift of the Spirit, then, is just as extensive as the offer of salvation itself. The Greek word for "gift" in v.38 is *dorea*, not *charisma*, which is the term Paul and Peter use for a charismatic or spiritual gift (see comments on Rom. 12:3-8; I Cor. 12:13; I Pet. 4:10,11). *Dorea* refers to the gift of salvation for all men in John 4:10; Heb. 6:4; and Eph. 2:8; to the gift of righteousness in Rom. 5:15,17; and to the gift of God's Son (II Cor. 9:15). *Dorea* is also the word that is used for God's gift of His Spirit in Acts 8:20; 10:45; and 11:17. Peter said in v.39 that the promise is "unto you" — to the Jews present on that first Day of Pentecost; "and to your children" — to their descendants, i.e., to all Jews since then; "and to all that are afar off" — to all Gentiles, who were considered by Jews as being "far off" from God and from the covenant promises made to Israel (Eph. 2:11-13,17; cf. Acts 22:21 Berkeley). He emphasized how broad this promise is by adding, "even as many as the Lord our God shall call." And every true Christian has been called or invited by God to come to His kingdom and glory (I Thess. 2:12; 5:24; II Thess. 2:14; Rom. 8:28,30; Eph. 4:1; I Pet. 2:9; 5:10).

Before going further, we must recognize that it is impossible to construct an exact biblical formula for receiving the Spirit. The instances of those who did as described in the Book of Acts are characterized by their variety.

According to Peter's words, God has set only two prior conditions for being baptized in the Spirit. The first is repentance which denotes a change of mind according to the Greek word *metanoia*. The *Amplified Bible* enlarges upon the meaning of "repent" in v.38 as follows: "Change your views, and purpose to accept the will of God in your inner selves instead of rejecting it." Repentance implies the previous work of the Holy Spirit to convict "of sin, and of righteousness, and of judgment" (John 16:8-11; see comments on John 14:15-18,26). The one who has no belief in God or has wrong beliefs concerning Christ as the eternal Son of God and Redeemer by His sacrificial death, must change his mind. The one who is harboring sin in his life must renounce it completely. This often may produce and be accompanied by a deep sorrow for one's past attitudes and deeds (cf. II Cor. 7:9,10). The Holy Spirit also awakens a longing for truth and goodness, a desire for God; in short, He creates a hunger and thirst for righteousness and spiritual life and power. This deep inner longing for reality and power can be satisfied only by repenting and turning to Jesus Christ with all of one's heart. Repentance and saving faith or trust in Christ are the two sides of the coin called conversion.

The other condition is baptism in water. The obedience of the new believer in Christ as a responsible person is indicated by Peter's command which narrows down this detail to the individual, "Be baptized every one of you" (v.38). The original translation given above of v.38 and 39 brings out the meaning of the Greek prepositions. Each convert is to be baptized "in the name of Jesus Christ" (Greek, *epi to onomati Iesou Christou*). In the Bible, the name of a person often stands for his character or his position, and thus symbolizes his authority. Therefore we have paraphrased the words as "upon the authority of Jesus the Messiah." The new Christian is to submit to baptism on the authority of the One who gave the threefold baptismal formula in Matt. 28:19: "baptizing them in (Greek *eis*) the name of the Father, and of the Son, and of the Holy Ghost." Peter's command, then, does not supersede trinitarian baptism but refers back to it.

The Book of Acts does not establish a new baptismal formula in the name of Jesus only. Actually Luke uses three different Greek prepositions before the term "name," and two ways of referring to Christ after the term "name." Here it is "in (*epi*, upon) the name of Jesus Christ"; in Acts 10:48 it is "in (*en*) the name of Jesus Christ"; and in Acts 8:16 and 19:5 it is "in (*eis*, into) the name of the Lord Jesus." F. F. Bruce explains that the Greeks used the latter expression to indicate that some property is transferred "into the name" of someone. Therefore the baptized person bore public witness that he has become the property of Jesus and that Christ is his new Lord and Owner. Bruce further comments that the longer expression in Matt. 28:19 is appropriate for Gentile disciples from all the nations who must turn from paganism to serve the living God, "whereas Jews and Samaritans, who already acknowledge the one true God, were required only to confess Jesus as Lord and Messiah" (*The Book of the Acts* [Grand Rapids: Eerdmans, 1959], p.181, n.32).

Our original paraphrase of v.38 also guards against the error of baptismal regeneration. This doctrinal error supposes that one is baptized "for the remission of sins" in the sense of "in order to obtain forgiveness of your sins." But the Greek preposition *eis*, usually translated "for" in this context, more exactly means "concerning," "with respect to," or "in reference to." This meaning of *eis* is evident in Acts 2:25; 16:9; Rom. 4:20 (NASB); Eph. 5:32 (NASB); and I Thess. 5:18. That this is the proper meaning of *eis* when used in the concept of baptism for the remission of sins, is quite clear in Mark 1:4 and Luke 3:3. These verses tell of John the Baptist who preached a baptism of repentance for the forgiveness of sins. John's stern message demanding fruits in keeping with their repentance before he would baptize them (Luke 3:7-14) shows that baptism was never performed to effect repentance and forgiveness but only to bear witness to their repentance (see comments on Matt. 3:11-17; Acts 22:16).

Having repented of his sins and acknowledged his faith in his new-found Savior Jesus Christ by water baptism, how may the convert receive the gift of the Holy Spirit? Returning again to our paraphrase, note that Peter exhorts his hearers to take an active part in receiving the outpoured Spirit. It is true that the KJV accurately translates the future tense of the Greek verb "receive": "and ye shall receive the gift of the Holy Ghost" (v.38). But the future indicative tense in Greek may have an imperative sense of command (A. T. Robertson, *A Grammar of the Greek New Testament in the Light of Historical Research* [Nashville: Broadman, 1947], pp. 874, 942), as in Mark 9:35, "If any man desire to be first, the same shall be last of all, and servant of all"; Luke 1:13, "Thou shalt call his name John." Therefore Peter is saying that receiving the Holy Spirit is not a passive acquisition, but demands active appropriation.

The interpretation of Peter's words at the end of v.38 is in keeping with Paul's insistence when he wrote to the Galatians that they had received the promise of the Spirit through faith (Gal. 3:14; see comments on Gal. 3:2-5,14). The miracle-working power of the Spirit is not an asset automatically provided to the believer in Christ, but must be claimed individually. The promise of the Spirit, like all other biblical promises (Heb. 6:12), must be received and inherited by faith. We do not gain the benefits of God's promises without consciously claiming them, any more than the Israelite invading Canaan under Joshua's command could possess his share of the Promised Land without actually treading upon it (Josh. 1:3). Just as one receives new life in the Son of God by a definite act of personal faith, even so he receives supernatural power in the Spirit of God by an act of conscious faith. Sometimes, as in the case of Cornelius (see comments on Acts 10:44-48), the two may be received simultaneously. Usually, however, both the N.T. and present-day experience indicate that there are two moments of faith, on separate occasions.

The simple acrostic READY may be an aid in remembering the various important steps in receiving the baptism in the Holy Spirit:

R — Repent. No one should seek to be baptized in the Spirit until he has first of all repented of any and all sin and accepted Jesus Christ as his Savior and Lord. As a Christian desiring the gift of the Spirit, he will not knowingly be disobedient to the

Lord, for the Holy Spirit is given to them that obey God (Acts 5:32; see comments there). He will gladly acknowledge Jesus as his Lord by submitting to water baptism.

The tremendous increase in recent years in astrology and spiritism makes it necessary to sound a warning to everyone seeking the baptism in the Spirit. If in the past he has been the follower of a false cult or has had any contact with the occult such as fortune-telling or spiritist seances, or if he has practiced magic (Acts 19:18,19) or played with Ouija boards or used the horoscope or dabbled in reincarnation, ESP, hypnotism, or witchcraft, he must renounce all connection with these Satanic practices. In some cases he may need to be set free from the grip of evil spirits before he is ready to receive the Holy Spirit. Attempting to be filled with the Spirit before he is delivered will only produce confusion or terrible conflict, and cause other people to doubt the validity of the baptism in the Spirit. See the chapter on this important matter, "Preparing to Receive the Baptism in the Holy Spirit," in the book by Dennis and Rita Bennett, *The Holy Spirit and You*, pp.36-55.

E — Expect. Because the Holy Spirit is appropriated by faith (Gal. 3:2,14), one must have an expectant attitude, believing that God will fulfill His promise to him. Knowing that the Holy Spirit has already been sent from heaven at Pentecost for all members of the Church throughout this age, the Christian may confidently anticipate the blessing of the Holy Spirit in his own life and ministry.

A — Ask. Jesus Christ is the Baptizer in the Holy Spirit (see comments on John 1:29-34). Therefore the candidate for this baptism should come to Jesus in prayer and ask *Him* and expect *Him* to pour out the Spirit upon him. Also, Jesus encouraged His disciples to ask their heavenly Father to give them the Holy Spirit (Luke 11:13), and to ask Him persistently (see comments on Luke 11:5-13). One prays this way when he senses his deep need for more of God and becomes desperately thirsty.

D — Drink. Jesus gave His great invitation, "If any man thirst, let him come unto me, and drink" (John 7:37) As Michael Harper has said, "If *thirst* is Jesus' condition for our coming to Him for power, then it follows that *drinking* will be the means of appropriation" (*Walk in the Spirit*, p.19). One is filled with wine by the act of drinking; even so one is filled with the Spirit by "drinking," i.e., by actively receiving the Holy Spirit through the prayer of faith (Gal. 3:2,14; Mark 11:22-24; see comments on John 7:37-39). Drinking a liquid is in some ways comparable to breathing in air. Therefore, some have found it to be an aid to their faith to take several deep breaths as symbolic of breathing in the Holy Spirit.

Y — Yield. The last step in becoming ready to receive the gift of the Spirit is the matter of yielding to God. The individual seeking to be baptized and filled with the Spirit must be willing to yield control of every part of his being to the Holy Spirit. To be filled with the Spirit means to be controlled by Him, for the Holy Spirit is a person, not a substance or an influence or a mere power (see comments on Eph. 5:15-21).

If you are a candidate for Spirit-baptism, you should yield yourself completely unto Jesus, as one who is alive from the dead, and also every member and faculty of your body as an instrument of righteousness unto God (Rom. 6:13,19; 12:1). Yield your will so that your motives are pure in seeking the baptism. Yield your members, especially your tongue as the organ of expression of the Holy Spirit through you (Acts 2:4). Because Satan can use the tongue, as he did Hitler's, to set a whole continent or world on fire (James 3:2-10), it is essential that you let the Spirit of God control your center of speech. Because of the great stress in our Western culture on the intellectual training of the mind and its expression in rational speech, many find that the ability to talk with understanding is the last stronghold they are willing to surrender to the Lord. So your being willing to speak in tongues involves total sacrifice of yourself as a whole burnt offering to God (Lev. 6:9-13; 9:22-24; Isa. 4:4,5). Then the glory of His presence may fall upon you and be seen in your life!

Remember that until you turn on the faucet, there is no flow of water from the pipe. And until you open your mouth to speak, there is not a free flowing of the Holy Spirit from your innermost being in worship to God and in ministry to others. Therefore when the indwelling Spirit of Christ begins to well up within your human spirit, yield to Him and allow Him to manifest Himself as He pours out into your soul and body. Do not resist the desire to praise and magnify God with whatever strange-sounding words that He may form on your lips and tongue. The N.T. shows that the natural result of being filled with the Spirit is to speak, whether in tongues or in prophesying or in praise and thanksgiving (see comments on Eph. 5:15-21).

It is impossible to prove that those who were baptized in the Spirit in the apostolic period immediately spoke in tongues on every occasion. Therefore it is better not to insist dogmatically that speaking in tongues is the invariable initial evidence. But we can say that the normal pattern in the N.T. was for this sign to be manifested when people received the gift of the Holy Spirit (see comments on Acts 8:5-25,26-39; 10:44-48; 19:1-7). Many have experienced an overflow of the Spirit through singing or worshiping in tongues at a subsequent time. Perhaps Paul was one of these (see comments on Acts 9:1-22). The important thing is not to refuse to speak words you do not understand. For as Michael Harper describes it, speaking in tongues is like a sacrament, an outward and visible sign of inward and spiritual grace (*Walk in the Spirit*, p.22). It is a rich blessing, not something to try to avoid. Because of the several wonderful purposes of tongues, Paul wanted all the believers in Corinth to speak in tongues as a continuing manifestation of the power of the Holy Spirit (see comments on I Cor. 14:1-33).

A final word to Christians who are earnestly desiring to receive the gift of the Holy Spirit yet feel hindered in one way or another. Many ask if it is possible to receive the baptism in the Spirit without speaking in tongues. Michael Harper's reply to this question is helpful: "The honest answer is that it is possible to receive this blessing and not *at the same time* speak in tongues. In the early Church it seems to have been the normal accompaniment of the receiving of the Holy Spirit. But there are factors in our day that were not present then and which obscure the matter for us. I refer particularly to ignorance, fear and prejudice" (*Power for the Body of Christ* [London: Fountain Trust, 1964], p.35). He goes on to explain that speaking in tongues was a well-known gift to the early Christians, and there was none of that prejudice and fear of this phenomenon that seems to cripple so many in our churches today when they think about this subject. Other hindrances may be self-consciousness or unbelief. The shy or inhibited person may be prayed for with the laying on of hands to receive the Holy Spirit at a public meeting, and begin to praise God in a new language when he is alone in the privacy of his home or while driving his car, etc. Remember that Jesus Himself said, "These signs shall follow them that believe. . . . They shall speak with new tongues" (Mark 16:17).

Acts 4:8 — PETER, FILLED WITH THE HOLY SPIRIT.
  "Filled with the Holy Spirit" and its companion "full of the Holy Spirit" are key phrases of the Book of Acts. In Acts 4:8, the Greek aorist participle implies that the Spirit at that moment took full control of Peter. The apostle sensed "an immediate sudden inspiration, giving the wisdom and courage and words which were needed at the time" (E. H. Plumptre, "The Acts of the Apostles," *Ellicott's Bible Commentary for English Readers,* VII, 21). It was the Holy Spirit who acted to put the telling words of defense into Peter's mouth. It was the first fulfillment of Jesus' promise for His disciples when on trial (see comments on Matt. 10:16-20).
  Luke uses the verb "filled" (*pimplemi*) thirteen times in his

Gospel and nine times in Acts. It occurs only twice elsewhere in the N.T. (Matt. 22:10; 27:48). Thayer in his *Greek-English Lexicon of the New Testament* ([Grand Rapids: Zondervan, 1956], p.509) says, "What wholly *takes possession* of the mind is said to *fill* it." In the aorist tense, the verb stresses the act of being filled, usually on that specific occasion. Men were filled with wrath (Luke 4:28), fear (Luke 5:26), rage (Luke 6:11 NASB), wonder and amazement (Acts 3:10), envy or indignation (Acts 5:17; 13:45), and confusion (Acts 19:29). In no case could this filling be said to initiate a permanent state of mind.

On the Day of Pentecost, the 120 Christians were all filled with the Holy Spirit (Acts 2:4). Again, a whole group of believers gathered with the apostles were filled with the Spirit after they united in prayer asking for boldness to witness (Acts 4:31; see comments on Acts 4:29-33). In each case they were fully possessed or completely controlled by the Spirit to manifest the power of the Lord in a situation and in a way completely beyond their own human abilities.

Likewise, Paul was filled with the Spirit when Elymas the sorcerer opposed him and Barnabas. Paul received sudden spiritual power to know the man's very character and then to pronounce the verdict of divine punishment on him (Acts 13:9-11). Similarly, Peter had exposed the hypocrisy of Ananias and Sapphira by the Spirit's revelation and not by any power of his own (Acts 5:1-11). These are clear instances of the charismatic gift of a word of knowledge.

The cases of Elisabeth and Zacharias bear out the normal use of the verb "filled" in the aorist tense to describe a certain incident and not a permanent condition. Luke writes that each was filled with the Holy Spirit (Luke 1:41,67) and goes on to record the prophecy that each one spoke forth. The only occurrence where the aorist of this verb may imply the beginning of a continuing state of fullness of the Spirit is in the statement of Ananias in Damascus to the newly converted Paul: "The Lord Jesus . . . has sent me so that you may regain your sight, and be filled with the Holy Spirit" (Acts 9:17 NASB). More likely, however, this is Ananias' way of referring to the act of being baptized in the Holy Spirit.

The other prominent expression in Luke's writings, "full of the Holy Spirit," does seem to describe the normal spiritual state of the person. The adjective "full" (*pleres*) used in this sense suggests the person is characterized by or thoroughly permeated with the Spirit or with spiritual attributes such as grace and truth (John 1:14), wisdom (Acts 6:3), faith (Acts 6:5), grace and power (Acts 6:8 NASB). Dorcas was "full of good works and almsdeeds" which she continually did (Acts 9:36). Luke characterizes the following as full of the Holy Spirit: Jesus (Luke 4:1), the seven to be chosen as deacons (Acts 6:3), and Stephen in particular (Acts 6:5; 7:55), and Barnabas (Acts 11:24).

The Greek verb, *pleroo*, which corresponds to the adjective "full," is used only two times in connection with the Holy Spirit. One is the important verse, "Be filled with the Spirit" (Eph. 5:18). The present tense of the verb, denoting a continuing action, and the fact that it is a command, indicate that the Spirit-baptized Christian needs continually to "stir up the gift of God" which is in him (II Tim. 1:6). There would be no need for such a command if every believer remained permanently full of the Holy Spirit after receiving the baptism. For further discussion, see comments on Eph. 5:15-21.

The other verse is Acts 13:52, which may be translated, "And the disciples continued to be filled with joy and the Holy Spirit." Here the verb *pleroo* is in the imperfect tense, describing a continuing condition in past time. In spite of persecution and the departure of Paul and Barnabas to Iconium, the joy of the new converts did not disappear, because they continued to be filled with the Spirit. Later Paul reminded these Galatians that joy, the true and deepest joy, is the fruit of the Spirit, not the result of circumstances (Gal. 5:22). In like manner, the Thessalonian Christians received the Gospel in much tribulation but with the joy inspired by the Holy Spirit (I Thess. 1:5). Being continually overflowing with the Spirit is the goal and privilege of believers in Christ at all times and in every situation.

ACTS 4:29-33 — PRAYER FOR BOLDNESS TO WITNESS.

Chapters 3 and 4 of Acts describe in detail one of the many apostolic signs and wonders mentioned in Acts 2:43, and the consequences of this particular miracle of healing. Going to the temple one afternoon to pray, Peter and John met a beggar lame from birth. When he asked for money, Peter responded, "Silver and gold have I none; but such as I have give I thee" — a gift of healing! So Peter commanded him in the name of Jesus Christ of Nazareth to walk. The moment Peter took his hand and raised him up, his feet and ankles were strengthened, and he entered the court of the temple leaping and praising God.

In a short time an amazed crowd of worshipers gathered. Peter used this opportunity as another occasion to bear witness to the healing power and saving grace of Jesus. He urged the people to turn from their wicked ways, saying, "Repent therefore and turn to Him, so that your sins may be blotted out, in order that times of respite from judgment may come from the presence of the Lord; and that He may send Jesus, the Messiah appointed for you, whom heaven must receive until the period for the restoration of all the things which God has spoken by the mouth of His holy prophets from of old" (Acts 3:19-21 original translation). Because judgment often took the form of drought and famine, "times of respite from judgment" includes the idea of times of refreshing or renewal in v.19.

Peter was not promising "universal restoration" (see NEB, TCNT, Williams, *Jerusalem Bible*, Phillips) in the sense of ultimate salvation for all beings, but the establishing of all that God had announced by means of the O.T. prophets. Israel will be restored to the Promised Land (Deut. 30:3-5; Isa. 11:11,12), and the theocracy will be restored under David's Son (II Sam. 7:16; Jer. 23:3-8; Ezek. 37:21-28; Zech. 14). Peter's term also includes the liberation of the whole creation from the bondage of corruption when Christ returns and the children of God are revealed in glory with Him (Rom. 8:19-23; Col. 3:4; II Thess. 1:7-10). That will be the period of the "regeneration" when the Lord Jesus will sit on the throne of His glory (Matt. 19:28). Then the new creation will reach its fullness or consummation. Through Christ, God will reconcile all things to Himself (Col. 1:20). Again, this does not mean the universal salvation or ultimate reconciliation of all men and of the devil and his angels, but that all rebellion will be quelled and the whole universe will be brought into peaceful harmony with God's perfect will.

Peter was calling upon the whole nation of Israel, as he did on the Day of Pentecost, to reverse their cry to crucify Jesus and instead to acknowledge Him as Messiah. "Had Israel as a whole done this during these Pentecostal days, how different the course of world history and world evangelization would have been! How much more swiftly (we may imagine) would the consummation of Christ's kingdom have come!" (Bruce, *The Book of the Acts*, p.92).

Many believed the message, but the Jewish authorities had Peter and John arrested for teaching that Jesus had been raised from death, which tended to prove to the populace that the doctrine of the resurrection of the dead is true, contrary to the teaching of the Sadducees (Acts 4:1-4; cf. 23:6-8). When the apostles were tried before the Sanhedrin the next day, the ruling elders and leading priests (who were Sadducees) recognized them as men who had been with Jesus because of their bold and authoritative manner of speaking. Since the man who had been healed was standing there with Peter and John right before their very eyes, they could not deny the miracle. They could do nothing but release them and command them not to speak or teach at all in the name of Jesus (Acts 4:13-22).

As soon as they were discharged, Peter and John returned "to their own company" (Acts 4:23), i.e., to the place where their fellow apostles were. How many other Christians were present we cannot be sure. The place could not have been the temple courtyard, for they had just come from the council-chamber of the Sanhedrin which was on the west side of the temple area. Because of surveillance by the temple police, the apostles almost certainly were gathered inside a private building, not in an open field near Jerusalem. Therefore, it does not seem likely that all five thousand male believers (Acts 4:4) were present, or that all those converted, subsequent to the Day of Pentecost, took part in the prayer meeting. It was not, then, a time when new believers met to receive the baptism in the Holy Spirit.

What follows is one of the remarkable prayers of the Bible. Moved by a common impulse, all who heard the report of Peter and John raised their voices in unison to God. The prayer was unrehearsed, yet it was with one accord. It consisted more of praise than of petition. They prayed to God as "Sovereign Lord" (Acts 4:24 RSV), acknowledging His absolute control as Creator and Ruler of all history. They recognized where they stood in terms of prophetic revelation, i.e., in the events of Ps. 2:1-3. Instead of begging for protection from persecution, they prayed for more power and boldness to witness: "And now, Lord, behold their threatenings: and grant unto thy servants, that with all boldness they may speak thy word" (v.29). They did not specifically pray to receive the Holy Spirit. When they finished, however, the assembly-place was shaken and "they were all filled with the Holy Spirit" (v.31 NASB).

Because the apostles were certainly among those who prayed and consequently who were filled with the Spirit, this filling cannot have been the initial baptism in the Holy Spirit. They had asked for boldness; the Holy Spirit filled them all afresh and sent them forth to speak the word of God with renewed confidence (v.31) and great power (v.33). They were enabled to continue their public preaching openly and freely in spite of the threats of the Sanhedrin. See comments on Acts 4:8 for discussion on "filled with the Holy Spirit."

Three reasons for the powerful, victorious witness of the early Christians may be noted in this passage. T. L. Osborn in his book, *Three Keys to the Book of Acts*, has pointed out that apostolic preaching was based on God's word (v.29), depended on the authority of the name of Jesus (v.30), and was empowered by the Holy Spirit (v.31). The Greek term *logos* occurs about thirty-five times in Acts in the sense of the word of God. His word convicted and convinced the most hardened hearts. The term *onoma,* as used of the name of Jesus Christ, is found thirty-three times in Acts. When asked for credentials, the apostles gave the name of Jesus (Acts 4:7-13). The Christians wielded it against diseases, demons, and difficulties, so that religious and political leaders were caused to tremble. The *onoma* of Jesus is not a magic formula but implies a faith relationship and full commitment to that "Name." What Christ has done and shall do, and what He means to us now can never be separated from His name. The word *pneuma,* as used of the Holy Spirit, occurs fifty-two times in Acts. These three terms, then — the word (*logos*), the name (*onoma*) of Jesus, and the Spirit (*pneuma*) — are the keys which unlock the door to the application of Acts in our lives today.

Those early disciples depended entirely on the Holy Spirit to work through their lives. Therefore whatever the opposition or trial, whether determined unbelief (Acts 9:27-29; 19:8,9) or intense bitterness (Acts 13:44,45; 14:2,3) on the part of their persecutors, or prolonged imprisonment such as Paul experienced (Acts 28:16,30,31), the Christians spoke out boldly in the name of the Lord. Because of such courage and steadfastness, they endured. Acts 14:3 is typical of their attitude and experience: "They spent a long time there speaking boldly with reliance upon the Lord, who was bearing witness to the word of His grace, granting that signs and wonders be done by their hands" (NASB).

Acts 5:32 — OBEDIENCE AND THE GIFT OF THE
HOLY SPIRIT.

Peter and the other apostles were again on trial before the
Jewish Sanhedrin. They had been given strict orders not to
continue teaching in the name of Jesus, and were now being
accused of filling Jerusalem with such teaching (Acts 5:27,28).
Peter stepped forward to answer the charges and said, "We
must obey God rather than men. The God of our fathers raised
Jesus whom you killed by hanging him on a tree. God exalted
him at his right hand as Leader and Savior, to give repentance
to Israel and forgiveness of sins. And we are witnesses to these
things, and so is the Holy Spirit whom God has given to those
who obey him" (Acts 5:29-32 RSV).

The issue at stake was which group truly obeyed God, the
Jewish rulers or the apostles? The leaders of the Jews had laid
violent hands on Jesus and in effect murdered Him, inflicting
the utmost disgrace on Him by having Him hanged on a tree
(see Deut. 21:23). On the other hand, God not only reversed the
effects of their crime by raising Jesus from the dead but honored
Him by exalting Him to His right hand. Furthermore, He
invested Him with the authority of Prince or Leader, and
Savior. Who, then, was right? Whose authority should the
apostles obey? Peter's final argument that the Christians were
the ones who obeyed God, and not the chief priests and elders,
was that God had given the Holy Spirit to the followers of Jesus,
not to the Sanhedrin members!

Is obedience a necessary condition for receiving the baptism
in the Spirit? Frederick D. Bruner has wrongly argued that the
obedience spoken of in v.32 is not a condition but the result of
the gift of the Holy Spirit. He believes the text means that the
Spirit has been given to those who are *now* obeying God. Thus
"obedience is the present *result* of the *prior* gift of the Spirit" (*A
Theology of the Holy Spirit* [Grand Rapids: Eerdmans, 1970],
p.172).

No one will deny that the gift of the Holy Spirit should make one a better, more obedient Christian. Bruner's interpretation, however, is based on a misunderstanding of the present tense Greek participle translated "obey." There is no participle in the imperfect (past) tense in Greek. The present participle expresses simultaneous action relative to the main verb, which here is "has given," an aorist (past) tense. The present participle may even be used to suggest antecedent time relative to the main verb. Therefore, Peter's statement means that those who were truly obeying God were the ones who received the Spirit on the Day of Pentecost. And it was obvious that day on whom the Spirit had been poured out, for the 120 believers in Christ spoke in other languages when they were filled with the Spirit.

But in what does obedience to God consist? A contrast with the attitude and customs of the high priest and elders and scribes may help clarify the matter. Those men scrupulously observed the Law of Moses and the traditions of the fathers. They followed religious observances, and many were zealous and very devout in their prayers and sacrifices and daily moral life. Yet, as Paul points out in Rom. 9:30-10:5, they did not pursue the righteousness of the law by faith. They sought to establish their own righteousness and did not subject themselves to the righteousness based on faith in the promised Messiah.

The attitude of the Jewish leaders was wrong, loving the praise and approval of men rather than the approval of God (John 12:43). They had no spiritual hunger or conviction of their spiritual barrenness. Like the Laodiceans, they felt they had need of nothing, when in God's sight they were wretched and miserable and poor and blind and naked (Rev. 3:17). Like the self-righteous Pharisee who went to the temple to pray in Jesus' parable (Luke 18:9-14), they had no humility, no sense of personal unworthiness, no cry of repentance. They did all their deeds to be noticed by men, and loved the chief seats in the synagogues. They were meticulous tithers, but neglected the weightier matters such as justice, mercy, and faithfulness. In short, Jesus said that while they outwardly appeared righteous to men, inwardly they were full of hypocrisy and lawlessness (Matt. 23:5,6,23,28).

Their lawless and hypocritical attitude toward God's perfect will culminated in disobedience to God's Son. In a word, this disobedience took the form of unbelief. "He who believes in the Son has eternal life; but he who does not obey the Son shall not see life, but the wrath of God abides on him" (John 3:36 NASB). The word "disbelieves" literally means "disobeys," as the RSV brings out in that verse. Such a person does not obey Christ, because he refuses to believe in and submit himself to Him. Therefore, he rejects Christ, not willing to come to the Light lest his deeds be exposed (John 3:18-20).

The fundamental act of obedience to God today is to believe in Him whom God has sent. This was Jesus' own answer to those who asked Him what they might do to work the works of God (John 6:28,29), because it indicates a willingness to obey God's will in every matter. Paul said the purpose of his preaching was to bring about "the obedience of faith among all the Gentiles" (Rom. 1:5 NASB). He urged men to yield themselves to the belief of God's saving message, which is the highest of all obedience. But true faith, saving faith, is faith which works by love in serving one another (Gal. 5:6,13). It eventuates in loving obedience to the known will of God. And full belief in Christ will not stop short of believing in and receiving God's promised gift of the Holy Spirit.

Therefore the answer is that the one essential condition for receiving the gift of the Spirit is to be a true believer in Jesus Christ, a born-again Christian. Such a person is obedient to the Gospel and to the faith (Acts 6:7; Rom. 10:16; II Thess. 1:8; Heb. 5:9). The converts of the Day of Pentecost continually devoted themselves to the apostles' teaching and to prayer (Acts 2:42). Their repentance was thoroughgoing, and as John the Baptist had required, they brought forth fruits in keeping with their repentance (Luke 3:8). True conversion means commitment to Christ as the new Lord of one's life. The true believer says, "Jesus is Lord," by the indwelling Holy Spirit (I Cor. 12:3).

As we continue to believe in Jesus as our Lord, we keep on obeying Him, and such obedience results in righteousness (Rom. 6:16,17). And as one yields the members of his body to righteousness, it makes for a holy life — it is "unto holiness" or sanctification (Rom. 6:19). Those who belong to Christ Jesus are characterized by the fact that they have crucified the flesh with its passions and selfish desires (Gal. 5:24).

Paul insists in his Epistle to the Galatians that Christians do not receive the gift of the Spirit by the works of the Law. *The Living Bible* brings this out very clearly: "Let me ask you this one question: Did you receive the Holy Spirit by trying to keep the Jewish laws? Of course not, for the Holy Spirit came upon you only after you heard about Christ and trusted Him to save you. Then have you gone completely crazy? For if trying to obey the Jewish laws never gave you spiritual life in the first place, why do you think that trying to obey them now will make you stronger Christians? . . . I ask you again, does God give you the power of the Holy Spirit and work miracles among you as a result of your trying to obey the Jewish laws? No, of course not. It is when you believe in Christ and fully trust Him" (Gal. 3:2,3,5).

Doing the works of the Law can never justify a man in God's sight (Gal. 2:16), because even if one could keep the letter of the Law, he offends when it comes to the true intent of the Law as the expression of God's holy will. Jesus explained this in the Sermon on the Mount when He taught, for example, that every one who even looks on a woman to lust for her has committed adultery with her already in his heart (Matt. 5:28). Therefore, Christian obedience is a product of the inner heart, not of outward duty. It springs from gratitude for grace already received (Rom. 12:1-8), not from the desire to gain merit and to justify oneself in the eyes of God. "Indeed, law-keeping from the latter motive is not obedience to God, but its opposite (Rom.

9:31-10:3)" (J. I. Packer, "Obedience," NBD, p. 904). For the Christian, then, obeying God means keeping the commandments of Christ and not consciously resisting what one knows to be His will.

In charismatic circles today, there is a danger of a substandard Pentecostal experience. One may himself desire, or be encouraged by others, to seek for a manifestation of tongues. If he speaks a few unintelligible syllables, he is told that he has been baptized in the Holy Spirit. But it may be a Pentecost without repentance, a Pentecost without Christ. If one bypasses obedience to Christ and His cross, if there is no repentance and remission of sins, the experience he receives may very well be counterfeit. Babbling in "tongues" to achieve status in a certain group may be prompted psychologically by one's "flesh" or self-nature, or even be activated by an evil spirit. See the warning under R — Repent — in comments on Acts 2:38-40.

Therefore our motive in seeking a Pentecostal experience is all-important. Is it the motive of love—love for Christ and love for other members of His Body (see comments on I Cor. 13). In a very revealing article, Harry Lunn writes, "Our motivation will determine what we seek, whom we seek, and what we receive" ("Beware the Christless Pentecost," *Logos Journal* vol. 39, no. 10 [Nov-Dec 1971]: p 47). One is always safe to seek the Lord Jesus, for He is the one who baptizes in the Holy Spirit. Let us keep our eyes on the Giver and not on the gifts. Let us be concerned about the gifts we can render unto Him — our time, our possessions, our very selves, in short, our obedience.

Acts 6:6 — THE LAYING ON OF HANDS.

This is the first reference in the Book of Acts to the laying on of hands. Here the account tells how seven qualified men were selected and set apart to the special task of administering the business affairs of the congregation in Jerusalem. In the N.T. period, the gesture of laying on of hands was used in three ways:

in the healing of sickness, in connection with the baptism in the Spirit, and in consecration or ordination to the ministry.

The touch of the human hand has been considered symbolic from the earliest times. It was often looked upon as a means of transferring powers or qualities from one individual to another. The head was usually the part touched because it is the noblest member of the body.

In the O.T., Jacob laid his hands on the sons of Joseph to convey his blessing (Gen. 48:13-20). On the Day of Atonement, the high priest placed his hands on the head of the scapegoat and confessed the sins of the people over it, thus transferring all their iniquities to the goat (Lev. 16:21,22). The worshiper always laid his hand on the head of the animal he was offering as a sacrifice, in order to identify himself with the animal dying in his place (Exod. 29:10,15,19; Lev. 1:4; 3:2; 4:4, etc.). When Levites were ordained to perform the service of the Lord, the Israelites laid hands on them to be their representatives (Num. 8:5-19). Moses invested Joshua with some of his authority by the laying on of his hand when he commissioned Joshua in the sight of the whole congregation (Num. 27:18-23).

Jesus Himself laid His hands on children to impart blessing to them by His touch (Matt. 19:13-15; Mark 10:13,16). More often we read that He laid His hands on the sick and touched them when He healed them (Mark 6:5; 8:23; Luke 4:40; 13:13; cf. Mark 5:23; 7:32,33).

We are not surprised to learn, therefore, that the early Christians frequently laid hands on the sick, and many were miraculously healed. Ananias placed his hands on the blinded Saul, and the latter immediately regained his sight (Acts 9:17,18). On the island of Malta, Paul laid his hands on the father of Publius and healed him of fever and dysentery (Acts 28:8). Of course, Peter touched the lame beggar sitting by the temple gate when he grasped the man's right hand and raised him to a standing position (Acts 3:7). Other references to miracles performed by the hands of the apostles and other Christians suggest that the laying on of hands may have been practiced (Acts 5:12; 14:3; 19:11). Anointing the sick with oil may be considered a specialized application of the laying on of hands for the purpose of ministering healing in the name of Jesus Christ (see comments on James 5:13-20). Paul found that he could extend his ministry of miraculous healing by sending to the sick pieces of cloth which he had touched (Acts 19:11,12). The practice of anointing prayer cloths to take to absent sick persons has developed from this, and it may be used effectively if done with pure motives.

The laying on of hands was also employed after water baptism with prayer for the reception of the Holy Spirit (Acts 8:14-19; 19:5,6; see comments on Acts 8:5-25; 19:1-7). It was not necessary, however, for an apostle or any other Christian to lay his hands on a believer that he might be baptized in the Spirit. It is obvious that at Pentecost and in Cornelius' house Jesus baptized them in the Holy Spirit without the ministration of human hands.

The third function of the laying on of hands in the N.T. Church was to ordain a man to a certain office or assignment in the service of the Lord. The meaning of this ceremony is clearly stated in Acts 13:2,3 to be that of setting apart the individual *from* the local body where he has received his training in ministering, and *for* the special work to which the Holy Spirit has already called him. The church at Antioch heard the voice of the Spirit, perhaps through a prophecy, that God had chosen Barnabas and Paul to perform a specific mission. The believers fasted and prayed a while longer to be certain this was the Lord speaking, and then acknowledged the divine commission by laying their hands on the two men. In this manner, the local congregation associated itself with the Holy Spirit in commissioning them and in delegating to them the authority of the entire body. Since the members of Christ's Body act as His ambassadors, their authority is His authority. Paul continued to recognize his membership in and responsibility to the church in Antioch (Acts 15:35), and felt duty-bound to report to the Christians there after a missionary journey (Acts 14:26-28; 18:22-23).

In both epistles to Timothy, Paul reminded his spiritual son of his ordination service in order to encourage him. Paul and the local elders, perhaps of the local church at Ephesus, had laid hands on the young man to consecrate him to the Christian ministry. On this occasion, Timothy received a charismatic gift to equip him further for his special task. Paul also recommended that Timothy not be too hasty in laying hands on a man (I Tim. 5:22). Since this verse occurs in a section about elders who fall into sin (I Tim. 5:19-22), it seems to refer to the ordination of elders rather than to the restoration of backsliders to church fellowship with a sign of blessing, as some have explained the verse.

In light of these three functions of the laying on of hands we may understand the statement in Heb. 6:2 which says that the doctrine of the laying on of hands was included among the foundational Christian teachings in the early Church.

ACTS 8:5-25 — THE PENTECOSTAL OUTPOURING IN SAMARIA.

"The blood of the martyrs is the seed of the Church." The persecution beginning with Stephen's bloody death served only to spread the fires of revival beyond the city limits of Jerusalem. Philip, the deacon, is an example of the many refugees who preached the Gospel as they were scattered throughout the districts of Judea and Samaria.

Philip went to the chief city of Samaria, the site of the old capital of the Northern Kingdom of Israel in O.T. times. Herod the Great had renamed the city Sebaste in honor of the Roman emperor when Herod rebuilt the city in a lavish way. As Philip proclaimed Christ, crowds listened intently because of the miraculous signs he was performing. Many demon-possessed

persons were set free, and many others who were paralyzed or
lame were healed. The result was that numbers of people, both
men and women, believed Philip's message and were submitting to Christian baptism (vv.12,16). There is no basis for
doubting that they were genuinely converted. Even Simon, a
clever magician and a great celebrity in that region, was
amazed by the miracles taking place. He, too, made a
profession of faith and was baptized.

The news of the revival in Samaria soon reached the church
in Jerusalem, forty miles to the south. The apostles felt
responsible for the new believers in Samaria and delegated
Peter and John to go to give any necessary supervision and
teaching. The practice of a representative of the Jerusalem body
going to a new Christian community was repeated when
Barnabas was sent off to Antioch (Acts 11:22).

It is a good two-days' journey on foot from Jerusalem to
Samaria. Thus a bare minimum of about five days elapsed, and
probably a longer period, between the first conversions and the
arrival of the two apostles. There was, then, a definite interval
between the regenerative work of the Spirit in the lives of the
Samaritan converts and their baptism in the Holy Spirit.

Peter and John realized at once that the Pentecostal gift of
the Holy Spirit had not been extended to Philip's converts.
They had received baptism in water but not the baptism in the
Spirit. Therefore the apostles prayed for them to receive the
promised gift of the Father. "Then they *began* laying their hands
on them, and they were receiving the Holy Spirit" (v.17
NASB). Williams' translation suggests that they received the
Spirit "one by one."

Luke does not directly describe the accompanying phenomena. But as F. F. Bruce comments, "The context leaves us in no
doubt that their reception of the Spirit was attended by external
manifestations such as had marked His descent on the earliest
disciples at Pentecost" (*The Book of the Acts*, p.181). A number of

Bible commentators agree that what Simon the Sorcerer "saw" or observed was the new converts speaking in tongues when hands were laid on them.* This ability or authority to impart the Holy Spirit with such evidence, Simon wanted to buy, for he knew he could not match it with his repertoire of magic arts. All of Philip's miracles of healing and exorcism had not impressed him like this sign!

A clue in the Greek text that tongues indeed were in evidence at Samaria may be found in v.21. In rebuking Simon for his wicked thought that he could obtain the gift of God with money, Peter exclaimed, "You have no part or portion in this matter, for your heart *is* not right before God" (NASB). The word for "matter" is Greek *logos,* "word," "speaking," or "kind of speaking" as in I Cor. 1:5 where Paul says the Corinthians were enriched "in all (manner of) utterance." Simon could have no part in this kind of speaking, because his heart was obviously crooked in holding such a materialistic view of the Holy Spirit and His gifts. What an object lesson regarding right motives in asking for the baptism in the Spirit and in desiring spiritual ministries! (see comments on I Cor. 13).

The fact that apostolic hands were laid on the Samaritan Christians and those at Ephesus (Acts 19:6) to bestow the Holy Spirit does not establish a precedent. There was no imposition of hands at Pentecost or in Cornelius' house. In the case of Paul, the man who laid hands on him was not an apostle (Acts 9:17). Paul does not include the power to impart the Spirit in the list of charismatic gifts in I Cor. 12:4-11. Perhaps the Samaritans, who were usually despised by the Jews of Jerusalem, needed to be assured by the apostles "that they were fully incorporated into the new community of the people of God" (Bruce, *The Book of the Acts,* p.182). The laying on of hands was as much a token

---

* For example, Johannes Munck writes: "Simon, who by virtue of his earlier life, closely observed all wondrous faculties and powers, was struck by the apostles' ability to make the baptized prophesy and to speak in tongues by the laying on of hands" (*The Acts of the Apostles,* Anchor Bible, vol. 31 [Garden City: Doubleday, 1967], p.75).

of fellowship and solidarity as it was a symbol of the imparta-
tion of the gift of the Spirit (see comments at Acts 6:6).

ACTS 8:26-39 — THE CONVERSION OF THE ETHIO-PIAN EUNUCH.

Philip's experience with the Ethiopian eunuch provides an
outstanding example of how the Holy Spirit helps in soul-win-
ning. Philip was in such close contact with God that he could
get the message from an angel (cf. Acts 5:19,20; 12:7-10) where
to go. He was obedient to this prompting and soon met a man
whose heart was already prepared. In spite of the man's high
rank and his fine vehicle, Philip listened to the Spirit, who said,
"Go up and join this chariot" (v.29 NASB). Philip sensed the
man's need when he saw him reading the Scriptures, and asked,
"Do you understand what you are reading?" The section
happened to be Isa. 53:7,8 about the Suffering Servant of the
Lord, a passage which men have interpreted in many different
ways. But Philip opened his mouth, and the Spirit filled him
and led him as he explained the Word and preached Jesus to
the foreign official. Philip must have taught him the great
doctrines about Christ and salvation, as well as the importance
of the ordinance of baptism, judging from the eunuch's
eagerness to be baptized (v.36).

When the eunuch was immersed, he evidently received the
gift of the Spirit, for "he went on his way rejoicing" (v.39). The
joy which filled his heart was undoubtedly the joy of the Holy
Spirit (Rom. 14:17; I Thess. 1:6; Acts 13:52). It is interesting to
note a curious addition which several Greek manuscripts and
Church Fathers inserted in v.39. With the added words, it
reads, "The Spirit of the Lord fell upon the eunuch, and the
angel of the Lord snatched Philip away." F. F. Bruce comments
that the "effect of the longer reading is to make it clear that the
Ethiopian's baptism was followed by the gift of the Spirit.
However, even with the shorter reading it is a safe inference
that he did receive the Spirit" (*The Book of the Acts*, p.190).

Acts 9:1-22 — THE CONVERSION AND BAPTISM OF
SAUL.

Where and when was Saul (Paul) actually converted? Was it
when he heard the voice of the Lord outside the city of
Damascus, or was it in Judas' house on the street called Straight
when Ananias came to him several days later?

Two facts clearly point to the earlier time. First, in relating
the details of his conversion later on, Paul stated that after the
One speaking from heaven had identified Himself as Jesus the
Nazarene whom Paul was persecuting, he himself responded,
"What shall I do, Lord?" (Acts 22:10). Paul was immediately
convinced by the glorious theophany who Jesus really is — the
Messiah, True Deity, the Lord of Glory. Therefore he at once,
though a strict Jew, confessed Jesus as Lord. This is tantamount
to conversion, as Paul later wrote, "If you confess with your
mouth Jesus *as* Lord, and believe in your heart that God raised
Him from the dead, you shall be saved" (Rom. 10:9 NASB).

Second, when Ananias came to the blinded man, he called
him "Brother Saul" (v.17). Because of the reputation of the Jew
of Tarsus as a persecutor of the Church, Ananias was at first
afraid when the Lord told him in a vision to go to Paul. He
never would have entered the house and addressed him as
"Brother" if he had not been fully assured that Paul was
already a true believer in Christ.

During the three days of blindness, therefore, Paul was
fasting and praying as a Christian. Only then did Ananias come
and lay his hands on him and say, "Brother Saul, the Lord
Jesus . . . has sent me so that you may regain your sight, and be
filled with the Holy Spirit" (v.17 NASB). At once his eyes were
healed, and he arose and was baptized. Without a word to the
contrary, we may assume that, as so often happened in the early
decades of the Church, Paul was filled with, or baptized in, the
Holy Spirit at the time of his baptism in water.

It is noteworthy that the human agent who mediated the
infilling of the Spirit to Paul was not an apostle, but simply an

otherwise unknown believer, and one in Damascus, not from the mother church in Jerusalem. As Howard Ervin brings out, it was not apostolic prerogative, but the authority of Jesus' name that validated the laying on of Ananias' hands. He acted in obedience to Christ's commission in Mark 16:15-18, which included authorization to lay hands on the sick, and the Lord wonderfully healed Paul and filled him with His Spirit (*These Are Not Drunken As Ye Suppose* [Plainfield: Logos, 1968], p.98).

The text does not specifically mention whether Paul spoke in tongues on this occasion. Thus we cannot be dogmatic as to whether this manifestation followed immediately or afterward. But that he did have the usual evidence is clear from his own testimony, "I thank God, I speak with tongues more than ye all" (I Cor. 14:18). We do know that right away Paul received power to witness and to proclaim Christ in the synagogues, saying, "He is the Son of God" (v.20). The purpose of the Pentecostal experience (see comments on Acts 1:4-8) began to be fulfilled without delay in this outstanding convert.

ACTS 10:44-48 — THE FIRST OUTPOURING OF THE SPIRIT ON GENTILES.

On the Day of Pentecost, Peter had quoted Joel's prophecy in which God says, "It shall be in the last days that I will pour forth of My Spirit upon all mankind" (Acts 2:17 NASB). On that occasion Peter had been the key to the salvation of thousands of Jews. Six or eight years later he became God's agent to open the door to the blessings of the new birth and Pentecost for all the Gentiles.

The first mission to the Gentiles was an event of fundamental importance in the fulfillment of Christ's command to preach the Gospel to all nations. It is apparent that God acted sovereignly in the conversion and Spirit-baptism of Cornelius and his household. The Lord first of all acted to prepare the Roman centurion and the Jewish apostle for their meeting. He gave each a vision, and He spoke to one by an angel and to the other by the Spirit. The long-standing and deep-seated Jewish prejudice against Gentiles was entrenched in Peter. Therefore, he had to be absolutely convinced that in Christ, God truly was abolishing Jewish ceremonial laws. The Lord made His will so clear to Peter that he gave lodging to the Gentile servants of Cornelius without any hesitation or misgivings, and went with them the next day to Caesarea. Peter was made to realize that "God is no respecter of persons," that He does not have favorites, but welcomes anyone who fears Him, regardless of his nationality or race (Acts 10:34,35).

When Peter arrived in Cornelius' house he found many people already assembled. There were relatives and close friends of the centurion (Acts 10:24,27), in addition to slaves and devout soldiers (Acts 10:7). Cornelius and his household were "God-fearers," semi-proselytes to Judaism who stopped short of circumcision, but who were "attracted by the simple monotheism of Jewish synagogue worship and by the ethical standard of the Jewish way of life" (Bruce, *The Book of the Acts*, p.216). Here was a large group of people who already believed in God and were acquainted with the doctrines and prophecies of the O.T. Living only fifty miles from the Sea of Galilee and only a little more from Jerusalem, they had heard much about the ministry of Jesus of Nazareth (Acts 10:37).

Peter's speech is undoubtedly summarized for us. He touched upon Jesus' baptism, miracles, crucifixion, resurrection, and commission to His disciples. Then Peter began to press for a decision: "Of Him all the prophets bear witness that through His name every one who believes in Him has received forgiveness of sins" (10:43 NASB). The prepared, eager hearts immediately accepted the Word with saving faith.

Then, before Peter could finish his sermon, Pentecost was repeated! The Holy Spirit fell upon all those who were listening to the message. This verb describing the action of the Spirit suggests that He gripped them and took possession of them, even as fear is said to "fall upon" man (Luke 1:12; Acts 19:17;

Rev. 11:11). This is not a description of His coming in
regeneration, but of the Pentecostal baptism in the Spirit for
power. It was unmistakable!

The six Jewish believers with Peter from Joppa (cf. Acts
11:12) were amazed, "because the gift of the Holy Spirit had
been poured out upon the Gentiles also" (v.45 NASB). How did
they know? Because "they were hearing them speaking with
tongues and exalting God" (v.46 NASB). Obviously someone in
the group knew one or more of the foreign languages. The
content was very similar to that of the messages in tongues at
Pentecost when the 120 were speaking "the wonderful works of
God" (Acts 2:11). Yes, the Gentiles were manifesting the same
sign of the baptism in the Spirit which had electrified the
crowds at the Feast of Pentecost (see comments on I Cor.
14:1-33).

Peter at once recognized that the Gentiles had truly been
saved and should receive the sign of the New Covenant for the
remission of sins. He therefore ordered Cornelius and his
companions to be baptized in the name of Jesus Christ. Because
of the suddenness of the Spirit's descent, in this case baptism in
water followed baptism in the Holy Spirit. It is to be noted that
the apostle did not consider the reception of the Spirit a
substitute for water baptism.

Afterward, Peter had to explain his conduct before the
Jerusalem congregation. They accused him of having broken
the ban on social intercourse with "unclean" foreigners, saying,
"You went to uncircumcised men and ate with them" (Acts
11:3 NASB). Peter defended himself by giving a straightforward account of his experience. When he reached the climax of
his story, he said, "And as I began to speak, the Holy Spirit fell
upon them, just *as He did* upon us at the beginning. And I
remembered the word of the Lord, how He [said], 'John
baptized with water, but you shall be baptized with the Holy
Spirit.' If God therefore gave to them the same gift as *He gave* to
us also after believing in the Lord Jesus Christ, *who was* I that I

could stand in God's way?" (Acts 11:15-17 NASB). The Jerusalem leaders then calmed down and praised God that He had obviously granted to the Gentiles repentance that leads to life (Acts 11:18).

Peter remained thoroughly convinced that when the Gentiles in Cornelius' house heard the Gospel they believed and God cleansed their hearts by faith before baptizing them in the Spirit. This was his argument ten or twelve years later at the Jerusalem council which convened to discuss the necessity of circumcising Gentile converts. Peter's proof that they were saved purely through the grace of the Lord Jesus, without any additional works of the Law, is given in these words: "And God, who knows the hearts, bore attesting testimony to them by having given them the Holy Spirit even as also to us. And He made no distinction at all between both us and also them, in answer to their faith having cleansed their hearts" (15:8,9 Wuest). The gift of the Spirit was God's seal that they had already believed in Christ (see comments on Eph. 1:13,14).

When Peter spoke of God having purified their hearts by faith (Acts 15:9), he almost certainly had in mind his dream. In it God had revealed to him that He was cleansing the ritually unclean so that they were no longer to be considered unholy (Acts 10:15). Therefore Peter was referring to the forgiveness of sins by the blood of Christ (I John 1:7) and to cleansing as aspects of justification, rather than to a further step of sanctification. Repentance as an integral part of conversion along with faith is a necessary condition for receiving the promised gift of the Holy Spirit, "but there is no suggestion that this blessing was promised on condition of a holy life, nor will its immediate result be a state of entire sanctification" (Harper, *Power for the Body of Christ*, pp.31f.). We may conclude that one may be baptized in the Spirit immediately after believing in Christ, regardless of his spiritual maturity. He must be fully justified (not wholly sanctified) to receive the gift of the Spirit.

Regarding sanctification, see comments on I Cor. 6:11.

Acts 16:6-10 — DIVINE GUIDANCE.

How does God lead His children? This passage describes two methods which the early Christians knew and which God still uses in this age of the Holy Spirit.

On his second missionary journey, Paul, along with Silas, revisited the Galatian churches to give further instruction and to strengthen them in the faith. Then they planned to travel due west into the province of Asia, undoubtedly to begin a ministry in Ephesus, the chief city. But in God's plan, Ephesus was not yet ready for Paul, nor Paul for it. Therefore, they were forbidden by the Holy Spirit to preach the word in Asia (v.6). Next, Paul and his group tried repeatedly to go northward into the province of Bithynia along the Black Sea, but "the Spirit of Jesus did not permit them" (v.7 NASB).

Luke does not tell how the Holy Spirit gave Paul and his companions these directions. But as F. F. Bruce suggests, in the first case He may have spoken through a prophet in the church at Lystra (*The Book of the Acts*, p.326). For example, as Paul was nearing Jerusalem on his third journey, different Christians ministered to Paul in the Spirit to warn him of the danger of setting foot in that city (Acts 21:11). They received a word of knowledge (Acts 21:4) and a prophecy (Acts 21:11) for Paul, but he bore the responsibility of what God wanted him to do with this knowledge. In that case he kept on with his plans. The comforting word which the Lord brought to Paul in the Jerusalem prison (Acts 23:11) proves that he had not been disobedient to the Spirit. Probably in Acts 21:4 the disciples added their own interpretation to the word of knowledge which revealed imminent danger for Paul, and concluded that he should not go up to Jerusalem.

In v.7 it is to be noted that the best Greek manuscripts have "the Spirit of Jesus." This is the only occurrence of this striking expression in the N.T., although it is closely paralleled by "the Spirit of Christ" in Rom. 8:9 and I Pet. 1:11; "the Spirit of Jesus Christ" in Phil. 1:19; and "the Spirit of His Son" in Gal.

4:6. Verses 6 and 7 of Acts 16, taken together, are especially important in establishing the fact that the two terms, "the Holy Spirit" and "the Spirit of Jesus," refer to one and the same Spirit, the same Third Person of the Trinity.

Just why Luke made a change in phraseology in referring to the Spirit in these two instances is not clear. Again F. F. Bruce's comment is helpful: "Possibly the methods used to communicate the Spirit's will on the two occasions were different; it may be that on the second occasion the communication took a form closely associated with the exalted Christ" (*The Book of the Acts*, p.327). During His earthly ministry, Jesus rebuked demons He was exorcizing and "would not allow them to speak" (Luke 4:41 NASB; the verb "allow" and the verb "permit" in v.7 are the same in the Greek). We may surmise, then, that the Lord Jesus Christ as Head of His Church issued one or more sharp commands by His Spirit to Paul not to enter Bithynia. The Lord seems to have revealed His will on this occasion in a more direct fashion than by adverse circumstances, but whether by a word of wisdom, by a prophecy, or by tongues and interpretation, we do not know. The guidance that Paul received is an example of the promise in Isa. 30:21, "And your ears will hear a word behind you, 'This is the way, walk in it,' whenever you turn to the right or to the left" (NASB).

God's strategy for world evangelization was Europe before Asia. Bithynia would have its chance later on. In fact, within fifteen years, Peter took the Gospel to that area, according to the salutation of his first epistle (I Pet. 1:1). By the beginning of the next century, Christianity was flourishing there, as we discover in a fascinating exchange of letters between Pliny, the Roman governor of Bithynia, and the Emperor Trajan.*

*Pliny to Trajan.

My Lord: It is my custom to refer to you everything that I am in doubt about; for who is better able either to correct my hesitation or instruct my ignorance?

I have never had anything to do with trials of Christians; consequently I do not know the precedents regarding the question of punishment or the nature of the inquisition. I have been in no little doubt whether some discrimination is made with regard to age, or

It was wise for Paul to make plans to go to Asia — and usually his plans were sensible and right. But, like him, we must be ready to lay our plans aside when God sends a new revelation of His will. Be orderly and systematic (see Paul's daily routine for two years at Ephesus, Acts 19:8-10) and use the wisdom of common sense, but be sensitive to the voice of the Spirit and subject to His change.

---

whether the young are treated no differently from the older; whether renunciation wins indulgence, or it is of no avail to have abandoned Christianity if one has once been a Christian; whether the very profession of the name is to be punished, or only the disgraceful practices which go along with the name.

So far this has been my procedure when people were charged before me with being Christians. I have asked the accused themselves if they were Christians; if they said "Yes", I asked them a second and third time, warning them of the penalty; if they persisted I ordered them to be led off to execution. For I had no doubt that, whatever kind of thing it was that they pleaded guilty to, their stubbornness and unyielding obstinacy at any rate deserved to be punished. There were others afflicted with the like madness whom I marked down to be referred to Rome, because they were Roman citizens.

Later, as usually happens, the trouble spread by the very treatment of it, and further varieties came to my notice. An anonymous document was laid before me containing many people's names. Some of these denied that they were Christians or had ever been so; at my dictation they invoked the gods and did reverence with incense and wine to your image, which I had ordered to be brought for this purpose along with the statues of the gods; they also cursed Christ; and as I am informed that people who are really Christians cannot possibly be made to do any of those things, I considered that the people who did them should be discharged. Others against whom I received information said they were Christians and then denied it; they meant (they said) that they had once been Christians but had given it up: some three years previously, some a longer time, one or two as many as twenty years before [i.e., significantly enough, under Domitian]. All these likewise both did reverence to your image and the statues of the gods and cursed Christ. But they maintained that their fault or error amounted to nothing more than this: they were in the habit of meeting on a certain fixed day before sunrise and reciting an antiphonal hymn to Christ as God, and binding themselves with an oath — not to commit any crime, but to abstain from all acts of theft, robbery and adultery, from breaches of faith, from denying a trust when called upon to honour it. After this, they went on, it was their custom to separate, and then meet again to partake of food, but food of an ordinary and innocent kind. And even this, they said, they had given up doing since the publication of my edict in which, according to your instructions, I had placed a ban on private associations. So I thought it the more necessary to inquire into the real truth of the matter by subjecting to torture two female slaves, who were called "deacons"; but I found nothing more than a perverse superstition which went beyond all bounds.

Therefore I deferred further inquiry in order to apply to you for a ruling. The case

The other means of divine guidance to be found in these
verses is by vision. In a vision, a man becomes oblivious of his
natural surroundings. The Spirit of God so controls his senses
that he seems actually to see, hear, and feel what is revealed to
him in the vision. The recipient of the vision may be awake
(Dan. 10:7; Acts 9:3,7; 10:3), in a trance (Acts 10:10,17; 11:5),
or dreaming (Num. 12:6; Job 4:13; 33:15; Dan. 4:9; 7:1). Paul
had a number of visions (II Cor. 12:1). He described the
appearance of Christ to him on the Damascus road as a
heavenly vision (Acts 26:19), and the Lord spoke to him one
night in Corinth by a vision (Acts 18:9). That young men
should see visions is one of the characteristics of the Pentecostal
outpouring of the Spirit (Acts 2:17).

The vision which came to Paul that night at Troas is often
termed the Macedonian call. We must note carefully that this
was not the time when he was called to serve the Lord. He
began to preach the Gospel in Damascus a few days after his

---

seemed to me to be a proper one for consultation, particularly because of the number of
those who were accused. For many of every age, every class, and of both sexes are being
accused and will continue to be accused. Nor has this contagious superstition spread
through the cities only, but also through the villages and the countryside. But I think it
can be checked and put right. At any rate the temples, which had been well-nigh
abandoned, are beginning to be frequented again; and the customary services, which
had been neglected for a long time, are beginning to be resumed; fodder for the
sacrificial animals, too, is beginning to find a sale again, for hitherto it was difficult to
find anyone to buy it. From all this it is easy to judge what a multitude of people can be
reclaimed, if an opportunity is granted them to renounce Christianity.

TRAJAN TO PLINY.

My dear Secundus:[1] You have followed the correct procedure in deciding the cases of
those who have been charged before you with being Christians. Indeed, no general
decision can be made by which a set form of dealing with them could be established.
They must not be ferreted out; if they are charged and convicted, they must be
punished, provided that anyone who denies that he is a Christian and gives practical
proof of that by invoking our gods is to win indulgence by this repudiation, no matter
what grounds for suspicion may have existed against him in the past. Anonymous
documents which are laid before you should receive no attention in any case; they are a
very bad precedent and quite unworthy of the age in which we live.[2]

[1] Pliny's full name was Gaius Plinius Secundus.
[2] The two letters are preserved in the *Epistles of Pliny*, x. 96 and 97.

conversion, as soon as he had been healed and filled with the Spirit (Acts 9:17-22). One does not need a vision or any other special divine guidance to call him to obey the Great Commission of our risen Lord (see comments on Matt. 28:18-20). Paul had already been serving God as a teacher and evangelist and apostle for a number of years, and he was now on his second missionary tour. This vision was given him to provide positive direction after the series of divine prohibitions.

The Lord also guides us by His written word. "Thy word is a lamp unto my feet, and a light unto my path" (Ps. 119:105). In addition, His direction may come in the form of an inner "voice" or strong impression of what to do in a certain situation. Furthermore, He permits circumstances beyond our control to alter the course we should take. For instance, God used the famine to bring Jacob and his sons to Egypt (Gen. 45:4-11; 46:2-4; 50:20). But He also expects us to seek wise human counsel (Prov. 11:14; 12:15; 15:22; 19:20; 20:18). He has created human beings with minds that can think and reason and plan, and He does not bless mental laziness on our part. Purposeful ignorance and slipshod organization bring no glory to God. We are commanded to seek wisdom and pray for it (Prov. 2:1-12; James 1:5), for by wisdom we may walk in upright paths, and our steps will not be impeded (Prov. 4:11,12 NASB).

God will not leave His children without direction. Being led by the Spirit of God is a characteristic mark of a true son of God (Rom. 8:14). He is our Redeemer, Jehovah our God, who leads us in the way we should go (Isa. 48:17). Because He is our Shepherd, He acts in compassion to lead us in paths of righteousness for His name's sake (Isa. 49:10; Ps. 23:1-3). In answer to our prayers, He will teach us His will and His way (Ps. 5:8; 25:4-10) as we commit ourselves completely into His hand (Ps. 31:3,5; Rom. 12:1,2; see comments on Rom. 8: 14-17).

ACTS 19:1-7 — TONGUES AT EPHESUS.

The third occasion when tongues are specifically mentioned in the Book of Acts took place at Ephesus twenty some years after Pentecost. This incident shows quite clearly that the Pentecostal experience is extended to include all believers in Christ.

Early in his third missionary journey, the apostle Paul returned to the chief city of the Roman province of Asia and happened on about a dozen men who were "disciples." In Luke's writings, when this term is not further qualified, it always designates disciples of Jesus. That they were Christians in some sense is borne out by Paul's reference to faith on their part — "since ye believed" (v.2). The verb "believe" is used about twenty times in Acts with no direct object. In every case, the context indicates that believing in Christ for salvation is meant.

Paul noticed, however, an obvious lack of power in their lives. God's evident seal or stamp of ownership, which is the Holy Spirit, was not upon them at this point (Eph. 1:13,14). Therefore Paul asked them a question, the very asking of which implies that it is possible to "believe" without thereby receiving the Spirit in Pentecostal fullness. "Having believed, did you receive the Holy Spirit?" (v.2 literal translation). The Greek here does not employ a temporal conjunction such as "after" or "when" to indicate the time relationship between believing in Christ and receiving the Spirit. But the aorist participle, "having believed," is the same as in Eph. 1:13. There the context more clearly brings out the fact that the gift of the Holy Spirit comes to one as a *consequence* of his believing in Christ, but that it is not necessarily *coincident* with his conversion. On the other hand, the N.T. consistently teaches that the fullness of the Gospel message embraces the news of the coming of the Spirit, and that normal Christian faith includes as one of the fundamentals the reception of the Holy Spirit.

In questioning the disciples, Paul discovered that their knowledge of Christianity was incomplete. They told him that they had been baptized into John's baptism. Their experience was very similar to that of Apollos before Priscilla and Aquila "explained to him the way of God more accurately" (Acts 18:26 NASB). Apollos already knew the O.T. Scriptures and had been instructed in the Way of the Lord, the teachings of the Lord Jesus. Enthusiastic and fervent in his spirit, he was able to speak and teach accurately the things about Jesus' life and to present Him as the Messiah, even though he was acquainted only with the baptism of John (Acts 18:25).

In addition to knowing O.T. references concerning the Spirit of God, disciples of John the Baptist would have known that he had spoken of a coming baptism in the Spirit (Matt. 3:11; see comments on Matt. 3:11-17), so that they could hardly have been ignorant about the existence of the Holy Spirit. These dozen men, however, like Apollos, had not known that the outpouring of the Spirit was an accomplished fact. Therefore their reply in v.2 should be interpreted as in the ASV or the margin of the NASB: "No, we have not even heard whether the Holy Spirit has been given." The same Greek construction occurs in John 7:39, where the translator must also supply the word "given" to make good sense in English.

Thus these men had not yet heard that Jesus had fulfilled His mission after His crucifixion, resurrection, and ascension by sending the Holy Spirit. Consequently, they had an incomplete knowledge of the Gospel. Furthermore, their pre-Pentecost type of baptism as the mark of their repentance, was no longer adequate after Peter had proclaimed baptism in the name of Jesus on the Day of Pentecost. John the Baptist himself had recognized his baptism was only temporary, "telling the people to believe in Him who was coming after him, that is, in Jesus" (v.4 NASB).

The order of the next events at Ephesus is very clear. It is the normal pattern of the baptism in the Holy Spirit. When the twelve men heard from Paul the whole truth about Jesus, they believed and received Christian baptism from him. If they had not been regenerated by the Spirit of God prior to Paul's arrival, certainly they were before they were baptized in water and before the Spirit fell upon them. Then Paul laid his hands on them, and they were baptized in the Spirit in Pentecostal fashion: "The Holy Spirit came on them, and they *began* speaking with tongues and prophesying" (v.6 NASB). In the early Church, the Spirit was normally communicated in His fullness at the time of one's baptismal ceremony. The disciples at Ephesus followed essentially the same instructions that Peter gave in Jerusalem — repent and believe, be baptized, and receive the gift of the Holy Spirit (Acts 2:38).

The speaking with tongues and prophesying were outward and visible signs of the presence and power of the Holy Spirit. Validation by means of these signs was just as important for these twelve disciples as for the believers on the Day of Pentecost. Their experience of manifesting the overflowing presence of the Comforter by speaking in tongues was consistent with that of the 120 at Pentecost and of Cornelius and his household, and probably of the Samaritan converts and of Saul of Tarsus.

ACTS 22:16 — BE BAPTIZED AND WASH AWAY THY SINS.

Does this verse actually teach baptismal regeneration? Ananias commanded the newly converted Saul of Tarsus, "And now why do you delay? Arise, and be baptized, and get your sins washed away, having called on His name" (literal translation). Saul (or, Paul) had confessed Jesus as Lord three days earlier on the road outside of Damascus (Acts 9:6; 22:10), so that he was converted or saved at that time. Were not his sins forgiven then also? Yes, he was forgiven instantly by God on the basis of the atoning sacrifice of Christ.

Water baptism, however, may be considered to wash off the

stain or stigma of one's past sins which still sullies his character and reputation. By the public confession of baptism, the new believer, who has already called on the name of the Lord Jesus in faith, now definitely renounces his past life, burying it once and for all, reckoning his old self to be dead and buried with Christ. Thus he puts off, lays aside, or washes away his old sins with the aid of a visible ceremony or "point of contact" for his faith. In the presence of God and of men, he announces that he is done with his sins. The guilt was forgiven by Christ at the moment of conversion; the influence and effect of one's sins, the drag on his reputation, can be dealt with decisively at baptism. He severs his connection with his sinful past and washes his record clean (see comments on Matt. 3:11-17; Titus 3:4-7; I Pet. 3:21).

ROMANS

ROM. 5:5 — LOVE POURED OUT.

The first ummistakable mention of the Holy Spirit in Paul's great doctrinal epistle to the Romans occurs in this verse. The apostle is describing the benefits which come to Christians because we have been justified by faith. In addition to being accounted righteous through faith in Jesus (Rom. 3:21-31; 5:1), we have peace with God as a settled fact. Also through Jesus our Lord, we have received the right of access into the very presence of God our King, because we stand before Him in a state of grace, not in our own merit (Rom. 5:2a). Not only so, but we can even rejoice in our afflictions, because we know that our troubles and trials are producing patience or perseverance. The chain reaction continues, so that perseverance produces proven character, and this in turn strengthens our hope of seeing and sharing the glory of God (Rom. 5:3,4,2b).

Paul continues: "Nor will this hope let us down, because God's love is poured out in our hearts through the Holy Spirit who has been given to us" (v.5, F. F. Bruce, *The Letters of Paul: An Expanded Paraphrase* [Grand Rapids: Eerdmans, 1965], p.197). We know that our hope of future glory is not illusory, because of our wonderful present experience of God's love. His love has been "shed abroad" (KJV) in our hearts, or better, "poured out," the very same verb used to describe the outpouring of the Spirit at Pentecost and in Cornelius' home (Acts 2:17,18,33; 10:45; Titus 3:6). According to the perfect tense of this Greek verb, not only has the Holy Spirit poured God's love into our hearts, but He continues to flood us and comfort us with that love and give us assurance of it.

In telling of God's boundless love for us demonstrated supremely in Christ's death in our behalf (Rom. 5:5-8), Paul refers to the fact that the Holy Spirit was given to us (end of v.5).

Historically, the Spirit was formally sent to the corporate Church at Pentecost, for all time and for all believers (Acts 2:33). Individually, however, He is given to each Christian in virtue of his faith to receive the promised Holy Spirit (Gal. 3:2,5,14; 4:6; I John 3:24; 4:13). Though the Spirit was given to all (Acts 2:38,39), each must receive Him personally. This is comparable to the fact that though Jesus died as a ransom for all (I Tim. 2:4; 4:10) and rose from the dead, once for all time (Heb. 9:25-28a), yet each one must believe in Christ and personally receive Him as Savior and Lord (John 1:12). One may note this duality of the corporate and the individual throughout both the O.T. and the N.T. Most of the promises are corporate promises to be appropriated by the individual as well.

Many can testify to a new realization and appreciation of God's love for them after the baptism in the Holy Spirit. Furthermore, they experience in a new way a divine flow of love through them to others who are in need.

Rom. 8:1-13 — LIFE BY THE SPIRIT.

Romans 8 has been called Paul's Pentecost. While it barely touches on the charismatic empowering, it is the greatest single chapter in the Bible about the inner working of the Holy Spirit in the life of the believer. This passage brings to a climax Paul's teaching on sanctification, and therefore is the peak-point of his major doctrinal epistle. The Holy Spirit is mentioned no less than seventeen times in the course of the thirty-nine verses.

In the sixth chapter, the apostle teaches that positionally the Christian died with Christ to sin and is alive unto God in Christ Jesus (Rom. 6:1-11). In the seventh chapter, he states that we have been released from the condemnation of the Law and now serve God in the new life of the Spirit (Rom. 7:6 RSV). Then Paul describes the fierce inner struggle which he as a born-again Christian experienced between his flesh (his old fallen human nature) and his mind (his new real self as a regenerated man). The cause of this conflict continues to exist throughout this present life, but God's provision for victory is proclaimed in chapter eight. A life of righteousness can now be an actuality through the sanctifying power of the indwelling Holy Spirit.

There is a new law, in the sense of a principle or dominating force, at work in the believer (v.2). Like every human being since Adam's fall, he was caught in the inevitable principle of sin and death. He could not keep from sinning, and he would eventually die (Rom. 5:12). He was not only legally condemned, but morally corrupt in the eyes of his righteous and holy Creator-Judge. But now in Christ Jesus his sentence of condemnation has been revoked (v.1), and a higher principle is operating in him to set him free from the stranglehold of sin. Sin had been choking off his life and causing certain death. The power of sin is like the force of gravity which pulls one down to destruction unless a greater force intervenes to hold him up. That new force is the Holy Spirit. He enters the heart to supply the life of Christ. He effects the "life of Christ Jesus" by forming a vital union of the believer with Christ. This may be likened to the union of a branch grafted into a tree.

The Spirit is in believers to reverse the direction of their "walk" and their thinking. In their natural state, they could only "mind the things of the flesh" (v.5). That is, they could only live by the dictates and promptings of their old selfish natures and think the thoughts which came naturally to them. But now they live in the sphere of the Spirit, because the Spirit of God dwells in them (v.9). Therefore the Spirit is prompting them to think His thoughts. Their whole attitude becomes spiritual under the Spirit's control because their minds are in tune with Him. Such a basic attitude of submission to God's law instead of the old hostility means life and inward peace (vv.6,7).

This new life in the Spirit is bound to have consequences for our whole being. Verses 10 and 11 describe how we are freed from the law of death (v.2). It is true that the body is still subject to death and can be counted on to die someday because of the aftermath of sin. Yet because of the Spirit who has His home within us, our mortal bodies will one day be quickened. The obvious meaning of the word "quicken" in this context is to restore to physical life by resurrection (as in John 5:21; I Cor. 15:22). At His second coming, Christians who have died will be raised from the dead just as Jesus was during His first advent. Those who are still alive and remain (I Thess. 4:15) will suddenly experience their mortal bodies being given new resurrection life. That will be the glorious day when "this mortal will have put on immortality" (I Cor. 15:54).

A mortal body, however, is one which is subject to death, but which has not yet died. This meaning is evident, for instance, in the command not to let sin reign in these mortal bodies (Rom. 6:12). Paul uses the term "mortal" again in II Cor. 4:7-11 when he states that our weak bodies are like earthen vessels, so that when the life of Jesus is manifested in our mortal flesh, the surpassing greatness of the power may obviously be of God and not from ourselves. It glorifies our God, then, to implore Him to strengthen and heal our mortal bodies when there is need. J. B. Phillips suggests in his translation of v. 11 that healing is a present benefit that is a foretaste of the resurrection : "Nevertheless once the Spirit of him who raised Christ Jesus from the dead lives within you he will, by the same Spirit, bring to your whole being new strength and vitality."

In vv.12 and 13, the apostle summarizes what he has been teaching from v.5 onward. We are not under obligation to the old nature, he says, to live habitually under its control. He implies that our obligation is now to the Holy Spirit. The paraphrase of F. F. Bruce aids us in understanding v.13: "If you live in conformity with the desires of the old nature, you are bound to die. But if by the Spirit you treat the body's former activities as dead, you will live." As Phillips renders it, "If . . . you cut the nerves of your instinctive actions by obeying the Spirit, you are on the way to real living." The Spirit is ever present to supply us with the power and determination to say no. It is the Spirit of Christ within who enables us to deny ourselves daily and take up our cross and follow the Lord Jesus. He motivates us to keep on mortifying the former deeds of the body as we exercise self-control. To illustrate the necessity of disciplining ourselves, Paul in another letter reminded the sports-minded Corinthians of how athletes even buffet their bodies (I Cor. 9:24-27). For this cause, God has given us the Holy Spirit, who in turn gives us a spirit of discipline (II Tim. 1:7 NASB; see comments on II Tim. 1:6-7).

From Romans 8:1-13, then, it is clear that the victorious life in Christ is more than a matter of mere self-control. It is living by an entirely different principle of being. Is is *life by the Spirit*. This explains why healing and other miracles can occur. A different order of creation is in effect. It is in the realm of the Spirit.

Rom. 8:14-17 — THE GUIDANCE AND WITNESS OF THE SPIRIT.

Living by the Spirit includes being led by the Spirit. The continual guidance of the Holy Spirit is one of the clearest marks of divine sonship. "For all who are being led by the Spirit of God, these are sons of God" (v.14 NASB). The blessed Holy Spirit not only guides us into all the truth that is in Jesus (John 14:3,26; 16:13), but His leading also relates to the practical business of daily living. God the Father wants us as sons to know His will at first hand and in detail. Samuel Chadwick once said, "Nothing is too trivial for omniscience. Come straight to God. Lay all questions naked before Him and He will make it plain to you what is His will" (*The Way to Pentecost* [New York: Revell, n.d.]).

The Book of Acts furnishes many specific instances of the Spirit's guiding in the hour of crisis and decision for the sake of the Gospel (see comments on Acts 16:6-10). But is there in addition a general direction in which the Holy Spirit is daily leading all Christians? There certainly is. Our common destination is holiness. "Follow peace with all men, and holiness, without which no man shall see the Lord" (Heb. 12:14). "For this is the will of God, even your sanctification" (I Thess. 4:3; see comments on I Cor. 6:11).

God has appointed the Holy Spirit to be the agent of our sanctification. Thus it is His duty to lead us away from sin. He leads us in paths of righteousness, for He is the Spirit of Christ our Good Shepherd. So He directs the obedient child of God to abandon the deeds of the flesh and to put down roots in the orchard of grace. There, under the Holy Spirit's expert care, the believer will bear His fruit (Gal. 5:18-23). The Spirit is ever leading us to fellowship with the Father through Jesus Christ, in whom we have our right of access into the Father's presence (Eph. 2:18).

You ask, How does the Spirit lead? Often it is by His "still small voice" (I Kings 19:12) appealing to one's conscience. On the other hand, sometimes the believer may be gripped by the Spirit and almost impelled against his will or better judgment. Luke says of Jesus that after His baptism He was led by the Spirit (Luke 4:1) — the same verb as in v.14. But as Mark writes about that incident, he makes this striking statement. "The Spirit immediately drove him out into the wilderness" (Mark 1:12 RSV). Similar to jet propulsion, the Spirit may drive the Christian from within. To be sure, He may draw him from without by external circumstances or by the advice of other members of the Body. He may plant suggestions in the mind. But on occasion He may lead by a strong inner compulsion that is as distinct as an audible voice. His direction, however, never leaves one in a state of anxiety or frustration, but produces a real sense of inner peace.

Another assuring factor in the leading of God's Spirit is that there is a ring of certainty to it. In connection with His guidance is His inner witness with our spirit. Now one of the marvelous transformations that occurs in salvation is the change in attitude of the human spirit. Jesus Christ died to redeem us that we might receive the adoption of sons (Gal. 4:5; Eph. 1:5). This means that by a divine act God legally placed us as sons in His household. We were given this status at the moment of our conversion, not as a result of special understanding or spirituality. By the new birth wrought in us by the Spirit of God, we became *children* of God with a new nature. By adoption, we were made *sons* of God with new rights and a new inheritance. As a result, our own spirits have a new outlook.

In both cases where the word "spirit" occurs in v.15 it should have a small "s." Williams paraphrases the verse in this manner: "For you do not have a sense of servitude to fill you with dread again, but the consciousness of adopted sons by which we cry, 'Abba,' that is, 'Father.' " There is no longer a slavery-spirit to bring us back into a state of fear, but our adoption spirit that makes us so aware of our sonship that we want to cry out, "Abba!"

This cry does not originate solely from the redeemed human spirit. Paul explained it more fully to the Galatians: "And because you are sons, God has sent forth the Spirit of His Son into our hearts, crying, 'Abba! Father!' " (Gal. 4:6 NASB). Thus there is a joint testimony of the Holy Spirit with our own renewed spirit that we are children of God. He is constantly bearing this inward witness so that in any and every situation we may *know* that we are saved. The apostle John has much to say about this inner conviction in his epistle. "And hereby we know that He abideth in us, by the Spirit which he hath given us" (I John 3:24). As God's love is perfected in us when we love one another, by this we know that we are abiding in Him and He in us, "because he hath given us of his Spirit" (I John 4:13; see also comments on I John 5:6-13).

The Spirit of God touches the human spirit in a mysterious but intensely personal way. He who inspired the holy Scriptures uses the Word of God to bring the revelation of God about His Son to one's inner consciousness. Then this same Spirit comes to provide an inner confirmation of the objective revelation. Thus when we believe, the truth of the Gospel is sealed in our hearts by the Holy Spirit. "We not only believe, but we have a conviction in our hearts that we have believed the truth" (Bernard Ramm, *The Witness of the Spirit* [Grand Rapids: Eerdmans, 1960], p. 68). The Spirit develops within the believer a spiritual perceptivity which is an intuitive ability to recognize God, understand His truth, and perceive His promises. The inner voice of the Holy Spirit, of which His witness with our spirit is one aspect, then becomes His chief means of leading the Christian in his daily walk.

Rom. 8:23-27 — THE INTERCESSION OF THE SPIRIT.

The verses leading up to this passage describe the present

sufferings of this creation. The Christian inevitably is affected by grief and pain along with everyone else. But even before the day when he will be glorified with Christ, he enjoys a number of advantages over other suffering human beings. For one thing, he is a joint-heir with Christ because he has already been adopted as a son into the family of God (Rom. 8:15-17). Therefore, he can pray and act and speak from a position of authority in the spiritual realm. Second, he has a wonderful hope that an end will come to the groaning and suffering that now prevails in the created universe (8:18-25). And thirdly, although he still has reason to groan much as does the creation around him, he has "the firstfruits of the Spirit" (v.23).

The believer is now with perseverance waiting out the time until his present adoption will be revealed (v.25). That will happen on the day he receives the redemption of his body (v.23), at the second coming of Christ and not before (I Cor. 15:22,23,35-54; Phil. 3:20,21; I Thess. 4:13-17). The manifestation or revealing of the sons of God (Rom. 8:19) will occur at the same time that the created world is set free from its slavery to corruption (Rom. 8:20,21). We are elsewhere told that our formal recognition will come when Christ returns and is revealed in glory (Col. 3:4; II Thess. 1:7-10). Therefore, any doctrine which claims there is a special group of manifested sons of God during this present age is in error.

Although he may be suffering, the believer already possesses the Holy Spirit as the firstfruits of that final, completed stage of his salvation. Paul's word for "firstfruits" (Greek *aparche*) appears frequently in the Septuagint (Greek O.T.) as the first part of a harvest. Thus the term was familiar to the Jews in the congregation in Rome. Here he seems to be referring intentionally to Pentecost, which was the feast of the firstfruits of wheat harvest (Exod. 34:22; see comments on Acts 2:1-4). The Holy Spirit is the sample of the future crop of glory and whets our appetite for what is yet to come. As A. Skevington Wood so beautifully puts it in his masterful treatment of Rom. 8, "The Holy Spirit adds incentive to the life of holiness by introducing us to a taste of heaven on earth" (*Life by the Spirit* [Grand Rapids: Zondervan, 1963], p.105). In writing to other predominantly Gentile churches with their interests more along commercial lines, Paul alludes to the "earnest" or first installment of the Spirit (II Cor. 1:22; 5:5; see comments on Eph. 1:13,14).

During this period of weakness and infirmity before we receive resurrected bodies, the Spirit is dwelling in us to help us (v.26). The verb for "help" is a composite word (*syn-anti-lamba-netai*) which suggests that He as the Comforter or Paraclete shares our burdens with us by taking our place. Wuest translates, "The Spirit lends us a helping hand with reference to our weakness." It is particularly in the matter of prayer that He comes to our aid, "for we do not know" — even after becoming Christians — "how to pray as we should" (NASB). Christ as our ascended High Priest is praying for us, in the sense that He makes us the object of His praying (Rom. 8:34; Heb. 7:25). The Holy Spirit, however, prays for us in the sense that He makes us the vehicle of His praying. There appears to be no suggestion in the Bible that the Holy Spirit ever prays except through the believer.

The Spirit, therefore, makes intercession for us and through us. Our very sense of helplessness and unworthiness before God is the first essential in true prayer. Only then do we let the Spirit intercede. He does so "with groanings which cannot be uttered." This translation represents the two Greek words *stenagmois alaletois*. The latter term describes our groanings or sighs as being inarticulate, not able to be expressed in understandable words.

Does Paul's terminology refer to or include praying in tongues? The Lutheran Bible commentator R. C. H. Lenski says, "Later writers state that the charisma of tongues was a speaking in non-human language and either identify these 'groanings' with this non-human language or conceive of them as a parallel to it" (*The Interpretation of St. Paul's Epistle to the Romans* [Columbus: Wartburg Press, 1945], p.547).

Even more telling are the following comments written by Frederic Godet in the nineteenth century, before the modern Pentecostal movement: "In every particular case, he who is the object of this assistance feels that no distinct words fully express to God the infinite good after which he sighs. The fact proves that the aspiration is not his own, but that it is produced in his heart by the Spirit of Him of whom John said, 'that He is greater than our heart' (I John 3:20). We here find ourselves in a domain analogous to that of the *glossais lalein, speaking in tongues,* to which I Cor. 14 refers; compare vv.14 and 15, where Paul says: 'When I pray in a tongue, my spirit (*pneuma*) prayeth indeed, but my understanding (*nous*) is unfruitful.' The understanding cannot control, nor even follow the movement of the spirit, which, exalted by the Spirit of God, plunges into the depths of the divine. Thus, at the moment when the believer already feels the impulse of hope failing within him, a groan more elevated, holy, and intense than anything which can go forth even from his renewed heart is uttered within him, coming from God and going to God, like a pure breath, and relieves the poor downcast heart" (*Commentary on St. Paul's Epistle to the Romans*, trans. by A. Cusin [Edinburgh: T. & T. Clark, 1881], II, 102).

It would be too much to claim that only when the child of God is consciously praying in tongues can the Holy Spirit make intercession from within. For surely the indwelling Spirit has interceded for Christians down through the centuries who have not known about this charismatic gift. But there is no doubt that praying in a tongue removes certain intellectual blocks by which the mind constricts the human spirit, so that the Holy Spirit has greater freedom to pray within the believer.

To be effective, we should always pray "in the Spirit." No matter whether it be in English or in a tongue or in an unuttered secret groaning, every prayer must be inspired by God's Spirit for it to reach heaven. Such prayers can never fail to be answered, because the Holy Spirit "intercedes for the saints according to the will of God" (v.27 RSV). We pray in the Spirit when we do not ask selfishly or wrongly, to consume it on our passions (James 4:3). The Holy Spirit enables us to align our will with God's, so that whatever we ask, it is for His glory and not to gain our own ends (John 14:13).

ROM. 12:3-8 — GIFTS THAT DIFFER.

This is one of the key passages in the N.T. describing the charismatic gifts. The Greek for "gifts" in v.6 is *charismata,* the same as in I Cor. 12:4,9,28,30,31 and I Pet. 4:10 (see comments on those passages). Paul had previously mentioned his desire to manifest some spiritual gift (*charisma*) to the believers in Rome, so that they might be established (Rom. 1:11).

While it is not within the scope of this study on the Holy Spirit to examine Romans 12:1-2 in detail, we should give heed to Paul's great exhortation in order to minister successfully in the spiritual gifts. We must present or yield our bodies, our very selves (NEB), as a living and holy sacrifice so that the Holy Spirit may control us completely. This is our "reasonable service" (12:1 KJV), our "spiritual service of worship" (NASB). It is essential to offer ourselves to God in complete dedication before we attempt to perform service to one another. Such a sacrifice is typified by the O.T. burnt offering (Lev. 1:3-9). Furthermore, we must continue to be transformed (Greek present tense) by the renewing of our minds so that we may be able to discern the will of God and approve it as being good and acceptable and perfect (12:2). According to Titus 3:5 (see comments there) such renewing is the work of the Holy Spirit. This renewal is the necessary spiritual preparation for a balanced and continuing charismatic ministry.

Using the illustration of the human body, as he does also in I Cor. 12, Paul goes on to remind us that its many members or parts do not all have the same ministry or manifestations (Rom. 12:4-5). Likewise, in the body of Christ and in the local Christian communities, we have charismatic gifts "that differ according to the grace given to us" (v.6 NASB). Paul is urging each Christian to show humility in the use of these gifts. No one should think more highly of himself than he ought to think. True, each of the gifts mentioned in Romans 12:6-8 has a natural counterpart which the Lord may heighten and use. But here the gifts under discussion seem to be supernaturally imparted. Even the measure of faith, which enables him to receive a charismatic gift is, in itself, an allotment from God (v.3). Therefore, he should avoid the feeling of self importance because of the gift he has, and instead cooperate with the other members of his church in mutual service.

There follows a list of seven representative gifts of the Spirit, with brief instructions as to how they should be exercised: (1) Prophecy — the ability to speak forth under divine prompting something which the Spirit has revealed to the one having this gift. It should be exercised "according to the proportion of his faith" (v.6 NASB), the measure of which is assigned by God (v.3). Paul's statement implies that the more faith one has, the greater will be his prophetic endowment.

(2) Ministry or service — the Greek word *diakonia,* which can refer either to the dispensing of the word of life (Acts 6:4) or to the administering of the temporal affairs of a local congregation (Acts 6:1-3). Gifts of serving are one of the two main categories of charismatic gifts in Peter's short discussion of this subject (see comments on I Pet. 4:10,11). A charismatic gift is surely in operation when one can keep on ministering to the saints with love and hard work (Heb. 6:10) until he fulfills that ministry (Col. 4:17).

(3) Teaching — not simply systematic instruction (II Tim. 2:2), but a manifestation of the Holy Spirit in the ability to make plain the meaning of the Word of God which He has inspired. As Donald Gee has written, "The main function of a

true teacher is to impart the knowledge that is the ground for wisdom" (*Spiritual Gifts in the Work of the Ministry Today* [Springfield, Mo.: Gospel Publishing House, 1963], p.47). One who has the gift of teaching may often manifest a word of knowledge, a flash of insight into truth that penetrates beyond the operation of his own unaided intellect (*ibid.*, p.42).

(4) Exhortation — the ministry of speaking words of comfort and encouragement (*paraklesis*) under the guidance and anointing of the Paraclete Himself (I Tim. 4:13; Heb. 13:22; Phil. 2:1 KJV "consolation"). This gift usually accompanies preaching (cf. Acts 13:15 with Paul's sermon that follows), teaching (I Tim. 4:13; 6:2; Titus 1:9; 2:15), and prophesying (I Cor. 14:3). Paul was careful to explain that his exhortation never was based on a desire to mislead nor made use of flattery (I Thess. 2:3-5).

(5) Giving — the exercise of private benevolence and sharing what one has. Giving should be done with "simplicity" (v.8 KJV) in the sense of sincerity and singleheartedness, i.e., with no self-seeking or ulterior motive. Or as the RSV and NASB render the word, giving should be done with "liberality." In II Cor. 8:2; 9:11,13 Paul uses this term to commend the Macedonian Christians for giving generously and cheerfully. A ministry of giving also needs wisdom and guidance from the Holy Spirit so that one does not contribute to unworthy causes or to selfish, grasping persons. Here again, a sudden word of wisdom or of knowledge may be the Spirit's way of alerting the donor.

(6) Leadership — a gift which implies ability to rule or manage or administer in a church. Every elder and deacon must have this ability, as proven first of all in his own household (I Tim. 3:4,5,12). Some elders were especially able along this line and were worthy of double honor (I Tim. 5:17). The members of their congregations were to obey them and submit to them (Heb. 13:17) and show due appreciation (I Thess. 5:12 NASB). This seems to be the same as the gift of governments (KJV) or administrations (NASB) which Paul lists in I Cor.

12:28. Here in Romans, Paul tells the leader to rule with diligence; or perhaps he means to cultivate the gift of leadership diligently. Certainly a ruling elder will often need a charismatic word of wisdom or knowledge in order to perform his task efficiently.

(7) Showing mercy — probably the same as the gift of helps (I Cor. 12:28). Every Christian in the local church, whether a leader or not, may — and should — have this gift of compassion and exercise it with cheerfulness. His special ministry may involve visiting the poor, the sick, or the sorrowing; it may be helping behind the scenes. In any case, he should do his work cheerfully. A person of a grudging or despondent mood obviously does not have the charismatic endowment for showing mercy to others.

In conclusion, it may be noted that Paul did not include the gift of tongues in this list. Since he encouraged the Corinthians to desire rather to have the gift of prophecy (I Cor. 14:1), and since that gift is listed here, it seems that speaking in tongues is not an essential ministry gift in a local congregation. When accompanied by the gift of interpretation of tongues, however, it may be used to edify others (I Cor. 14:4,5).

Rom. 12:11 — AGLOW WITH THE SPIRIT.

Commentators and modern translations differ over the meaning of the three words "fervent in spirit" found in the KJV at v.11. It may refer to one's human spirit, as in the case of Apollos in Acts 18:25 where the same Greek expression occurs, or it may mean the Holy Spirit, as in the translation in the above title, which is taken from the RSV. The Greek participle *zeontes* literally means "boiling." In either case, "The spiritual temperature is to be high in the Christian community" (EGT, II, 692), and it is certainly the Holy Spirit who lights the fire within each believer, as Dean Alford pointed out long ago (*The Greek Testament*, II, 444).

This exhortation of the apostle appears in a series of short commands concerning Christian behavior (Rom. 12:9-21). These are to characterize the life of the Spirit-filled believer in his relation to other Christians.

Paul's first word has to do with Christ's great commandment to His followers, to love one another with God-given *agape* love (verse 9a). An original paraphrase is given here to bring out the meaning of certain expressions in this passage:

> 9 Let your Christian love be unhypocritical, always turning in horror from what is evil, joining yourselves to what is good.
>
> 10 In your brotherly love to one another, be tenderly affectionate; take the lead in showing honor and respect to one another.
>
> 11 In earnest diligence, never be lagging behind; be aglow with the Spirit, rendering service as a slave to the Lord.
>
> 12 By the blessed hope of Jesus' return, keep joyous and cheerful, enduring steadfastly in the time of trouble and persecution, and persevering in your prayer-life — constantly devoting yourself to prayer.
>
> 13 Contribute to the needs of the saints (God's people), seeking eagerly for opportunities to show hospitality.
>
> 14 Bless those who persecute — stop cursing them, bless them!
>
> 15 Share the joy of those who rejoice, and share the grief of those who weep.
>
> 16 Live in harmony by being like-minded with one another; do not be high-minded or have a haughty attitude, but associate with the lowly members and accept humble duties. Do not consider yourself wise in your own conceited estimation of yourself.

Rom. 14:17 — THE KINGDOM OF GOD.

What is the kingdom of God like in its present phase, before the Lord Jesus Christ comes again to rule in person? Until His return, the rule of God on earth is effective only among those who have been delivered from the dominion of darkness and transferred into the kingdom of God's well-beloved Son (Col. 1:13). God's kingdom exists today where Christians are formed into a community of redeemed men who live in subjection to the will of God. His kingdom does not consist in mere words or talk (I Cor. 4:20 RSV), but is an actual demonstration of His Spirit moving in moral and spiritual power (I Cor. 2:4) to change lives and conform them to the image of Christ.

Therefore, as Paul argues in Rom. 14 and 15, the kingdom of God is not a matter of getting what you like to eat and drink and in the process forgetting to love your brother and to consider his conscience (Rom. 14:13-17). Rather, it is a matter of righteousness and peace and joy in the Holy Spirit. Paul is saying that the reign of God is seen in Christian living — in uprightness of conduct, in peace and harmony with other believers, and in joy inspired by the Holy Spirit (cf. I Thess. 1:6). This is the joy which comes from the indwelling of the Spirit of God in the community of Christians as He produces unity and fellowship, gladness, and sincerity of heart (cf. Acts 2:42-46).

Paul is evidently combating the materialistic ideas which the Jews held concerning the expected messianic kingdom. Similarly, the Moslem conception of paradise taught in the Koran is a luxuriant garden where the faithful recline on soft brocaded couches while they dwell with dark-eyed virgins and are served by immortal youths from silver dishes filled with wine and choice foods.

But Paul is describing a *now* kingdom, a kingdom where righteousness prevails. Jesus our Lord commands us to seek it (Matt. 6:33; Luke 12:31,32). Paul's prayer at the close of this section gives assurance of God's grace for such kingdom living: "May the God of hope fill you with joy and peace in your faith, that by the power of the Holy Spirit, your whole life and outlook may be radiant with hope" (Rom. 15:13 Phillips).

I CORINTHIANS

I COR. 1:4-9 — NOT LACKING IN ANY SPIRITUAL GIFT.

The apostle Paul begins his first epistle to the members of the church at Corinth with a word of thanksgiving to God on their behalf. He is especially thankful that they have been enriched with all (forms of) utterance or speech and with all (gifts of) knowledge (v.5). He continues, ". . . because in you the evidence for the truth of Christ has found confirmation" (v.6 NEB). Then he says, "so that you are not lacking in any spiritual gift, as you wait for the revealing of our Lord Jesus Christ" (v.7 RSV).

The word for "gift" or "spiritual gift" (RSV) in v.7 is *charisma* and refers to a special gift freely and graciously given by God to His children. Specific teaching regarding the Christian's charismatic gifts may be found in Rom. 12:3-8; I Cor. 12-14; and I Pet. 4:10,11. Here the term shows what Paul means by "all utterance" and "all knowledge" in v.5. "All utterance" evidently refers to the various charismatic or spiritual gifts of speech, such as prophecy, tongues, and interpretation of tongues, as well as teaching and preaching the Gospel. "All knowledge," then, would cover the gifts of revelation, such as the word of wisdom, the word of knowledge, and the discerning of spirits. The Corinthian believers lacked none of these gifts (see also II Cor. 8:7, where Paul says they abounded in faith and utterance and knowledge, as well as in earnestness [NASB] and love). Paul expected them to keep using the charismata until the coming again ("the revelation" NASB) of our Lord Jesus Christ. This is a clear indication that he did not believe the gifts of the Spirit would cease before Christ's return.

In these opening lines of greeting and thanksgiving, Paul beautifully expresses his love for the Christians at Corinth and his confidence that God would go on confirming them to the end. When one also reads Luke's account of the Spirit's work at Corinth (Acts 18:1-18,27,28) and Paul's second letter to the Corinthians, he gets the impression that in spite of their divisions and carnality and other disorders, they were a church dear to the heart of God. After the trouble in the synagogue at Corinth, the Lord had told Paul in a night vision, "I have much people in this city" (Acts 18:10). It would be unfair to judge them as the worst of the churches simply because the apostolic correctives for their problems were given in writing and have been preserved for us in fuller measure than for other congregations. To their everlasting credit, we may note that they did heed Paul's stern reprimands and repented (II Cor. 7:5-16). It is necessary to say all this lest some tend to despise the church at Corinth and then to disparage the gifts it possessed — in effect, a form of guilt by association.

It is clear that the basic problem at Corinth was not the misuse of the gifts of the Spirit but disunity, pride, and even immorality or incest. Carnal weaknesses manifested themselves in almost every area. Because Paul does not deal with spiritual gifts until late in his letter, we may be sure that the abuse of these gifts was the result and not the cause of the Corinthians' more serious problems.

I COR. 2:10-16 — THE SPIRIT REVEALS GOD'S WISDOM.

Among cultured, intellectual people, there is the tendency to indulge in the speculations (Rom. 1:21 NASB; II Cor. 10:5 NASB) and vain reasonings of human philosophy (Col. 2:8 NASB; cf. I Tim. 6:20). Paul resisted this temptation to his pride when he came to Corinth, and instead stuck to a message which seemed foolishness to the highly civilized Greeks (I Cor. 1:18-25). He preached Christ crucified — the Christ who is both the power of God and the wisdom of God (I Cor. 1:24,30). Rather than using a show of oratory and persuasive words of man's wisdom, he depended on the demonstration of the Spirit and the power of God to produce conviction (I Cor. 2:4,5).

Not that Paul opposed all wisdom in itself: Not at all! He opposed *pride* in wisdom, philosophy, and human knowledge (Col. 2:8; I Tim. 6:20). When among mature believers, he spoke about a wisdom from God which once was hidden from human understanding but is now revealed. This wisdom is God's "secret purpose framed from the very beginning to bring us to our full glory" (I Cor. 2:7 NEB). It covers things which man can never learn through scientific investigation — all the things which God has prepared for those who love Him (I Cor. 2:9). In order for us as human beings ever to be able to know these wonderful things, it was necessary for God to *reveal* them to us through His Spirit. Thus Christianity is a *revealed* religion, not a natural religion. There are objective, absolute truths about God, made known by Him during the course of history, for the Christian to learn. The theologians call this, "propositional revelation." While God has revealed Himself in nature and in His acts (e.g., in the Exodus), His objective revelation which we may receive today is primarily and fundamentally verbal communication — the written Word of God. His greatest revelation of Himself in history, however, has been in Christ, His Son (Heb. 1:3), the living Word (Greek *logos*, John 1:1-18). In its present aspects, this revelation is chiefly personal and subjective as the Holy Spirit makes Christ known to us (John 16:13-15).

Looking again at I Cor. 2:10, we find Paul explaining that just as it takes a man's own spirit to perceive his inner thoughts and reveal them by putting them in words, so it takes the Holy Spirit to search out and make known the "deep things of God." This expression designates the very essence or nature of God and then His attributes, His will, and His plans (Frederic Godet, *Commentary on St. Paul's First Epistle to the Corinthians*, trans. from the French by A. Cusin [Edinburgh: T. & T. Clark, 1889], I, 148). Therefore no man can comprehend the thought of God and all the things that pertain to Him, apart from the help of God's Spirit (vv.10,11).

In his excellent book on the internal witness of the Holy Spirit, Bernard Ramm makes this statement: "The Spirit establishes the direct connection from the mind of God to the mind of the Christian" (*The Witness of the Spirit*, p.54). He reminds us that the reformer John Calvin maintained that the same Spirit who spoke through the prophets must "penetrate into our hearts" and *repeat* the message to us, convincing us of its divine origin. "The objective revelation, the testimony of God, is revealed in our hearts *directly* by the Holy Spirit, who is the actual effector, the actual executive of that inward illumination which finds its originating impulse in God the Father" (*ibid.*, p.53). Calvin and other theologians called the Spirit's inward revelation or illumination the *testimonium* (see comments on Rom. 8:14-17).

How does the Holy Spirit impart His revelation to men? F. F. Bruce has paraphrased vv.12-16 for us and in so doing has cleared away most of the difficulties in understanding this important passage about the work of the Spirit. "And the Spirit we have received is not the spirit of the world but the Spirit of God, that we may know the things which God by His grace has bestowed upon us. So, when we speak of these things, we do not use words taught us by human wisdom, but words taught us by the Spirit, giving a spiritual form to spiritual truth. The unspiritual man cannot take in the things which the Spirit of God imparts; they are folly to his way of thinking, and he is unable to apprehend them because they are assessed by the spiritual faculty. But the spiritual man is able to assess everything, while he himself is subject to no one's assessment. For 'who has come to know the Lord's mind, so as to give Him instruction?' (quoted from Isa. 40:13). But we — we who have received the Spirit of God — possess the mind of Christ" (*The Letters of Paul*, p.73).

This passage throws light both on the matter of the inspiration of the Scriptures, and perhaps also on the guidance which the Holy Spirit gives in prophesying, teaching, etc., in the manifestation of a gift of utterance even today. The latter must be included unless the "we" and "us" pronouns of vv.10-16 are limited to refer only to the apostles and prophets who wrote the O.T. and the N.T. But this way of interpreting these verses is against Paul's argument that all Christians have received the Spirit so they can know God's wisdom.

Verse 13 is perhaps the clearest text in the Bible to show that the Spirit guided Paul and the other writers of Scripture in the choice of the very words when they were writing the Bible — what we call the doctrine of verbal inspiration. They were inspired or superintended by the Spirit at the unique level of perfection in their writing. At the same time, He who is the bringer of freedom (II Cor. 3:17) respected the personality of each writer, so that the individuality and writing style of the biblical authors shines through the process of divine inspiration (see comments on II Pet. 1:19-21). But v.13 also describes the charismatic Christian who is speaking under an anointing of the Holy Spirit. He speaks, whether in an unknown tongue or in his native language, in words taught by the Spirit, "combining spiritual *thoughts* with spiritual *words*" (NASB). Frederic Godet phrases it aptly: "This hidden wisdom God has revealed to us by His Spirit, and we speak it with words formed in us by this same Spirit. He gives us the form, after having given us the matter." And again: "The same Divine breath which lifted the veil *to reveal*, takes possession also of the mouth of its interpreter when it is *to speak*" (*I Corinthians*, pp.153f.).

Here we must humbly recognize that any given utterance by the Spirit's power may be less than perfect, depending on the degree of yieldedness of the one speaking. Furthermore, Paul specifically says that at present our knowledge is incomplete (only "in part"), and so is our prophesying (I Cor. 13:9). We must state forthrightly that no genuine charismatic utterance will ever oppose or supersede the written Word of God, for the

Holy Spirit is the Author of both, and He will never contradict Himself. God's revelation in the Bible is final. His word to us through the spiritual gifts is only supportive or corroborative.

I Cor. 3:16,17 — GOD'S TEMPLE.

Beginning with the last words of I Cor. 3:9, Paul has been describing the Corinthian believers as God's building. He is sounding a warning to the various workmen engaged in its construction. He himself had laid the foundation, which is Jesus Christ (I Cor. 3:10,11), and other men have been building upon what he had started. Their work in the sense of their teachings was of three types: (1) some employed enduring materials such as "gold, silver, precious stones" — the wisdom of the Gospel which is divinely revealed truth; (2) others built with flammable materials such as "wood, hay, stubble" (or, sticks, grass, straw) — more human wisdom, perhaps coupled with worldly church practices; and (3) some tended to destroy God's temple by causing division within the local congregation.

It is wise to take a careful look at vv.16 and 17. *The Amplified Bible* is a real aid in doing this:

> 16 Do you not discern *and* understand that you [the whole church at Corinth] are God's temple (His sanctuary), and that God's Spirit has His permanent dwelling in you — to be at home in you [collectively as a church and also individually]?

> 17 If any one does hurt to God's temple or corrupts [it with false doctrines] *or* destroys it, God will do hurt to him *and* bring him to the corruption of death *and* destroy him. For the temple of God is holy — sacred to Him — and that [temple] you [the believing church and its individual believers] are.

In connection with how one might wreck a local church, R. C. H. Lenski's comment on v.17 is quite suggestive: "We shall not go far wrong when we say that, if the Corinthians themselves are God's sanctuary because of the indwelling of the

Spirit, he destroys this sanctuary, be he teacher or layman, who by lies and deceptions drives the Spirit out of the hearts of the Corinthians and fills them with the spirit of the world" (*The Interpretation of St. Paul's First and Second Epistle to the Corinthians* [Columbus: Wartburg Press, 1946], p.148).

God's temple (Greek *naos*, the sanctuary itself, as contrasted with the *hieron*, the overall temple with its courts and gates) is a figure in this passage for the local congregation at Corinth, but also as the local manifestation of the one true "temple" of God, the Church Universal, composed of all true believers in Christ. The same meaning is attached to the figure of the temple in II Cor. 6:16; Eph. 2:20-22; and I Pet. 2:5,9 (see comments on I Pet. 2:5-9).

In I Cor. 6:19, however, Paul likens the body of each individual believer to "a temple of the Holy Spirit" (NASB; not "*the temple*," KJV). Each Christian, therefore, must keep his own body pure and holy, especially from the sin of sexual immorality. Fornication, more than any other sin, desecrates the very sanctuary of God because of the physical union consummated in its act. Yet Christ and the Christian have a mystical spiritual union, or as Paul describes it, "The one who joins himself to the Lord is one spirit with Him" (I Cor. 6:17 NASB). Therefore he should never join himself to a harlot (6:15-18).

The Church as the Body of Christ and as the Temple of God is unique in God's dispensations or periods of governing His creation: It is in this age alone that God dwells on earth only *in the hearts* of His believing people by His Spirit, both corporately and individually. In the past, He dwelt in the tabernacle and in the temple *among* His people, and in the future there will again be a temple in Jerusalem when Jesus Christ returns in person to reign as king.

I COR. 6:11 — SANCTIFIED BY THE SPIRIT.

To sanctify is to make holy. To be holy as God is holy is the goal of the Christian. Jesus and the apostles emphasize this over and over again. "Be ye therefore perfect, even as your Father which is in heaven is perfect" (Matt. 5:48). "Perfecting holiness in the fear of God" (II Cor. 7:1). "He hath chosen us in him . . . that we should be holy and without blame before him (Eph. 1:4). "For this is the will of God, even your sanctification" (I Thess. 4:3). "That *we* might be partakers of his holiness" (Heb. 12:10). "Follow peace with all *men*, and holiness, without which no man shall see the Lord" (Heb. 12:14). "As He which hath called you is holy, so be ye holy in all manner of conversation; because it is written [in Lev. 11:44,45; 19:2; 20:7], Be ye holy; for I am holy" (I Pet. 1:15,16).

God commands us to be holy because He originally made man in His likeness, and holiness is the basic attribute or characteristic of His being. In the new creation, His purpose is to conform us to the image of His Son (Rom. 8:28,29), and Jesus Christ is the holy Son of God (Luke 1:35), the sinless, spotless Lamb of God (I Pet. 1:19). Holiness, then, is the characteristic mark of the believer. For holiness is more than goodness or innocence or freedom from sin. Holiness is something infinitely higher because it is godliness, Godlikeness and Christlikeness. As we all see, holiness is possible only through having the Holy Spirit. It should never be considered apart from the person of the Holy Spirit. This is the greatest sin of all, trying to be good without God. This was the problem of the Pharisees.

Basically, the word "sanctify" means to set apart, to consecrate, to reserve something or someone for sacred use. Therefore sanctification in the Bible has both a negative and a positive side (II Cor. 6:16-18). We must be separated from sin, from the world, from our old selfish ways (the negative side); we must be set apart unto God, unto Christ to serve Him, unto a life of holiness and moral purity (the positive side). But because we are born with a sinful nature and sin has such a grip on us, none of us can make himself holy. Praise God, however, for He is performing His work of sanctification in each Christian, and He will not stop until the day we see Jesus (Phil. 1:6; 2:13).

God's work of sanctification, like salvation of which it is one aspect, is in three stages. It has three tenses — past, present, and future: imputing divine holiness, progressive growth in personal holiness, entire holiness in spirit, soul, and body. A number of Scripture passages clearly teach that positionally the believer in Christ has already been sanctified. For example, Paul discusses the wisdom of God and how He has chosen the foolish things of the world to shame the wise, so that no man can boast about his own goodness or ability before God. Paul concludes by saying, "But by His doing you are in Christ Jesus, who became to us wisdom from God, and righteousness and sanctification, and redemption" (I Cor. 1:30 NASB). He considers that the Corinthian Christians are already saints ("holy ones"), for they have been sanctified in Christ Jesus (I Cor. 1:2, past tense, the Greek perfect tense). Yet the rest of the epistle deals with sins and problems in their lives, showing that Paul can only mean positional sanctification.

God considers Christians as already holy and free from the defilement of sin because He identifies them with His Son. In this sense, at the moment of our conversion we receive both sanctification (in its objective, external sense) and justification (in which God accounts us righteous from condemnation by the Law). We were sanctified by the blood of Jesus, the blood by which He ratified the New Covenant (Heb. 10:29). Therefore, because Jesus Christ has washed us from our sins by His blood (Rev. 1:5) and has sprinkled our hearts clean from an evil conscience (Heb. 10:22; cf. 9:14), we as Christians are entitled to forget our past sins.

The Holy Spirit began His work of santification to draw us to Christ and separate us from the world even before we were saved. Note how Peter says that the Christians to whom he is writing are "chosen and destined by God the Father and sanctified by the Spirit for obedience to Jesus Christ and for sprinkling with His blood" (I Pet. 1:2 RSV).

Similarly, Paul writes to the brethren at Thessalonica that "God chose" them "from the beginning to be saved, through sanctification by the Spirit and belief in the truth" (II Thess. 2:13 RSV). It is in this sense that Paul tells the Christians at Corinth, most of whom were converted out of deep sin (I Cor. 6:9-11a), that they have already been washed and sanctified and justified "in the name of the Lord Jesus, and by the Spirit of our God" (v.11). Therefore, as K. F. W. Prior writes, "The Christian may regard himself as being on the Godward side of the gulf which separates God from human sin" (*The Way of Holiness* [Chicago: Inter-Varsity Press, 1967], pp.34f.). Thus sin has lost its power to separate and condemn the believer. It has not lost its power to plague and torment him, however.

The Holy Spirit's work in us is far more extensive than convicting us (John 16:8-11), bringing us to a saving relationship with Jesus Christ, and regenerating us (John 3:5). He is also the member of the Trinity who effects the present-tense stage of our sanctification. This is to make our eternal status in Christ an inward reality. He is the Sanctifier, while Christ is our sanctification, our holiness. In the current process of making us holy, the Spirit remains in the background, yet directs and energizes the entire work. His part is disclosed in II Cor. 3:18: "But we all, with unveiled face beholding as in a mirror the glory of the Lord, are being transformed into the same image from glory to glory, just as from the Lord, the Spirit" (NASB). Paul means that the Lord, specifically the Spirit in this case, is the divine agent of the work going on within us that transforms us into Christ's very likeness. This process takes place as we keep our eyes fixed on Jesus our glorious Lord (cf. Heb. 12:2 NASB). Let us remember that the Spirit makes much of Jesus Christ, for He was sent to glorify the Son (John 16:14). He imparts the resurrection life and the *agape* love of Christ to us.

Sanctification is God's gracious work whereby our whole nature is being renewed or renovated into the image of God through Jesus Christ, and we are enabled to put to death the tendency to sin and to live unto righteousness. Paul describes this as putting off the old man and putting on the new (Eph. 4:22,24). The "old man" is the corrupt human nature with which every man is born; it is the old pattern of life, the capacity he has to please self and to commit sin freely and to be enslaved to Satan. By "putting off" the old man, Paul does not mean destroying it, but displacing it from its control center, putting it out of the driver's seat. The "new man" is the new, holy nature which we receive through the new birth, created by God "in righteousness and true holiness" (Eph. 4:24). It is the seat of the Spirit in the regenerated man, the inner sanctuary where the Spirit dwells within the believer's body as His temple. The "new man" is the capacity which the Christian has to love and serve both God and man and to practice righteousness. But he must "put on the new man" in the sense of consciously exercising the graces of which this new nature consists (Col. 3:12,13). The "new man" is more than a mere capacity, however. It is Christ Himself living His life through my whole being (Gal. 2:20). The *agape*-love of the new man, for instance, is Christ loving the unlovable through my personality and my service.

In order to grow in grace and to progress in holiness, the child of God needs freedom and power. He must be liberated from sin's bondage and dominion over him in order to be free for Jesus to rule him and lead him. But he must also have the power to resist further temptations, to say no to sin's entice-ments, to stand against the attacks of the devil. This is where the work of the Spirit becomes so important. Paul could shout triumphantly: "The law of the Spirit of life in Christ Jesus hath made me free from the law of sin and death" (Rom. 8:2). The written law can no longer condemn him, for he is in Christ Jesus, justified, pardoned, and accounted righteous (Rom. 8:1).

The unwritten law or principle of sin and death can no longer hold him in its vicious circle, because the new dominating principle of the Holy Spirit — the principle of that life which is his in Christ Jesus — has set him free. Satan does his utmost to hide the fact of this deliverance from believers. But "where the Spirit of the Lord is, there is liberty" (II Cor. 3:17). It is by the Holy Spirit as He empowers and teaches and leads us that this freedom from sin's dominion becomes our actual possession.

Our part, then, in progressive sanctification is that of faith and obedience. We believe the truth about God's provision (II Thess. 2:13) and have faith in Christ (Acts 26:18), and we practice obedience resulting in righteousness (Rom. 6:16 NASB). For as we present our members as slaves to righteousness, the end result is sanctification or holiness (Rom. 6:19). It is the Spirit of God who overcomes our fleshly, selfish nature by His indwelling life. Our responsibility is to "be filled with the Spirit," to "walk in the Spirit," and to "pray in the Spirit." Then our victory over self will come spontaneously, just as the ascending sap in the tree pushes off the dead leaves which cling to the branches all winter.

Yet progress in holiness is not inevitable or automatic. We can grieve the Holy Spirit by complacency and yielding to temptation and heeding the desires of the old nature. Following Christ and walking in the Spirit day by day is the only path of holiness. This involves denying oneself, "giving up all right to himself" (Matt. 16:24 Phillips). As the *Living Bible* paraphrases Rom. 8:5,6, "Those who let themselves be controlled by their lower natures live only to please themselves, but those who follow after the Holy Spirit find themselves doing those things that please God. Following after the Holy Spirit leads to life and peace, but following after the old nature leads to death."

You as a believer are under obligation, not to the old nature to live according to its desires, but to the Holy Spirit. "For if you are living according to the flesh, you must die; but if by the Spirit you are putting to death the deeds of the body, you will live". (Rom. 8:12,13 NASB). Paul says categorically in Gal. 5:16, "Walk by the Spirit, and you will not carry out the desire of the flesh" (NASB). You will not yield to self-indulgence, nor will any other deeds of the flesh become evident, if the Spirit is in control and producing a harvest of love, joy, peace, etc. (see comments on Gal. 5:22-23).

Through constant submission to the Lord as His willing bondservants, we are set free from all lesser masters and may experience a practical victory over former sinful appetites and habits, haunting fears and hateful thoughts. For the Holy Spirit is actively engaged in renewing our minds and giving us right attitudes (Titus 3:5; Rom. 12:2; Eph. 4:23). He implants the mind and attitude of Christ in us, which is the attitude of humility (Phil. 2:5-8). He is ever faithful in His task of conforming us to the image of Christ. In training us in righteousness, He makes much use of the Scriptures (II Tim. 3:16), for we are sanctified and cleansed through heeding the truth of God's holy Word (John 17:17; 15:3).

And when will His task be completed? When will God have sanctified us wholly? Our spirit and soul and body will be preserved complete, without blame *at the coming of our Lord Jesus Christ.* And God will bring it to pass because He is faithful (I Thess. 5:23,24). He will make us stand in the presence of His glory blameless and with great joy (Jude 24). Then the Bride of Christ will be holy and blameless, having no spot or wrinkle (Eph. 5:27). This is our ultimate sanctification — Paul calls it our glorification (Rom. 8:30) — when we shall be like Christ, pure as He is (I John 3:2,3). Then our personal spiritual state will be brought up to the level of our present standing in Christ, our actual practice will be in perfect accord with our position that we already enjoy as members of His Body.

I Cor. 12-14 — CONCERNING SPIRITUAL GIFTS.

These three chapters comprise a unit in the apostle Paul's discussion of the various problem areas in the life of the

Christians at Corinth. Beginning with chapter 7, he apparently was answering questions which they had asked him, perhaps in a letter brought by the men he named in I Cor. 16:17. He introduced his reply to each question by the expression, "Now concerning" (Greek *peri de*) or "Now" (see at I Cor. 7:1,25; 8:1; 11:2,17; 12:1; 15:1 [cf. 15:12]; 16:1). Linking chapters 12-14 with chapter 11, we have Paul's discussion of problems relating to the public worship of the church. So if we consider his instructions regarding the Lord's Supper (I Cor. 11:17-34) to be relevant to twentieth century church life, we cannot logically relegate the question of spiritual gifts to the first century only, as some try to do.

An outline and brief discussion is given here as an aid in the study of these three key chapters about the gifts of the Spirit in the local church.

Outline and Summary

1. The Test of Spiritual Gifts (12:1-3). In the worship of their pagan gods, the Greeks were sometimes carried away in a frenzy by demonic forces. These were the real powers behind the dumb idols (cf. I Cor. 10:19-21). The demons often seized people by their evil power, even prophesying or speaking in tongues through the priests and priestesses, as in the oracle at Delphi. Therefore, the proper test of the genuineness of a spiritual gift is the acknowledgment of Jesus as Lord by the person manifesting the gift. Only the one who truly expresses from his heart genuine submission to Christ is operating in the power of the Holy Spirit (see comments on Matt. 7:21-23).

2. The Common Source of the Various Gifts (12:4-11). While we note the diversities or different varieties of charismatic gifts, we must recognize that they all come from the same triune God. All these gifts are the work of one and the same Spirit, who distributes to each individual Christian just as He wills (v.11).

3. The Analogy of the Body (12:12-26). The relation of

Spirit-baptized believers to one another and to Christ as the Head is illustrated by the human body with its many parts. Every member is essential to its proper functioning, so there should be no division or jealousy within the body.

4. The Order of the Gifts (12:27-31a). We must be willing to recognize that our individual place and function in Christ's Body is a matter of God's appointment. Three ministries are listed in order of importance, but there is a question whether the gifts which follow are ranked in any particular order. In v.31 Paul speaks of "the best gifts" (KJV), which should be translated as "the higher gifts" (RSV) or "the greater gifts" (NASB). Nearly all English translations and Bible commentators follow the KJV which interprets the verb *zeloute* in v.31a as an exhortation or command: "But covet earnestly the best gifts." This may be incorrect, however, because the Greek imperative can also be translated as an indicative: "But you are striving after, zealous for, the greater gifts." Paul's whole argument in this chapter is that God decides which gift to give to each member of a church, and that no member should think of himself as greater or more important than the others. But the Corinthians all wanted to be an apostle or a prophet or a teacher. They were also seeking the gifts of a more miraculous nature: the working of miracles, gifts of healings, speaking with tongues and interpretation (v.29,30). Arnold Bittlinger points out that apparently they were not interested in the less dramatic gifts of helps and governments mentioned in v.28 (*Gifts and Graces: A Commentary on I Corinthians 12-14* [London: Hodder and Stoughton, 1967], p.74). As Michael Harper explains it, "Paul is not encouraging the Corinthians to grade the gifts, but rather he is rebuking them for doing so, and so neglecting 'the more excellent way' of manifesting them. Clearly the gift of tongues was high on the list in the estimation of the Corinthians, and Paul wants to put it in its proper place, and urges them to desire all the gifts, especially the ones which edify others" (*Walk in the Spirit*, pp. 68f.).

5. The Incomparable Way of Love in Conjunction with Seeking and Using the Gifts (12:31b-13:7). Paul now describes that most excellent way of life (Greek *hodos*) in which the spiritual gifts can function properly and fulfill their purpose of edifying others in the church. He is not so much stating the proper *manner* (which would be the Greek word *tropos*) of using the gifts — i.e., with the motive of love. Rather he is showing that this is the only correct *route* to follow (cf. 14:1, "Follow after charity"), the perfect way for all of life, including the ministry of one's gift. This leads him to that most beautiful portrayal of love in all of literature.

6. The Duration of Spiritual Gifts (13:8-13). Christians have differed widely as to whether the spiritual gifts and ministries of 12:28-30 and 13:8 continued after the apostolic age and down to the present. Obviously, the office of apostleship has been withdrawn in the primary sense. There is no warrant given in Scripture for an apostolic succession beginning with the original twelve apostles of Jesus. In the secondary sense of "apostle" found in the N.T. (Eph. 4:11), however, many missionaries and others have founded churches or done other pioneering work, manifesting extraordinary gifts and blessing from God. Again, the gift of prophecy in its specialized sense of speaking forth and writing down the inspired, infallible Word of God has been sovereignly withdrawn; but believers may still speak forth a message revealed by God when they are under an anointing of the Spirit.

Here Paul teaches that whereas love will never fail, the charismatic gifts will stop "when that which is perfect is come" (v.10). Some have taught that by *to teleion*, "that which is perfect," Paul means the completed canon of holy Scripture. Paul's statement in v.12, however, which says that then we shall see face to face and know fully even as now we are fully known (NASB), indicates that he is looking forward to the perfect state of things to be ushered in by the return of Christ from heaven (Thayer's *Greek-English Lexicon*, p.618). A study of church history reveals that many of the charismatic gifts continued to be manifested long after the N.T. was written and the apostles were all dead (see Adolf Harnack, *The Mission and Expansion of Christianity* [N.Y.: Harper Torchbooks, 1962], pp.129-146, 199-205).

7. The Relative Value of the Gifts of Tongues and of Prophecy (14:1-25). The apostle points out the several purposes of speaking in an unknown tongue and its limitations in a meeting of the congregation. Prophesying is preferable, because the one who prophesies edifies the church (see separate comments on I Cor. 14:1-33).

8. The Proper Ministration of Spiritual Gifts (14:26-35). Paul issues careful instructions regarding the orderly exercise of the gifts of utterance in church meetings in order to promote edification and to prevent confusion. Women should not interrupt meetings to be among those who pass judgment on prophetic messages. Instead they should address their questions to their own husbands at home (see comments on I Cor. 14:33b-35).

9. Final Instructions on Church Order (14:36-40). The apostle indignantly asks the Corinthians if they suppose that they, in contradistinction to all other churches, have the right to maintain such irregularities as women wearing unsuitable hairstyles in defiance of their position, gluttony and drunkenness at the Lord's Supper, speaking in tongues without interpretation, prophets refusing to give place to one another, and women speaking out to contradict or ask foolish questions. Paul insists what he is writing is by divine command and summarizes chapter 14: "Desire earnestly to prophesy, and do not forbid to speak in tongues" (v.39 NASB). Verse 40 acts as an overall conclusion to chapters 11-14: "But all things should be done with regard to decency *and* propriety *and* in an orderly fashion" (TAB).

I Cor. 12:4-11 — SPIRITUAL GIFTS DESCRIBED.

I. Definition. A spiritual gift is a supernatural capacity or power bestowed on a Christian by the Holy Spirit to enable him to exercise his function as a member of the Body of Christ. These gifts are not to be thought of as natural abilities nor as permanent possessions, but are supernatural and often sudden manifestations of the Spirit Himself (v.7). A gift is not given primarily to benefit the one through whom it is manifested but is "for the common good" (v.7 NASB), for the profit of the whole congregation in a local church.

Spiritual gifts are not to be confused with spiritual graces or fruits of the Spirit — aspects of Christ's character which every Christian is to cultivate (Gal. 5:22,23). Nor are they identical with spiritual offices — positions in the churches whether for spiritual or temporal oversight of their affairs (elders, deacons, I Tim. 3:1-13) or for ministries both within and beyond the confines of the local assembly (apostles, prophets, evangelists, pastor-teachers, Eph. 4:11). God appoints only certain believers to these spiritual offices (I Cor. 12:28a,29a) in line with specific spiritual gifts already manifested in their lives. These persons are Christ's gifts (*domata*) to His Church (Eph. 4:8).

In I Cor. 12-14 three Greek words are translated as "gifts" or "spiritual gifts." The first is *pneumatika* (I Cor. 12:1; 14:1; see also Rom. 1:11). Literally, it simply means "spirituals," a term which always bears the connotation "supernatural" in the epistles of Paul, according to a careful study made by Dr. Howard Ervin (*These Are Not Drunken As Ye Suppose*, pp.227-233). Therefore we can be certain that the spiritual gifts are supernatural powers or manifestations of the Holy Spirit, not natural abilities. The *pneumatika* are "gifts which exceed the natural, and may, therefore, be freely bestowed on members of a church irrespective of natural talents" (Harper, *Walk in the Spirit*, p. 64). A second word translated "spiritual gifts" is *pneumata* (I Cor. 14:12), literally, "spirits." This term also draws attention to the fact that the gifts are manifestations of the

Spirit. Therefore, both these terms emphasize that their source is the Spirit (*pneuma*).

The most frequently used term in these chapters and in the N.T. for the gifts of the Spirit is *charismata*, "charismatic gifts." Since our English adjective "charismatic" (as it appears in such expressions as the "modern charismatic renewal") stems from this word, we should examine it closely. The Greek noun *charisma* occurs seventeen times in the N.T. It is related to the noun *charis*, "grace," and the verb *charizomai*, "to give freely" (e.g., Rom. 8:32; I Cor. 2:12). In general, *charisma* refers to any gift of divine grace, whether it be of salvation and eternal life (Rom. 5:15,16; 6:23) or of the covenant privileges of the Israelites (Rom. 11:29; cf. 9:4,5); or to a special grace given to an individual, such as the gift of continency enabling one to remain unmarried in order to perform a specific work for God (I Cor. 7:7); or to a miraculous deliverance from great peril (II Cor. 1:11).

The current religious usage of our English adjective "charismatic" is derived, however, from the technical sense of *charisma*, especially as it is found five times in the plural in I Cor. 12 (in vv.4,9,28,30,31). The *charismata* are "gracegifts," special gifts of a non-material sort, freely conferred by the grace of God on individual Christians. This word, then, emphasizes that the spiritual gifts are *gifts* and not rewards or wages. As Michael Harper says, "They are not prizes or badges given for special merit. They are freely bestowed upon the people of God according to the sovereign will of the Holy Spirit" (*Walk in the Spirit*, p.65).

Charismatic gifts enable individual believers, when needs arise, to minister to other members of the Body of Christ as well as to people who are not saved, in ways beyond mere human capability and ingenuity. It is a manifestation of the Divine Presence when an ordinary human suddenly is given illumination of unknown facts and wisdom how to meet a difficult problem, or can discern what is an evil spirit, or can believe for a miracle, or can administer healing to an incurable, or can speak forth a message from the Lord in his own language or in one he has never learned, or interpret an utterance given in an unknown language.

The Lord permits every congregation to experience needs from time to time which will require the exercise of the various charismatic gifts. These will be operative wherever the exalted Christ is present in power and freedom. Sometimes they are not recognized, many times they are not wanted or are blocked. Lack of unity and lack of faith can inhibit the gifts that God has given for His Church. False doctrine, indifference, and racial and denominational pride or divisions may often be holding back the manifestation of charismatic gifts.

The *charismata* were not isolated phenomena occurring only in the Corinthian church. Paul instructed the Roman believers to make full use of their charismatic gifts (see comments on Rom. 12:3-8), and urged Timothy not to neglect his *charisma* (see comments on I Tim. 4:14) but to stir it up (see comments on II Tim. 1:6,7). Peter likewise exhorted each reader to manifest his charismatic gift for the benefit of someone else, as a good steward of God's manifold grace (see comments on I Pet. 4:10,11). The entire early Church knew the power of the Spirit of God (e.g., Gal. 3:5; Heb. 2:4), just as Gideon and Samson experienced it in an earlier age. This same Spirit is restoring His gifts to the Church today wherever members of Christ's Body are willing to receive them.

In addition to the three words translated "gifts" or "spiritual gifts," the apostle Paul uses three other Greek words to reveal various facets of their nature. (1) In v.5 (NASB) we read that there are varieties of "ministries" (Greek *diakonion*). Translated "administrations" in the KJV, this term means "services" in the sense of opportunities to serve or to minister to others. Paul is saying there are different kinds of ministries in which the gifts become real in practice.

(2) "And there are diversities of operations" (v.6). Here the

Greek word *energematon,* "energies" or "effects," signifies the activities or results produced by the imparted spiritual energy. It is the same word translated "working" in v.10 in the phrase "working of miracles." In this sense, the gifts are not regular, permanent abilities; instead, they are momentary powers to effect a miracle, to bring healing, to know something in a flash. And it is the same God who energizes or activates all these gifts in those who act as agents and in those on whom the effect is produced.

(3) The third descriptive word revealing the nature of the spiritual gifts is *thanerosis,* "manifestation," in v.7. When a gift is displayed, it is a manifestation of the Holy Spirit. It is a visible act which can be seen or heard or felt, not an invisible grace like the fruit of the Spirit. In each believer, then, the Holy Spirit can be expected to manifest Himself. It is not to be only for that man's own spiritual advantage, but "to profit withal," for the common good, for the benefit of others.

II. Purpose. There are several reasons for the continuing manifestation of the gifts of the Spirit from the first century until now. Each generation must be convinced afresh of the reality of God, that He is not dead but living and loving. Furthermore, the gifts are needed today because the world is not yet evangelized. *All* Christians, as well as missionaries and evangelists, need supernatural equipment to do their part in proclaiming Christ to a lost and dying world. More specifically, the purpose of spiritual gifts may be stated as follows:

1. To manifest the power of God in the Body of Christ on earth. Men must be confronted with the reality of the invisible God. When the secrets of a man's heart are disclosed through a prophecy or word of knowledge, he is bound to declare "that God is certainly among you" (I Cor. 14:25 NASB). God's purpose is to confound all mere worldly wisdom (I Cor. 1:27; 2:6-10). That is why Paul was led to repudiate his training in Judaism and his natural advantages (I Cor. 2:1-5; Phil. 3:3-8) and to tell only what Christ had accomplished through him in

the power of signs and wonders (Rom. 15:18-19). This has been demonstrated in the Indonesian revival beginning in 1965, where large numbers of Muslims have been converted to Christ as a result of the manifest power of God.

2. To aid in carrying out the Great Commission. Before His ascension, the Lord Jesus promised that supernatural signs would give confirmation to the Gospel wherever His believers would go to preach it (see comments on Mark 16:9-20). The apostles combated heathenism, not by convincing oratory and superior education, but by gifts of healings and miracles (Acts 14:8-18; 16:16-18; 19:11-20; 28:1-10). Again and again down through history, God has rescued His servants and brought sinners to their knees when a miracle or a sudden revelation was given in response to faith. In this way, Christians have been enabled to withstand bitter persecution and to wage spiritual warfare against the enemies of the Gospel. By the word of knowledge and the word of wisdom and by the gift of the discerning of spirits, they have detected the subtle devices of the unseen foe and have exposed the "angels of light," as Peter did with Ananias and Sapphira.

3. To edify and perfect the Church. The members of the local church are edified and exhorted and consoled by gifts of inspired utterance such as prophecy (I Cor. 14:3,12,26; Acts 9:31). Each individual also may edify himself through speaking in tongues privately (I Cor. 14:4). On the universal scale, the entire Church will be built up and brought to the unity of the faith through the work of service or ministering (same Greek word as in I Cor. 12:5) performed by every member or saint (Eph. 4:12,13). They in turn have become effective workers through the diligent training and leadership given by the apostles and prophets, evangelists, pastors and teachers in whom the gifts of the Spirit are operative.

4. To effect the deliverance of God's people. God's purpose in this Messianic age announced by John the Baptist is beautifully summed up in the prophecy of his father Zacharias: "To grant

us that we, being delivered from the hand of our enemies, might serve Him without fear, in holiness and righteousness before Him all our days" (Luke 1:74,75 NASB). Jesus was sent and anointed with the Spirit of the Lord in order to bind up the brokenhearted and to proclaim liberty and deliverance to the captives (Isa. 61:1; Luke 4:18). He baptizes us in the same Holy Spirit in order to carry on His work. It is our responsibility to rescue the lost as well as our brothers and sisters in Christ from the grip of Satan and his demons (Acts 26:18). Such was the ministry of Philip at Samaria, where many who had unclean spirits were set free (Acts 8:5-7). We have Jesus' solemn promise that when we as members of His Church take the offensive against Satan's strongholds, "the gates of hell shall not prevail against it" (Matt. 16:18). When we contend with the super-natural forces of wickedness in the spirit-realm, it is obvious that we should be equipped with the necessary gifts of the Spirit.

God's purpose in bestowing charismatic gifts, then, is that through their operation Christians might be the functioning Body of Christ on earth.

III. Classification and Description. Paul does not seem to have listed the gifts in any particular order in vv.8-10. Therefore, they have been grouped together in various ways, but the following threefold classification is adopted by many:

A. Discerning Gifts — gifts of revelation (the power to *know*)
  1. A word of wisdom.
  2. A word of knowledge
  3. Discerning of spirits
B. Dynamic Gifts — gifts of power (the power to *do*)
  1. Faith
  2. Gifts of healings
  3. Workings of miracles
C. Declarative Gifts — gifts of inspired utterance (the power to *speak*)
  1. Prophecy

2. Tongues

3. Interpretation of tongues

A. The first three gifts listed above are given to Christians to enable them to know what to do or say in specific situations. Jesus manifested a word of wisdom when, to the Pharisees who were intent on trapping Him with their question about paying a tax to Caesar, He gave His famous reply: "Render to Caesar the things that are Caesar's; and to God the things that are God's" (Matt. 22:21 NASB). He promised us similar wisdom for times of emergency, "for the Holy Spirit will teach you in that very hour what you ought to say" (Luke 12:12 NASB; see comments on Matt. 10:16-20). Acts 6:1-7 is an outstanding example of the need of a word of wisdom to settle particular problems that arise in governing a church congregation. The answer of the twelve apostles manifests wisdom of the highest degree—deep spiritual principles coupled with sound common sense. The Spirit's blessing is evident in that their statement found approval with the entire congregation and enabled the word of God to keep on spreading so that many more became obedient to the faith. James, acting as moderator of the first church council at Jerusalem, manifested a word of wisdom (Acts 15:13-21) which was accepted by all and which settled the controversy regarding legalism. The possibility of receiving a word of wisdom, however, should never cause one to stop seeking wisdom for life in general (James 1:5). We cannot depend on this charismatic gift for every situation because it is only *a word* of wisdom. As Donald Gee says, it is "a spoken utterance through a direct operation of the Holy Spirit at a given moment, rather than an abiding deposit of supernatural wisdom" (*Concerning Spiritual Gifts* [Springfield, Mo.: Gospel Publishing House, n.d.], p.26).

Dennis Bennett defines a word of knowledge as a "supernatural revelation of facts past, present, or future which were *not learned through the efforts of the natural mind.* It may be described as the Mind of Christ being manifested to the mind of the believer, and is given when needed in a flash of time (I Cor. 2:16). This gift is used to protect the Christian, to show how to pray more effectively, or to show him how to help others" (*The Holy Spirit and You*, p.155). A word of wisdom often is given in conjunction with the word of knowledge in order to show how to apply the information God has revealed. In the O.T., Nathan the prophet received a word of knowledge regarding David's affair with Bathsheba, as well as wisdom to know how to bring the king to repentance (II Sam. 12:1-14). The prophet Elisha knew in his heart about Gehazi's greedy act and therefore was able to expose his hypocrisy (II Kings 5:20-27). Jesus our Lord knew the evil thoughts of the scribes (Matt. 9:2-6) and the marital history of the Samaritan woman (John 4:17-19). A word of knowledge enabled Peter to rebuke Ananias and Sapphira for their lying wickedness (Acts 5:1-9).

The word of knowledge is also a teaching gift in the Church. The British Pentecostal Bible teacher Donald Gee stresses this point in his books (*Concerning Spiritual Gifts*, pp.27-34, 110-19; *Spiritual Gifts in the Work of the Ministry Today*, pp.33-52). By comparing the list of gifts in vv.8-10 with the lists of offices and gifts in I Cor. 12:28 and Rom. 12:6-8, one soon realizes that the commensurate spiritual gift for the office of apostle is the word of wisdom, and that the gift corresponding to the office of teacher is the word of knowledge. In this sense, a word of knowledge may be manifested when the teacher receives a new insight into the knowledge of God or of the Christian faith, and at the same time is given new ability to express it and explain it to others. This aspect of the word of knowledge seems to be what Paul has in mind when he talks in I Cor. 13:2 of knowing all mysteries and all knowledge. In Eph. 1:17, Paul prayed that God would give each Christian a spirit of wisdom and of revelation in the sphere of a fuller knowledge of Himself. By a word of knowledge, the teacher may be quickened upon occasion to impress on his hearers the knowledge of the hope of God's calling, of the glorious riches of God's inheritance in the saints, and of the surpassing greatness of God's power toward the believer (Eph. 1:18,19).

The third gift which operates by a direct revelation from God is the "distinguishing of spirits" (v.10 NASB margin). It goes without saying that this is not a critical spirit in the natural or even the true intellectual discernment of the child of God that is developed through Christian fellowship and through study of the Bible. Yes, it is essential for us to partake of the word of righteousness and to train our senses or faculties to discern good and evil, i.e., to make moral decisions (Heb. 5:13,14). The spiritual gift of discernment, however, does not come through training but is imparted in the moment when it is needed. The Greek word for "discernment," *diakrisis,* literally means a "judging through," a seeing right through to the inner reality with a judgment based on that insight. Dennis Bennett explains that by this gift the believer is enabled to know immediately what is motivating a person or situation (*The Holy Spirit and You,* p.143). Those responsible for the orderly progress of a meeting of the brethren need to know whether a person is operating under the inspiration of the Holy Spirit, whether he is expressing his own thoughts or feelings, or whether he is controlled by a wrong spirit. The Holy Spirit will manifest Himself by this gift through those who pass judgment on the messages of the prophets in the assembly (I Cor. 14:29). Usually the discerning of a false or evil spirit brings a sense of heaviness, unrest, or even sickness, whereas the sense of the presence of the Holy Spirit is one of joy and peace and love. This gift, then, is the gracious provision of the Head of the Church to arm her against the subtle deceptions of the enemy.

A striking example of the gift of discerning of spirits in operation is found in Acts 16:16-18. A slave-girl having a spirit of divination met Paul and his party in Philippi, evidently desiring to follow them to the place of prayer. Even though her shouts to the crowds about Paul seemed lofty and spiritual, yet Paul detected the true nature of the motivating spirit and at last commanded it to come out of her. Probably he waited until the day she was ready to be saved so that when he exorcized the demon it would have no right to reenter her (see comments on I John 4:1-6).

B. The three dynamic gifts provide extraordinary powers to effect changes in the lives and circumstances of both saints and sinners. The gift of faith is not saving faith, which a man exercises when on the basis of God's word he trusts in Christ to redeem him. Nor is it the faith of Gal. 5:22, one of the fruits of the Spirit, which develops in the believer as faithfulness or fidelity. The gift of faith, according to Dennis Bennett, is "a sudden surge of faith, usually in a crisis, to confidently believe without a doubt, that as we act or speak in Jesus' Name it shall come to pass" (*The Holy Spirit and You*, p.134). This is the wonder-working faith that Jesus said can move mountains (Matt. 17:20; 21:21; Mark 11:22-24; Luke 17:6; I Cor. 13:2). As Lenski says, by means of this charisma, things that are otherwise impossible are actually accomplished in the course of our service unto the Lord (*I and II Corinthians*, p.501). This gift frequently operated through Elijah and Elisha in the O.T. Think of Elijah's faith when he prepared for the fire to fall from heaven and when he announced that rain would come! (I Kings 18:22-38, 41-45). Daniel had the gift of faith when he "stopped the mouths of lions" (Heb. 11:33; Dan. 6:22). George Mueller's orphanages at Bristol, England, for 2000 children, and Hudson Taylor's obtaining 100 missionaries to evangelize the interior of China are modern-day examples of the gift of dynamic faith in action.

The next two gifts appear in the Greek as plurals: literally, "charismatic gifts of healings" and "workings of powers." The plurals indicate that all healings and all miracles are in each separate case a supernatural operation of the Spirit. As Bittlinger says, "Every healing is a special gift. In this way the spiritually gifted individual stands always in new dependence upon the divine Giver" (*Gifts and Graces*, p.37). Lenski explains:

"In each instance a specific intimation came to them from the Spirit that the act should be performed, and not until that moment did it occur, but then it always took place without fail" (*I and II Corinthians*, p. 502). Peter and John, for instance, had passed the lame beggar at the Gate Beautiful many a time, but not until a certain day did the Spirit prompt them to channel healing to him (Acts 3:1-8). This principle explains why a Spirit-filled Christian cannot go into a hospital and administer healing to every sick person he sees. The plural nouns also indicate the different kinds of diseases and afflictions, requiring different sorts of healing. The implication may be that a certain person is especially used in bringing healing to those suffering from a certain disease or a group of diseases.

Dennis Bennett makes an important clarification regarding the matter of healing as a spiritual gift. He says: "A Christian does not have to have the baptism with the Holy Spirit in order to pray for the sick, nor is the fact that a person has prayed effectively for the sick a sign that he or she has received the baptism with the Holy Spirit. Jesus said: 'These signs shall follow them that *believe* . . . they shall lay hands on the sick, and they shall recover' (Mark 16:17,18 KJV). Any believer can pray for the sick and see them healed by the power of Jesus. Generally speaking, however, it is after the baptism in the Holy Spirit that increased faith for healing comes, and the Christian begins to minister to the sick. Like the other gifts, healing seems to be released with a far greater intensity and reality after the receiving of the Holy Spirit" (*The Holy Spirit and You*, p.112). For the prayer of faith and anointing the sick with oil, see comments on James 5:13-20.

The "working of miracles" covers those wonderful works which are not strictly healings. Included under the category of miracles would be the exorcizing of demons and the restoring of persons from death, such as Dorcas and Eutychus (Acts 9:36-41; 20:6-12). Quite a number of authenticated cases of the raising of the dead have taken place recently in Africa and

Indonesia, as well as in America. The creation of new bodily parts or organs might better be explained as an instance of this gift in operation instead of one of the gifts of healings. Since the beginning of the Indonesian revival in 1965, the Christians have repeatedly trusted God to turn water into wine for their communion services. Some have walked across deep, flooded rivers, or have seen voracious crocodiles stop and swim away, or have walked dry-clothed through jungle downpours, or have fed fifty people with a few small tapioca roots, or have been given deadly poison to drink with no ill effects (Cf. Mel Tari, *Like A Mighty Wind* [Carol Stream: Creation House, 1972]). In bestowing this gift of miracles, the Spirit of Jesus enables His followers to do His works, yes, and even greater works (see comments on John 14:12-14).

C. The third group of spiritual gifts are those through which God may declare Himself when the Holy Spirit prompts men to speak forth publicly. Here in chapter 12, the apostle is listing gifts which are used within a church meeting to minister blessing to one another. Therefore in this list and in I Cor. 12:28-30 the gift of speaking in various kinds of tongues is to be considered from the standpoint, not of its private devotional value, but of its function to edify the other members of the congregation when followed by the twin gift of interpretation of tongues.

The gift of prophecy or prophesying is not the same as a God-given ability to preach and teach the Gospel effectively. The N.T. has a number of distinctive words which refer specifically to preaching and proclaiming the known word of God, as differentiated from speaking forth a new revelation from the Lord. The most important are *kerysso*, to proclaim or announce a message as a herald does (used 61 times); *euangelizo*, to tell good news, to evangelize (over 50 times, and the noun *evangelion*, "gospel," over 70 times); *katangello*, to tell thoroughly or proclaim clearly (15 times); *laleo ton logon*, to speak the word (6 times); *martyreo*, to bear witness, to testify (over 60 times); and *didasko,* to teach (about 90 times). Preaching, then, is telling and explaining what one already knows, what he has learned. Prophesying, however, is directly proclaiming the mind of God, by the inspiration and prompting of the Holy Spirit, and not from one's own thoughts. It is supernatural speech in a known language, as Dennis Bennett tersely describes it. The gift of prophecy is one to be greatly desired (I Cor. 14:1,39). See comments on I Cor. 14:1-33 for further discussion of the gifts of prophecy and tongues.

IV. Reception of the Gifts. Every Christian must first of all recognize that spiritual gifts are sovereignly manifested. The Spirit divides or distributes them to each person individually as *He* wills (v.11b). As the word *charisma* indicates, such a manifestation of the Spirit is freely given, and cannot be earned or purchased (as Peter so bluntly told Simon the Sorcerer, Acts 8:18-23). God's plan is to equip us thoroughly (Heb. 13:20,21 Phillips) to enable us to perform the specific ministry to which God has called us and for which He has placed us in the Church. On this matter, it is worthwhile to listen to the advice of Gordon Lindsay, who was one of America's foremost Full-Gospel Bible teachers:

"In these days, too often we see men trying to copy the ministry of another. The attempt to wear Saul's armor can never make for a satisfying ministry. We believe that every young minister who feels the call of God should first of all, by waiting on God in prayer and fasting, and with heart open, seek to learn what ministry God has set him in the Church to accomplish. *The great question then is not how we shall use God, but how can God use us"* (*All About the Gifts of the Spirit* [Dallas: Christ for the Nations, 1962], p.25).

The human reception and ministration of the gifts is primarily dependent on our faith. Paul instructed the Roman believers that if one's gift was prophecy, he should exercise it according to the proportion of his faith (Rom. 12:6; see comments on Rom. 12:3-8). As members of Christ's Body, we have a right — yes, an obligation — to desire earnestly to receive and manifest the gifts of the Spirit (I Cor. 14:1,13,39). We should long to be spiritual heirs of the early Christians, just as intensely as Elisha wanted to be Elijah's successor (II Kings 2:9-15). Such earnest desire is evidence of an active faith. In some instances, as in the case of Timothy, the individual's faith to receive a spiritual gift was strengthened through the laying on of hands (see comments on I Tim. 4:14; Acts 6:6).

There are other important factors to observe for the gifts to operate smoothly and for the glory of God. The individual should first receive the gift of God's Spirit and keep filled with Him (see comments on Eph. 5:15-21). The baptism in the Holy Spirit is vital to a normal operation of the gifts. Even Jesus Christ the Son of God did not perform His mighty works until He was baptized with the Spirit.

Since pride is the greatest pitfall for a person who has been the channel for gifts of the Spirit to flow out to others, he must continually humble himself at the feet of his Lord. God has chosen the weak things of the world to shame the things which are strong, so that no man should boast in the sight of God (I Cor. 1:26-29). Moses was a very humble man (Num. 12:3), and he wrought many miracles; but when he lost his temper and intimated that he and Aaron were the ones whose power could bring forth water out of the rock, he lost the full blessing of God (Num. 20:10-12).

The example of the apostles and other early Christians is one of total dedication of themselves to the Lord. Barnabas is said to have been a good man and full of the Holy Spirit and of faith (Acts 11:24). Elsewhere we read of how he gladly shared his possessions with the rest of the church in Jerusalem (Acts 4:36,37). The prophets and teachers at Antioch, including Barnabas and Paul, were obedient to the voice of the Holy Spirit when He spoke to them (Acts 13:1-4). Thus it is not surprising to read that later on in a moment of crisis Paul was filled with the Spirit so that he discerned the spirit in Elymas, and wrought a miracle of judgment to blind the wicked sorcerer (Acts 13:8-12).

Christians in that first century were uncompromising and willing to pay the price, as Stephen was, even to a martyr's death (Acts 7:55). Therefore the Spirit gave them a holy, supernatural boldness and confidence to proclaim the word of God (Acts 4:8,29-31). Their consecration, while not a sinless perfection, displayed a balanced holiness that gave evidence of Christ in them just as much as His gifts operating through them.

I COR. 12:13 — BAPTIZED IN ONE SPIRIT.

This is the key verse in rightly understanding the doctrine of the baptism in the Spirit. Yet English-speaking Christians have misunderstood it for centuries because of the faulty translation in the KJV and all those modern versions which have followed in its tradition. The problem lies primarily in the incorrect rendering of the prepositions, especially the first one, which is "by" in the KJV. Before studying further into the context and meaning of v.13, let us look at an original literal translation: "For in *one* Spirit also we were all baptized with reference to (the) *one* Body, whether Jews or Greeks, whether slaves or freemen — yes, we were all given *one* Spirit to drink."

By taking v.13 out of its context, many Bible expositors have taught that it is descriptive of our conversion experience, telling how the Holy Spirit incorporates us into Christ's Body through the new birth. In chapter 12, however, the apostle is not giving instruction about salvation and how to enter the New Covenant but is discussing the functioning of supernatural gifts in the Church. There is no need for him to make a statement about how to receive Christ or how one is to get into the Body. Rather he is emphasizing the unity of the Spirit, the Giver of the various spiritual gifts. In v.13 he is explaining the *relation*, the unity or common bond, which pertains in the one-and-the-same Spirit for all who are already believers. Paul is talking about the continuing seal of the New Covenant which is for all members of Christ's Body in order to identify them as truly belonging to Christ. The baptism in the Spirit is the great unifying factor in a body of such diverse members. In the entire chapter, Paul is talking about the oneness in diversity of the Church.

I Cor. 12:13 is the last of the seven verses in the N.T. which specifically mention baptism in the Spirit. Four of the verses record the prophecy of John the Baptist (Matt. 3:11 [see comments on Matt. 3:11-17]; Mark 1:8; Luke 3:16; and John 1:33 [see comments on John 1:29-34]). The other two passages are in Acts (1:5 [see comments on Acts 1:4-8] and 11:16). That Paul is referring to the Pentecostal baptism *in* the Spirit, and not to some other type of baptism *by* the Spirit, is evident; for he alludes by his words, "whether we be Jews or Gentiles, whether we be bond or free," to the term "all flesh" in Joel's prophecy (cf. Acts 2:18).

Even some of those who oppose the doctrine of a baptism in the Spirit subsequent to conversion may be of help to us in correctly interpreting certain aspects of v.13. Such a one is the Anglican rector John R. W. Stott of London, who has presented a clear but simple exegesis of the verse. He writes, "The Greek expression is precisely the same in all its seven occurrences, and therefore *a priori*, as a sound principle of interpretation, it should refer to the same baptism experience in each verse. The burden of proof rests with those who deny it. The natural interpretation is that Paul is echoing the words of John the Baptist as first Jesus and then Peter had done (Acts 1:5; 11:16). It is unwarrantable to make Jesus Christ the Baptizer in six instances, and the Holy Spirit the Baptizer the seventh. . . . If it is because the words *en heni pneumati* (RSV "by one Spirit") come at the beginning of the sentence, the reason for this is surely that Paul is stressing the oneness of the Spirit in whom we share, not that the Spirit is the baptizer" (*The Baptism and Fullness of the Holy Spirit* [Chicago: Inter-Varsity Press, 1964], p.14).

Mr. Stott goes on to explain that four things can be said about every kind of baptism: its subject (the baptizer), its object (the baptized), the element with or in (Greek *en*) which, and the purpose for or with reference to (*eis*) which the baptism takes place. See the chart on page 256 explaining the occurrences in the N.T. of the Greek verb *baptizo* in connection with the prepositions *en* and *eis*.

When the preposition *eis* appears with the verb *baptizo* in the N.T., it normally defines the relationship to which baptism introduces the person (G. G. Findlay, *I Corinthians*, EGT, II, 890). Therefore, in these verses it should be translated "in relation to" or "with reference to" and not "into." For instance, in I Cor. 10:2 we read that all the Israelites were baptized *eis* Moses in the cloud and in the sea. What Paul is referring to is a relationship to Moses as their deliverer and mediator of the Sinaitic covenant. But their connection to Moses began when they obeyed the Passover instructions by faith and left their homes to follow him out of Egypt. Their experience of the Red Sea and the continuing pillar of cloud only sealed this already existing relationship. Similarly, we are saved through faith in the atoning benefits of Christ's death, and baptism in water is merely the visible sacramental sealing of our relationship to Jesus which began when we first trusted Him (John P. Baker, *Baptized in One Spirit* [London: Fountain Trust, 1967], pp.17-20.

No baptizer is mentioned in Acts 1:5 and 11:16 or in I Cor. 12:13 because the verb *baptizo* is passive. Therefore, the emphasis lies on either the people who receive the baptism or on the one Spirit with whom they are baptized. It is very clear that although Jesus Christ is not named in v.13, He must be regarded as the Baptizer.

Mr. Stott asks, "If [in v.13] the Holy Spirit were Himself the Baptizer, what would be the 'element' in which He baptizes? That there is no answer to this question is enough to overthrow this interpretation, since the baptism metaphor absolutely requires an 'element,' or the baptism is no baptism. Therefore, the 'element' in the baptism of I Corinthians 12:13 must be the Holy Spirit, and (consistently with the other verses) we must supply Jesus Christ as the Baptizer. Similarly, at the end of the verse, it is the Holy Spirit of whom we drink, and consistently (with John 7:37ff.) it must be Christ by whom we are 'made to drink' of Him. . . . The being baptized and the drinking are clearly equivalent expressions" (*The Baptism and Fullness of the Holy Spirit*, p.17).

In v.13 two aspects of the gift of the Holy Spirit are indicated in the two verbs "baptized" and "made to drink." The sovereign, divine act of *giving* is depicted in Christ's having baptized us in the one Spirit, whereas the human *receiving* of the gift by faith is intimated in the picture of our drinking the Spirit (see comments on Acts 2:38-40). The Greek verb *epotisthemen*, usually translated in v.13 "made to drink" in the more literal versions, would better be rendered "given to drink." The idea in the verb *potizo* is that a drink is offered to someone, but he must drink it or reject it himself (Matt. 10:42; 25:35,37,42; Rom. 12:20; I Cor. 3:2). When our Savior was about to die on the cross, He was given a drink of sour wine soaked in a sponge (Matt. 27:48). This He received (John 19:29,30), although He had earlier refused to drink wine mingled with gall after tasting it (Matt. 27:34). The verb "given-to-drink" in v.13, then, points to a conscious, voluntary reception of the Spirit on the part of each Spirit-baptized Christian, not something which automatically happens to him.

Arnold Bittlinger, German theologian of evangelical Lutheran persuasion, confirms this interpretation of v.13 when he says, "The expression 'baptize' always means 'to be dipped or immersed into something.' The Spirit surrounds and covers the believer as water does at baptism. The expression 'drink,' however, gives the impression that the believer receives the Spirit into himself as he does the bread and wine at the Lord's Supper. . . . In both cases the form of the verb in Greek suggests that receiving the Spirit is a single experience which happened at a specific time in the past" (*Gifts and Graces*, p.57).

If v.13 speaks of Spirit baptism and not of the new birth, then how are the two occurrences of the expression "we all" in this verse to be interpreted? Many commentators hold that these words refer to all true believers, and that therefore the verse teaches that every Christian enters both his new life and the Church by means of baptism by the Spirit.

John Baker of Cheltenham, England, replies most convincingly to that view by pointing out that the question of how we become Christians is irrelevant to the subjects under consideration in I Cor. 12-14. He writes: "In prosecuting his subject in chapter 12, the Apostle centers his thoughts around two points, the unity of the Body of Christ, and the diversity of its members with their differing gifts and ministries. He has described these gifts as differing manifestations of the same one Holy Spirit (verses 4-11), and he is about to explain their varied exercise within any one church in terms of the different functions of the various different organs or 'members' in the human body (v.14ff.). In verses 12 and 13 he is underlining the thought of the unity both of the Body of Christ, and of the Spirit who animates, inspires and fills its many members in the exercise of their differing ministries and gifts. Therefore, the emphasis of the Apostle's thought in verse 13 is not at all concerned with how we *become* Christians, but with the unity or one-ness of those who *are* Christians, as members of the one Christ, empowered and filled by His one Spirit, to function effectively in His one Body here on earth. So the object of verse 13 cannot be to assert how many of the Corinthians have been baptized in the Spirit and how many have not, but to emphasize that *all* who were so baptized, were baptized in the same one and only Holy Spirit, who produces all these different manifestations, within the one Body of Christ" (*Baptized in One Spirit*, pp.16f.). The words to be emphasized in reading the verse, then, are not "we all" but "one Spirit" and "one body." Note Paul's stress on the oneness of the Body in v.12.

At the same time, it is well to remember that it was normal in the apostolic age for every believer to be baptized in the Spirit, to receive the gift of the Holy Spirit soon after his conversion. Peter had cried out to the multitude of worshipers on the Day of Pentecost that the promise of the Spirit is for *all*, "as many as the Lord our God shall call" (see comments on Acts 2:38-40). The full work of salvation was seldom short-circuited in those days, so that the convert to Christ received not only life but power. The experience at Ephesus reveals that it was unusual for a professing disciple *not* to have the marks of the Spirit on his life (see comments on Acts 19:1-7). In the early Church, it no doubt frequently happened that when a new convert arose from the water of baptism, the Holy Spirit came upon him, so that he was baptized in water and in the Spirit at the same time. Thus it could be said that Christian baptism was one (see comments on Eph. 4:3-6).

I Cor. 13 — THE INCOMPARABLE WAY OF LOVE.

Love is not a gift. Love is the motivation for giving: "God so loved . . . That He gave. . . ." Love is an act of the will, an act of self-surrender and the giving of oneself to others. Edward J. Carnell said that love is fellowship between persons (*Baker's Dictionary of Theology* [Grand Rapids: Baker Book House, 1960], p.332). Therefore, love has always existed, even before creation, within the Trinity.

The Bible never gives a theological definition of *agape*-love. Instead, God chose to demonstrate His love in Christ (Rom. 5:8) and told us love's attributes. In this famous love chapter, we find only two adjectives which describe *agape* positively. "Love is patient, love is kind" (v.4 NASB). And in the Greek, these two descriptive terms are verbs, suggesting that love is active, not static. This sort of love is the antidote which Paul prescribes for the disease of carnality infecting and dividing the church at Corinth.

The ancient Greeks used four different words for love: *eros*, sexual desire or sensual longing (not used in the N.T.); *storgē*, natural affection or mutual love of family members or friends for one another (Rom. 1:31; II Tim. 3:3); *philia*, love, friendship, fondness (James 4:4; cf. "friend," Acts 19:31; etc.); and *agape*. I Cor. 13 refers to *agape* only. This was a more or less neutral word in classical Greek into which the Spirit poured the meaning of the unique quality of God's love.

Because love is long-suffering or patient, it harbors no jealousy. It would not envy another's spiritual gift. It does not allow one to brag about himself, nor let him exaggerate or become conceited about his own gift, or become inflated with pride because of how the Spirit has used him. Thus love never acts arrogantly or rudely or unbecomingly (as some Corinthians were doing at the Lord's Supper [I Cor. 11:17-34], and by speaking out of turn in the meetings, 14:26-40). Therefore, it never tests the patience of others. It does not seek its own; that is, it does not insist on its own way or its own rights, for such insistence is selfish, a "work of the flesh" (Gal. 5:19). In the exercise of spiritual gifts, the loving man seeks to edify others, not to gratify himself. Love is never provoked ("easily" of v.5 in the KJV is not represented in the Greek text), meaning that it is not irritable or touchy or quick to take offense. It thinks no evil, i.e., it "does not take into account a wrong suffered" (NASB), it "keeps no score of wrongs" (NEB), it does not nourish resentment or try to get even. Love forgets when it forgives and begins afresh with every new encounter (Bittlinger, *Gifts and Graces*, p.86). Love does not rejoice in unrighteousness or when injustice befalls someone else, but rejoices when truth prevails. It finds no pleasure in seeing a brother "get what's coming to him" and never says, "It serves him right."

Because love is kind, it bears all things — it conceals the faults of others and throws a cloak of silence over what is offensive in another person (W. F. Arndt and F. W. Gingrich, eds. *A Greek-English Lexicon of the New Testament and Other Early Christian Literature* [Chicago: Univ. of Chicago Press, 1957], p.773). Love believes all things, without doubting God. For example, when someone you prayed for is not healed, love believes all persons, without becoming suspicious, but thinking the best about other Christians unless facts prove otherwise. Love hopes all things, so that for it there are no hopeless cases. It endures all things, without weakening or retaliating or becoming critical. Such love never fails. It abides on and on forever.

No wonder, then, that Paul wrote to the Galatian believers that love is the fruit of the Holy Spirit (Gal. 5:22). Only the Spirit of God can produce love in you, because love is what God *is* in His nature. Therefore love is the evidence of divine, eternal life, of genuine abundant life, lived by the Spirit in you. Love is not a spiritual or charismatic gift, for the *charismata* are what God *does* by His power.

Understanding what love is assists us in interpreting I Cor. 12:31. The last half of that verse is the transition to chapter 13, which describes the correct way of life, the proper atmosphere, for the gifts of the Spirit to operate attractively and efficiently. Some have thought Paul's statement, "And yet shew I unto you a more excellent way," implies that love supersedes the gifts, rendering them unnecessary. A more accurate translation, however, dispels this misunderstanding. The text really says, "And furthermore (*kai eti*) I am going to show you (the) way par excellence (*kath' hyperbolen*)." He is about to further his discussion of spiritual gifts by explaining to the Corinthians the incomparable way of love, rather than offering love as a superior alternative to charismatic gifts.

Nor in chapter 13 itself does the apostle say that if one has love, it displaces the gifts. He does not question whether the manifestations themselves are genuine — gifts of tongues, or prophecy, of (words of) knowledge, and of faith — if he shows no love (vv.1,2,8). The deficiency is not in the gifts or in the Spirit, but in the man endowed with the gift. He does not say that the gifts are nothing, or that charitable deeds do not help the recipients, but that "*I* am nothing" and "it profits *me* nothing." As Godet says, "What such a man has done may be of value to the Church; to himself it is nothing, because there was no love in it" (*I Corinthians*, II, 240). No, Paul does not propose love without gifts. It is rather love *plus* the gifts of the Spirit, for he concludes in I Cor. 14:1 with this exhortation: "Make love your aim, and earnestly desire the spiritual gifts" (RSV).

Love is the best safeguard against pride in Christian service. Desiring the gifts in order to bless and help others will enable the believer to conduct his charismatic ministry in a humble way. Humility and love go hand in hand. In fact, they are like a coin: love is the obverse side and humility the reverse. Display of love rather than of power should be the goal of one's ministry in the gifts of the Spirit. Since God is love, this will be the most characteristic sign of His presence and His working.

I Cor. 14:1-33a — TONGUES OR PROPHECY?

A major aspect of the disorder in the church at Corinth involved the misuse of the phenomenon of speaking in tongues. Evidently some of the members of that church did not recognize that there are distinct ministries of tongues, not all of which are intended for the assembly meetings. For instance, an offender might interfere with the worship of others by uttering praise and prayer to God out loud in his unknown tongue, instead of speaking silently to himself and to God (cf. v.28). Many of them showed no concern if their utterances in tongues were not interpreted. They seemed less informed of the value of the gift of prophecy and using it to edify the congregation than of being free to voice their worship in tongues audibly. Others in the church reacted strongly against such excesses and tried to forbid speaking in tongues. Perhaps these were members of the Gnostic-style faction who, alarmed at the threat of exposure of their own wrong beliefs and attitudes through the operation of the revelatory gifts, were looking for an excuse to rule out the gifts altogether (see Ervin, *These Are Not Drunken As Ye Suppose*, pp.175-208).

Nature of tongues. What is speaking in tongues — which is also called glossolalia (from *glossa*, "tongue," and *laleo*, "to speak")? Paul employs the Greek term *glossa* throughout his discussion in I Cor. 12-14. He says there are various kinds of tongues (I Cor. 12:10,28). In nearly every case in the N.T., these seem to have been languages never learned and thus unknown to the speaker. In mentioning the tongues "of men and of angels" (I Cor. 13:1), however, Paul may be suggesting both existent spoken languages and ecstatic utterances unintelligible anywhere on earth. In another letter, he alludes to personal ecstatic experiences, but only in his privacy with God ("For whether we be beside ourselves [*exestemen*], it is to God" [II Cor. 5:13]).

On the Day of Pentecost, the 120 believers upon whom the Holy Spirit had just been outpoured spoke in "other tongues" (*heterais glossais*). The Greek means "different languages." These were known human languages, different than their own Hebrew and Aramaic and Greek spoken in Galilee. Jews of the Diaspora or Dispersion who had come to Jerusalem for the annual Feast of Weeks, recognized these "other tongues" to be their native languages or dialects (Acts 2:4-11). Each of the Jews in the temple area, where the 120 Christians had faithfully assembled for the Mosaic observances, suddenly heard his own language or tongue wherein he was born (*dialektos* in both v.6 and v.8). A list of fourteen different peoples and countries is given to show that the disciples spoke in at least that many different languages. The Greek word *dialektos* refers in every case to a language of a nation or a region (cf. Arndt-Gingrich, *Greek-English Lexicon*, p.184). Luke also uses *dialektos* to describe the Aramaic name Aceldama (Acts 1:19) and to tell how the ascended Christ spoke intelligibly to Saul of Tarsus on the Damascus road (Acts 26:14) and how Paul defended himself "in the Hebrew tongue" (Acts 21:40; 22:2). See comments on Acts 2:1-4, 14-21, 38-40.

It seems safe to conclude that whenever an utterance in an unknown tongue was given audibly in an assembly under the prompting of the Holy Spirit, it was in a human language. Dr. S. Lewis Johnson, Jr., of Dallas Theological Seminary explains that since Luke was a close companion of Paul and wrote the Book of Acts after Paul had written his Corinthian epistles, it would seem logical for Luke to have noted the distinction between the tongues at Pentecost and those in Corinth, if any existed. "In other words, I Corinthians should be interpreted by Acts, the unknown by the known, a good hermeneutical principle. . . . It is quite unlikely that the phenomena, described by the two writers in identical terms, would be dissimilar" (I Cor., *Wycliffe Bible Commentary* [Chicago: Moody Press, 1962], p. 1253).

In modern times, many utterances in tongues have been understood by those standing near who knew the foreign language in question. On the night of September 26, 1965, for example, the Holy Spirit sovereignly came in power on believers in the Presbyterian church in the town of Soe on Timor Island in Indonesia. An illiterate woman knowing only the Timorese language was heard to be worshiping Jesus Christ in perfect English, and an uneducated man of Soe was magnifying God in German (Tari, *Like A Mighty Wind*, pp. 26–27). There have been numerous incidents similar to this in America and other countries as well.

To understand the nature of genuine speaking in tongues by the Spirit, we need to study v.2 in conjunction with v.5. Verse 2 describes speaking in a language unknown to the speaker or any listeners without interpretation following. Paul says the one who speaks in a tongue in this way speaks to God, not to men. That person is using a language which he himself does not rationally understand, in order to communicate the deep thoughts and feelings of his spirit to God. In his spirit, he speaks "mysteries," mysterious things not understood by his mind or by those who may overhear him. As Godet long ago stated it, speaking in a tongue is a sort of spiritual soliloquy (*I Corinthians*, II, 265). Therefore, speaking in a tongue is a supernatural manifestation of the Holy Spirit whereby the Christian speaks in a language he has never learned but which expresses his innermost thoughts and feelings, a language which God hears and understands (Laurence Christenson, *Speaking in Tongues* [Minneapolis: Bethany Fellowship, 1968], pp.22,27).

In v.5, however, the apostle places speaking in tongues followed by the gift of interpretation, in parallel with prophesying as far as its value in edifying the church is concerned. Now prophecy edifies, because through this gift God is giving a revelation and speaking to the church. Therefore, we may conclude that also in tongues with interpretation, God is speaking to men. Occasionally, however, the tongues speaker may be praising God or praying to Him, as the interpretation makes clear. This public manifestation of tongues is apparently what Paul refers to in chapter 12:10,28,30 as the charismatic *gift* of tongues for the ministering of one member of the body to the others.

Extent of tongues. The charismatic gift of tongues was a new manifestation of the Spirit never displayed by any of the O.T. prophets and saints. Isaiah 28:11, quoted by Paul in v.21, is not primarily a prophecy foretelling the Pentecostal gift. In its own context, Isaiah's verse refers to the seemingly "stammering lips" and alien tongue of the Assyrians and their mercenary troops of various nationalities, whom God would bring to "speak" to His people as a divine judgment. The people of Judah had refused to listen to God's prophets when He had offered His rest and refreshing (Isa. 28:12), and so were to be hardened in their unbelief by the tongues of the foreign invaders. Likewise, in the church at Corinth, tongues were a "sign" to "them that believe not" or "unbelievers" (the *apistoi*) and to the "unlearned" (the *idiotai*, vv.22-24). The *apistoi* were probably not unsaved outsiders but perhaps were false teachers who professed to be Christians and whom the Corinthian believers were admitting to their services; and the *idiotai* would then have been novices who gullibly listened to the false teachers. These were in the habit of accusing the tongues speakers of being "mad," hardening their own hearts in unbelief and disobedience in the very process of mocking. While tongues without interpretation could only be a sign of God's displeasure with their unbelief, prophecy could disclose the secrets of their hearts and bring some of them to repentance (vv.24,25; see Ervin, *These Are Not Drunken As Ye Suppose*, pp.201-8). Even Joel's prophecy (Joel 2:28-32) did not specifically foretell tongues, but promised other forms of spiritual revelation, such as prophesying, visions, and dreams.

To speak with "new tongues" was an unprecedented experience for Spirit-anointed men of God. Thus it is a miraculous sign unique to the Church Age (Mark 16:17,20). [Even if the last verses of Mark's Gospel are not original to him but added early in the second century A.D., it would be primary evidence that the practice of tongues was not limited to the first few decades of the Church (see comments on Mark 16:9-20).] Tongues will cease or come to an end "when that which is perfect is come," at the second coming of Christ (I Cor. 13:8-10).

Speaking in tongues is reported to have occurred after Pentecost when the Holy Spirit was poured out upon Cornelius and his household (Acts 10:45,46). Peter claimed later that the Spirit had fallen upon the Gentiles at Caesarea "just as" (*hosper kai*) He did at Pentecost (Acts 11:15), intimating that the Gentiles also spoke in one or more tongues recognizable as languages (see comments on Acts 10:44-48). Tongues were in evidence again at Ephesus when Paul laid his hands upon twelve newly baptized disciples (see comments on Acts 19:1-7). Many commentators believe that glossolalia also happened at Samaria when the recent converts were receiving the Holy

Spirit (see comments on Acts 8:5-25). Paul sooner or later spoke in tongues and continued to do so (v.18). His initial experience may have taken place when he was filled with the Holy Spirit in Damascus (see comments on Acts 9:1-22).

The term "speaking in tongues" does not appear in any epistle other than I Corinthians. Certain expressions, however, indicate that the gift of tongues was not confined to the church at Corinth. Paul's instructions in I Cor. 14 evidently were meant for "all the churches of the saints" (14:33,34). He urged the Ephesian and the Colossian believers to worship God with "spiritual songs" (Eph. 5:19; Col. 3:16). These are Spirit-given songs, identified by many with Paul's "singing with the Spirit," i.e., singing in tongues. Yet the absence of glossolalia in the list of charismatic gifts in Rom. 12:3-8 (see comments there) shows that we cannot claim Paul's authority that tongues are a *necessary* part of the public ministry in every local church.

Purposes of tongues. In the N.T., glossolalia does not seem to have been an instrument of evangelism. On the Day of Pentecost, the disciples were heard speaking "the wonderful works" (*ta megaleia*, "the greatnesses") of God (Acts 2:11). In Cornelius' house they likewise were praising and magnifying (*megalunonton*) God (Acts 10:46). In neither case did they proclaim the Gospel, nor did interpretation accompany the manifestation of tongues. It was Peter's sermon in a language commonly known by all the assembled Jews (in Aramaic or Greek) that wrought conviction in the hearts of the 3000 who were converted at Pentecost. The following uses of tongues seem apparent in the N.T. (verses marked v. or vv. are in I Cor. 14):

1. A sign of the promised outpouring of the Spirit and the believer's consequent reception of Him, known as the baptism in the Holy Spirit. The one common immediate consequence of the coming of the Spirit in power at Jerusalem, Caesarea, and Ephesus was speaking in tongues. Speaking with "new tongues" is listed as one of the signs that will accompany those who have believed the apostolic message (Mark 16:17). This initial

speaking in a tongue following the baptism in the Spirit is not proof, however, that one has received the *gift* of tongues for public use in the congregation.

2. A private devotional exercise (vv.2,4,14-18,28). In this use, glossolalia becomes a means of personal edification through the communication of one's spirit with God in praise and prayer. This is an act of spiritual worship not controlled or limited by one's intellect. It was practiced in great measure by Paul himself (vv.14,15,18), and he wanted all his readers to be speaking in tongues in this way (v.5 RSV). Praising God was the purpose that the 120 disciples had on the morning of Pentecost (see above), although at the same time, the miracle served as a sign to the hearers. Paul stresses, however, that usually this function of tongues should be performed in private or under one's breath. Some have linked the intercession of the Spirit "with groanings too deep for words" (Rom. 8:26,27 NASB) and "praying in the Spirit" (Eph. 6:18; Jude 20) to praying in tongues, but these passages cannot be limited to glossolalia (see comments on Rom. 8:23-27). Many are discovering that praying in tongues opens the door for the Holy Spirit to deal with one's spirit in the area of his subconscious attitudes and desires. Here is an aid in bringing every thought of one's mind captive to the obedience of Christ (II Cor. 10:5).

3. Congregational worship in spiritual songs (Eph. 5:18,19). This is the beautiful, unrehearsed, extemporaneous singing in the Spirit by all or many of the believers assembled in worship. Often it takes the form of singing praise to God in various tongues, which need not be interpreted because all are participating in the adoration. If only one person sings aloud in a tongue, then an interpretation should follow, perhaps also in song.

4. A message to fellow believers (vv.5b,13,26,27). This use is the gift of tongues *per se*, listed in I Cor. 12:10,28 as one of the charismatic gifts, all of which are to be used to minister to other members of the Body of Christ. Whereas Paul wanted all to

speak in tongues devotionally (vv.2-5a), not all speak with tongues to the congregation of the church (I Cor. 12:30). Usually in this function, Christ is speaking by His Spirit to the assembled people. In order for the message from God in an unknown tongue to edify the church, the gift of tongues must operate with the sister-gift of interpretation. The one who interprets may be the one who has spoken in the tongue (vv.5,13), or it may be another person (vv.27,28). The interpretation is not necessarily an exact translation of the utterance in tongues, but may be a rendering in the vernacular of the main content of the message in the unknown language (Christenson, *Speaking in Tongues*, p. 116). The response in English may be longer, because the interpretation itself may have been followed by words in prophecy. Or it may be that the speaking in tongues was actually a prayer, and the presumed interpretation an answer by prophecy (Bennett, *The Holy Spirit and You*, p. 89). The tongues utterance plus the interpretation may edify the church equally as much as prophesying (v.5b), lending a distinct note of the supernatural to the meeting.

5. A sign to strangers and unbelievers. Speaking in tongues may be either praise *to* God or a message *from* God. In either case, at the same time, it may act also as a sign: a) of the Divine Presence when the language is identified and understood; b) when the tongue is not understood, but nevertheless is recognized to be evidence of the living God at work; and c) of unbelief when the tongue is mocked and its divine character is denied. The tongues at Pentecost which produced amazement in the Jews from other lands are an example of the first type. The glossolalia served to get their attention, so that they might listen with open ears to Peter as he preached the Gospel. In some cases of recent record, a message has been given directly to a person of foreign birth in his or her mother tongue. The result is often that the heart of the hearer is convicted and melted, and he receives Christ as his Savior and Lord. The speaking in tongues by Cornelius and his associates may not have been

understood by Peter and the Jews with him, but they knew the tongues were exalting God (Acts 10:44-46); this would illustrate the second type. In cases of the third type, unbelieving critics and scoffers may consider glossolalia to be mere gibberish and become hardened in their attitude. Their very mockery of tongues becomes the sign of their unbelief (vv.22,23; see p. 157 for discussion of Isa. 28:11).

Regulation of tongues. Paul recognized the abuses of speaking in tongues along with its values. Because a number of persons in the church at Corinth were overemphasizing tongues, he set forth certain principles and rules for their proper use. No one should boast that his rather dramatic gift is more supernatural or more important than another less conspicuous one (I Cor. 12). The only right motive for desiring the gifts, including tongues, and the only right attitude in which they function profitably, is love (I Cor. 13). A message in tongues must be followed with an interpretation; otherwise the one manifesting the gift of tongues should remain silent. Only two or at the most three should speak in tongues in any given meeting, and these in turn (vv.28,29). These instructions were given to prevent glossolalia from dominating the entire meeting and thus hindering persons with other gifts from ministering to the church.

Nature of prophecy. Prophecy is one of the charismatic gifts manifested in the Christian by the power of the Holy Spirit (I Cor. 12:10,11). Much can be learned about the gift of prophecy through a study of the O.T. prophets. The clearest illustration of the role of a prophet is to be found in Exod. 7:1,2. The Lord told Moses that He would make him as God to the Egyptian king, and that his brother Aaron would be his prophet. "You shall speak all that I command you, and your brother Aaron shall speak to Pharaoh that he let the sons of Israel go out of his land" (NASB). Moses was God's prophet or spokesman to tell all that God revealed to him, and Aaron in turn was Moses' spokesman to relay the divine message, unchanged, to the Pharaoh. Num. 12:6,7 states that ordinarily God made Himself known to a prophet in a vision or a dream, although He spoke more directly to Moses in order to give the Law in all its detail (see comments on II Pet. 1:19-21). The careers of Jeremiah, Ezekiel, and Daniel frequently demonstrate the obedience which God required of them—and the persecution they often had to endure because of their obedience.

One result of the Pentecostal outpouring of the Spirit during the Church Age is that *all* of God's children might be able to prophesy (see comments on Acts 2:14-21). Paul evidently believed that every Spirit-baptized Christian potentially can manifest the gift of prophecy, as the Spirit wills, for he wrote, "I want you all to speak in tongues, but even more that you would prophesy" (v.5). Therefore, he ended his entire discussion on the spiritual gifts by exhorting, "Covet to prophesy" (I Cor. 14:39). He considered prophecy to be the most important of the gifts of utterance, and perhaps of all the gifts (v.1). Of course he recognized that not all members of Christ's Church have the *ministry* of prophet (I Cor. 12:28,29).

Indwelt and empowered by the Spirit of God, a believer of this dispensation since Pentecost may receive an inner revelation and be prompted to speak by the Holy Spirit, without the aid of a dream or vision. When he is yielded to the Spirit's control and realizes that a few thoughts or words of inspiration are coming to his mind, he should act on faith and give forth these words directly as an utterance of God to the church (I Pet. 4:11), and expect that the Spirit will supply the rest of the message even while he is speaking.

Purpose of prophecy. Over and over in I Cor. 14 it is stated that the purpose of the gifts of utterance is to edify the other members of the church. There are three ways in which prophecy ministers to Christians, according to v.3: edification, exhortation, and comfort or consolation. The first term means building up, as one builds a house with strong, good materials. The words of God spoken in prophecy, like the written "word of

His grace" (Acts 20:32), serve to establish and strengthen the church and to add new members to it. The second term, "exhortation," is the Greek word *paraklesis*, from the same root as Paraclete or "Comforter," Jesus' expression for the Holy Spirit (see comments on John 14:15-18,26). Thus through the gift of prophecy, the Spirit can carry out His work of comforting and encouraging and counseling in the local church. The third term, "consolation" (*paramythia*), is closely related to the second. It refers specifically to the solace afforded by love (Phil. 2:1), often at the time of bereavement, as in the case of the Jews coming to console Mary and Martha (John 11:19,31). It means to calm and pacify. Thus prophecy can calm our doubts and fears and help us to rest in the presence of Jesus.

Another result of prophecy may be the conversion of an unbeliever or deluded Christian, as seen in vv.24,25: "But if all prophesy, and an unbeliever . . . enters, he is convicted by all, he is called to account by all; the secrets of his heart are disclosed; and so he will fall on his face and worship God, declaring that God is certainly among you" (NASB). Here is an instance of the gift of knowledge functioning together with the gift of prophecy to reveal the condition of the sinner's heart and turn him from the error or delusion of his way (James 5:19,20).

Regulation of prophecy. In addition to the rules for the use of tongues in a meeting, the Lord gives two main instructions regarding the gift of prophecy: "Let two or three prophets speak, and let the others pass judgment" (v.29 NASB).

Only two or three prophets should speak during a worship service so that the meeting does not become overbalanced with charismatic utterances, with no time left for singing and prayer and teaching and preaching the Word. When one gave a prophecy, he evidently stood on his feet. If another member who was seated received a fresh revelation, he was to stand up to indicate this. Then the first brother (who perhaps by then was going beyond the Spirit's anointing in his own words!) was to become silent and sit down. Each member had the right and the potential in the Spirit to prophesy, so that every other member might learn from him and be exhorted. Each could have an opportunity, if they prophesied one by one in successive meetings, no more than three to a service.

The other regulation is to test each prophetic utterance: "Let the others weigh what is said" (v.29 RSV). Prophets must be tested, because prophesying is the cooperative working together of the Holy Spirit with the human spirit. While the Spirit of God prompts and superintends, the spirit of man is alive and free, and therefore responsible for the rational thoughts of the mind and the words of the tongue. All are to judge, but especially those with the gift of the discerning of spirits are to be alert to detect any trace of false teaching. There is to be a witness of the Spirit in the hearts of the other brethren that the message is right and in agreement with the authoritative Scriptures. Prophecy must never contradict the written Word of God. All believers, but especially the elders, are responsible to be on guard against false prophets and teachers, who may arise even from within the congregation, "speaking perverse things, to draw away disciples after them" (Acts 20:28-30).

Finally, order is to be maintained in the meeting by the observance of good manners and consideration of others. Paul forthrightly says, "The spirits of prophets are subject to prophets" (v.32 NASB). This reminds us, says Dennis Bennett, that the gifts of the Spirit come by inspiration, not compulsion, and provide no excuse for erratic behavior (*The Holy Spirit and You*, p.104). If the Holy Spirit is truly in control, the meeting will be peaceful, loving, and orderly; "for God is not the author of confusion, but of peace" (v.33a).

Tongues or prophecy? According to the apostle Paul, it is not a matter of one versus the other, but of both practiced in humility as the Spirit wills and as each member is in subjection to the others in the local church. "Therefore, my brethren, desire earnestly to prophesy, and do not forbid to speak in tongues" (I Cor. 14:39 NASB).

I Cor. 14:33b-35 — THE ROLE OF WOMEN IN
CONGREGATIONAL WORSHIP.

"The women should keep quiet in the churches, for they are
not authorized to speak, but should take a secondary and
subordinate place, just as the Law also says. [Gen. 3:16]" (v.34
TAB). Paul refers apparently to women sitting in judgment
over men and teaching them or giving authoritative direction
in the churches, as roles which are unfit for women (Findlay,
I Corinthians, EGT, II, 915).

In chapter 11, the apostle had already reproved the irregular
behavior of certain Christian women at Corinth with regard to
their worshiping with their hair loose and disheveled. This
seems to be the true meaning of *akatalypto* (translated "uncov-
ered" or "unveiled" [ASV, RSV] in I Cor. 11:6,13), a rendering
determined by the use of this Greek term in the Septuagint
translation of Lev. 13:45. That O.T. passage required the leper
to let the hair of his head "go loose" (ASV) or be left
"disheveled" (NASB margin; New JPS) as a sign of his
uncleanness. Under the Mosaic Law, a woman's hair hanging
loose and unkempt was the public sign of an accused adulteress,
the sign of moral unrestraint and unfaithfulness to her husband
and rejection of his authority over her (Num. 5:13-20 NASB).
Therefore women at Corinth who exhibited their new so-called
"liberty in Christ" by wearing unfeminine hair styles were
probably motivated by a rebellious spirit, for they were not
following the prevailing practice of the other churches (I Cor.
11:3-16).

According to the best understanding of that difficult section
of Paul's epistle, the proper sign of a godly wife's submission to
her husband was not a veil or some other type of artificial head
covering, as usually supposed. Rather it was a neat, modest
hairdo that was not overly ornate (cf. I Tim. 2:9). Paul
explained that a woman's long hair was a glory to her, and was
given to her instead of (Greek *anti*) a covering or veil (I Cor.
11:15). Therefore the Christian woman should wear her hair in

a becoming feminine style that is longer than the prevailing style of men's hair, in order clearly to distinguish between the sexes and to be the divinely given sign of her role. (See James B. Hurley, "Did Paul Require Veils or the Silence of Women? A Consideration of I Cor. 11:2-16 and I Cor. 14:33b-36," *Westminster Theological Journal*, XXXV [1973], 190-220).

Now in chapter 14 it seems to be the women's speaking out in judgment of prophetic messages (cf. 14:29) that Paul is reproving. Verses 33b-35 are best taken in conjunction with the whole section of 14:26-35, rather than making a separate topic of these two and a half verses. Again Paul insists that women who thus speak out are flouting a principle that is standard in all the churches of the saints (14:33b), not merely a local custom at Corinth.

The silence which Paul commanded was probably conditional, not absolute, in order to prevent the women from monopolizing the service and certainly from usurping the authority of the men. He was not prohibiting the women from manifesting gifts of the Spirit, for his words in I Cor. 11:5 infer that women as well as men normally participated in the corporate worship in prayer and prophesying. After all, the Spirit was poured out upon both "your sons" and "your daughters," upon both male and female bondslaves (Acts 2:17,18). Howard M. Ervin is no doubt correct in saying, "Paul is not, as some have contended, forbidding women to speak in tongues in the congregational services. From the context, he seems rather to prohibit undisciplined discussion that would interrupt the service, for, counseled Paul, 'if they would learn anything, let them ask their own husbands at home' " (*These Are Not Drunken As Ye Suppose*, p.148).

Elsewhere the apostle explicitly forbids a woman to teach or to exercise authority over a man (I Tim. 2:12). Ervin concludes that Paul's reference is to the *ministry* of teacher, "which carried with it the authority and responsibility for authoritative pronouncements on doctrine" (*ibid*, p.146). Carl W. Wilson believes that women were allowed to prophesy, because the prophetic gift involves having a direct *objective message* from God so that the individual acts simply as God's spokesman and does not convey his or her own message, but God's. "On the other hand, the gifts of government and teaching involve the individual's giving subjective judgment under guidance of the Holy Spirit, and these are always differentiated in Scripture from prophecy (Mal. 2:4-8; 3:11; Jer. 18:18; I Cor. 12:28; Eph. 4:11,12)" (Carl W. Wilson, "Women, Ordination of," *Baker's Dictionary of Theology*, p.557).

While women might prophesy in a worship service as a charismatic manifestation of the Holy Spirit which was open to every Christian, no women in churches of the N.T. legitimately held the prophetic office (Ervin, *These Are Not Drunken As Ye Suppose*, pp.146ff.). The N.T. gives no record of any genuine prophetess in any of the apostolic churches. Anna (Luke 2:36) belonged to the dispensation of the Old Covenant, while Jezebel (Rev. 2:20) was obviously a false prophetess. The NASB and Williams miss the point in translating Acts 21:9 so as to say that Philip's daughters "were prophetesses." TAB, TLB, NEB, and others bring out the idea involved by saying they "had the gift of prophecy." Luke implies merely that they prophesied, as Agabus and others did (Acts 21:10,11; 20:23; 21:4), that Paul would meet with trouble in Jerusalem.

Not only addressing the meeting or judging a word of prophecy on the part of a woman would be an act of authority exercised over the congregation, but even asking a question would give a woman opportunity to evade her proper role of submissiveness. A question may be only a veiled objection to what is being preached or taught or prophesied, or even a contradiction of it. Paul knew how easily, under the pretext of stating a question, a woman could elude his command to refrain from posing as a teacher in the church. Neither men nor women should ask questions and debate and argue with the

God-appointed ministers of the Christian community in such a way that the authority of the leaders is undermined.

Admittedly, the question of the role of the Christian woman is a difficult one. It is necessary to hold in balance both the truth that in Christ there is neither male nor female (Gal. 3:28) and the biblical restrictions placed upon women. Certainly Jesus did more than anyone else in history to ennoble the status of women. In the ancient Greek world, women were considered inferior to men, and wives lived in seclusion and practical slavery. In Judaism their position was markedly better, but the real turning point came when the Virgin Mary became the mother of the Son of God and was called blessed (Luke 1:35,48). Nevertheless, the divine order beginning with creation, and unchanged by the fall of man and by redemption, is that headship and authority are assigned to the man (Gen. 3:16; I Cor. 11:7-9; I Tim. 2:12,13). Therefore it is the responsibility of the Christian husband to cherish and encourage his wife to such an extent (Eph. 5:28,29) and to rule his household with such love and wisdom (I Tim. 3:4) that she feels released in her spirit to engage in her God-given ministry of prayer (I Pet. 3:7) and helping him (Gen. 2:18; I Cor. 11:9). Only then can she submit gladly to her role and feel fulfilled in it.

II CORINTHIANS

II Cor. 1:21,22 — THE EARNEST OF THE SPIRIT.

Paul is explaining to the Corinthians that he is not a vacillating person in being prevented from visiting them sooner. His own word is consistent, not a yes today and a no tomorrow. His example is Christ Jesus, the Son of God, in whom yes means yes. For all the promises of God, who is ever true and faithful, receive the answer of yes in Christ (II Cor. 1:15-20). Paul then describes God as the One who is constantly establishing our position in Christ and who gave us the earnest of the Spirit in our hearts: "It is God who gives us a firm standing in Christ, along with you; it is God who has anointed us for our service, who has set His seal upon us and given us His Spirit in our hearts as His sure pledge" (vv.21,22, F. F. Bruce, *The Letters of Paul*, p.127).

According to Paul, our present common experience as Christians is confirmed by the three simultaneous and decisive acts of anointing, sealing, and receiving the Spirit that took place in the past. But when? At regeneration? At the baptism in the Holy Spirit? If the time of any one of these acts can be determined, it will set the time of all three.

Let us examine the first of these three acts. Paul's statement, "anointed us," means that God made us like the Anointed One, Christ, in the sense that both Christ and we are anointed with the same Spirit. But we were anointed with the Spirit — we received the anointing from the Holy One (see comments on I John 2:20,27) — when we received the promised gift of the Holy Spirit. According to Acts 2:38-40 (see comments there) the gift of the Spirit, in the sense of His enduing the believer with power, is offered to the Christian subsequent to his conversion. The reception of this gift by faith is known as the baptism in the Spirit.

Anointing, sealing, and giving the Spirit, therefore, in the sense of vv.21,22, all occurred in a single event, when the Christian disciple was baptized in the Holy Spirit. The "anointing" points to the power of the Spirit to perform the works of Christ (Isa. 61:1; Acts 10:38) and to the capacity given to believers by the Spirit to know the truth (I John 2:20,27). The "sealing" emphasizes the gift of the Spirit as the seal of the New Covenant which God has made with His people through Christ the Mediator. The seal also serves as a sign of ownership, for by sealing believers with His Spirit, God marks them as His very own. He did this by "giving" the Spirit "in our hearts." It is true that the Holy Spirit first entered our being as Christ's agent to bring us His resurrection-life. The N.T., however, never equates our new birth with God's *gift* of His Spirit to us. Jesus made it clear that not until after He would return to the Father would He send the Spirit of truth as Comforter to abide in them (John 16:5,7; 14:16,17; 15:26; see comments on John 14:15-18). He fulfilled the promise on the Day of Pentecost, ten days after His ascension to the right hand of the Father. Therefore, when Paul writes in v.22 that God *gave* us the Spirit in our hearts, he is referring to the baptism in the Spirit and not to conversion.

The Greek word *arrabon*, translated "earnest" in the KJV, means the first down payment by which the recipient is assured of final payment in full. It is derived from the Hebrew word *erabon*, which appears in Gen. 38:17-20 as the pledge which Tamar demanded of Judah. In modern Greek, *arrabon* means an engagement ring, the token of future marriage from the lover to his prospective bride. The Spirit Himself is this earnest, or pledge (NASB), or guarantee (RSV), as Paul says again in II Cor. 5:5. The Spirit is God's pledge to us of our inheritance (Eph. 1:13,14; see comments there), even of that full and perfect knowledge of God and of His Son Jesus Christ which is eternal life (John 17:3). The Spirit is a fitting seal, pledge, and down payment because He is a *present* experience. He is God's way of saying, "See, this is what I am talking about!"

II Cor. 3:8 — THE MINISTRY OF THE SPIRIT.

Every Christian is a servant of Jesus Christ. As a servant of Christ, he is a servant or minister of the New Covenant instituted by Christ. Whereas the ministry of the Old Covenant or Law of Moses was a ministry which tended to death, glorious as it was with the Lord's presence at Mount Sinai, the ministry of the New Covenant is a ministry of the Spirit (II Cor. 3:6-8). We do not serve under the old written code, but in the new life of the Spirit (Rom. 7:6 RSV). Therefore, the ministry of this present dispensation, from Pentecost until the return of Christ, is under the authority and direction of the Holy Spirit.

The chief characteristic of this ministry is that the Spirit gives life (II Cor. 3:6). The Holy Spirit is the Life-giver (John 6:63). By His quickening power, the resurrection life of Jesus is planted in the human heart, and the person is born again (John 3:5).

Having imparted spiritual life to us — the new life of Christ — the Spirit's subsequent and continuing work is to change us into the very image or likeness of Christ, from one degree of glory to another (II Cor. 3:18). In II Cor. 3:16, Paul paraphrases Exod. 34:34 to read, "But whenever a man turns to the Lord, the veil is taken away" (NASB). In II Cor. 3:17, he explains that the term "the Lord" must be interpreted as the Spirit, in making application of that passage to an individual seeking God during the present dispensation. He then adds that wherever the Spirit of the Lord is present, there is liberty. Men's souls are set free, as J. B. Phillips paraphrases it. The NEB translation enables us to understand the rich meaning of the words in II Cor. 3:18: "And because for us there is no veil over the face, we all reflect as in a mirror the splendour of the Lord; thus we are transfigured into His likeness, from splendour to splendour; such is the influence of the Lord who is Spirit."

Only the Spirit of Christ dwelling within us can change us into the likeness of our precious Lord and Savior. It is not possible for the believer to become conformed to the image of Christ by external imitation of Him. A. J. Gordon, a Baptist clergyman in Boston during the nineteenth century, explained the divine process in a beautiful way: "Christ, who is 'the image of the invisible God,' is set before him as his divine pattern, and Christ by the Spirit dwells within him as a divine life, and Christ is able to image forth Christ from the interior life to the outward example" (*The Ministry of the Spirit* [Philadelphia: American Baptist Publ. Soc., 1896], p.114). And as the

Comforter makes us more and more like Christ, He imparts to us the fruit of the Spirit (Gal. 5:22,23), which really consists of various aspects of Christ's holy character. This is His continuing work of sanctification in its present stage (see comments on I Cor. 6:11).

Another phase of the Spirit's ministry is to make us able ministers of the New Covenant (II Cor. 3:6). We are not adequate or qualified in ourselves. We are not capable on our own initiative of conceiving a single wise thought or performing a single helpful deed that would benefit Christ's kingdom; our adequacy is from God (II Cor. 3:5). It is the Spirit of God who teaches us, directs us, empowers us, and distributes His gifts to us. In this way, He equips us to be able to perform our duties as servants of Christ. Paul recognized this enabling once again in his list of characteristics of the ministry of reconciliation (II Cor. 6:6). The saintly Andrew Murray of South Africa pointed out that the power of the ministry on the divine side is the Spirit, while on the human side it is faith (*The Spirit of Christ* [London: Nisbet, 1888], p.247). Paul said that he had the same "spirit of faith" that the writer of Ps. 116 had (II Cor. 4:13). He is not referring directly to the Holy Spirit, but to the human spirit which is in fellowship with the divine Spirit and therefore is characterized by the attitude of faith. It is this spirit or attitude of faith, which is a fruit of the Holy Spirit, that sustained Paul in his severe trials and afflictions (II Cor. 4:8-11). Faith is necessary throughout the entire Christian life. Whatever is of the Spirit, is by faith on our part. Through weakness or severe trials, God brings us to the death of self, i.e., to the end of trusting in ourselves, so that the resurrection-life of Jesus may be manifested in our mortal flesh. Andrew Murray concluded his teaching from II Cor. 4 by saying: "And this is the Ministry of the Spirit, when faith glories in infirmities, that the power of Christ may rest upon it. It is as our faith does not stagger at the earthiness and weakness of the vessel, as it consents that the excellency of the power shall be, not from ourselves, or in anything we feel, but of God alone, that the Spirit will work in the power of the living God" (*The Spirit of Christ*, p.250).

II Cor. 12:7,8 — PAUL'S THORN IN THE FLESH.

"Because of the surpassing greatness of the revelations, for this reason, to keep me from exalting myself, there was given me a thorn in the flesh, a messenger of Satan to buffet me — to keep me from exalting myself! Concerning this I entreated the Lord three times that it might depart from me" (NASB).

Bible commentators and other writers in recent times for the most part have assumed that Paul's "thorn in the flesh" was some physical handicap, illness, or bodily weakness. Numerous diseases have been suggested, such as epilepsy, acute ophthalmia or eye trouble, malarial fever, hysteria or melancholy, sick headache, or some nervous disorder. They have supported their interpretation by the words "in the flesh" and by equating Paul's problem with his phrase "infirmity of the flesh" in Gal. 4:13,14. But the only similarity in the two expressions is the word "flesh" (Greek *sarx*), which Paul uses scores of times and in a number of different ways in his epistles. Furthermore, whatever was the nature of his thorn, it did not prevent his continuing in an extremely active ministry which included long journeys on foot. Still others have suggested Paul's "thorn" was the feeling of guilt in his conscience stemming from having formerly persecuted the Church. While Paul often mentioned the crime, yet he knew that the grace of Jesus Christ had fully absolved him (I Tim. 1:13-16).

A study of the phrase "thorn in the flesh" (*skolops te sarki*) and of its context in Paul's defense of his apostleship (II Cor. 10-13), indicates that it refers to a person, not an illness. According to the O.T., this phrase is a rather common idiom for a human enemy. In Num. 33:55 the Israelites are told that if they do not drive out the Canaanite inhabitants of the land, the latter will become "pricks in your eyes, and thorns in your sides, and shall vex you in the land." In the Septuagint (Greek translation of the O.T.), *skolops* is the word for "pricks." In Ezek. 28:24 the enemies surrounding the house of Israel are referred to as "a pricking brier" (Greek *skolops pikrias*, "a thorn of bitterness") and "any grieving thorn." Josh. 23:13 has similar idiomatic terminology (although the Septuagint does not employ the word *skolops* to translate any of the words): "They shall be snares and traps unto you, and scourges in your sides, and thorns in your eyes, until ye perish from off this good land." Ezekiel's opponents are called "briers and thorns" (Ezek. 2:6), and Micah complained that the best of the wicked rulers and judges were "as a brier" (Mic. 7:4).

In v.7 the "thorn in the flesh" is characterized as "a messenger of Satan" (*angelos satana*). The Greek word *angelos* occurs 188 times in the N.T., translated 181 times in the KJV as "angel" and seven times as "messenger." In no other verse does *angelos* refer to anything but an earthly or a heavenly personal being. Therefore the "messenger" in v.7 most likely has reference to an actual person. It is possible that it could refer to the oppressing spirit or demon operating through such a person. In that case a literal translation, "an angel of Satan," would be correct.

Paul rehearsed in chapter 11 the gist of his struggle with false teachers at Corinth. He sarcastically called them "most eminent apostles" (NASB, II Cor. 11:5; 12:11), but then described them in all seriousness as false apostles, deceitful workers, persons who are disguising themselves as apostles of Christ (II Cor. 11:13). "And no wonder," he said, "for even Satan disguises himself as an angel of light (*angelon photos*)" (II Cor. 11:14 NASB). Satan, himself, masquerading as an angel or messenger of light, was being represented by humans who were called false apostles and his "ministers" (*diakonoi*). These were probably Judaizers who attempted to require Law-keeping of converts to Christianity, and thus were perverting the Gospel of God's grace. They were similar to Paul's adversaries in the Galatian churches and at Colossae. They liked to pose as "ministers of Christ" (II Cor. 11:23), but they could not begin to show the credentials that Paul could as a true apostle of Christ.

When, therefore, in v.7, Paul spoke of a messenger of Satan, it is reasonable to conclude that here, too, he was referring to an enemy of the Gospel. (The discussion above has been based to a great extent on the article of Terence Y. Mullins entitled, "Paul's Thorn in the Flesh," JBL, LXXVI [1957], 299-303).

Paul's particular opponent evidently kept dogging his steps from place to place. Prior to setting out on his current trip to Corinth, Paul had been ministering for more than two years in Ephesus (Acts 19:8,10,22). Quite probably it was in that city where this false teacher repeatedly vexed Paul and sought to undermine his apostolic authority.

If Paul's thorn in the flesh was the continual aggravation caused by a hostile person and not a sickness, then one cannot claim support from this passage that there are some illnesses which God may refuse to heal.

GALATIANS

GAL. 3:2-5,14 — RECEIVING THE SPIRIT THROUGH FAITH.

Paul wrote this epistle to the churches he had founded in Galatia in order to teach them the correct way to live the Christian life. The error of Jewish legalism which was subverting the faith of the Galatians pertained as much to the means of their sanctification as of their justification. They had known clearly how to be saved. He had taught them what he and the apostles in Jerusalem had agreed upon, namely, that neither Jew nor Gentile is justified by the works of the Law but through faith in Christ Jesus (Gal. 2:16). Then, however, Jewish

Christians had come after he left, teaching that one could not enjoy the covenant blessings given to Abraham unless he submitted to circumcision (Gal. 5:2-12) and observed the Jewish feasts and special days (Gal. 4:10).

Chapter 3, v.3 is the key to the entire book of Galatians. Paul asks the believers why, since they had begun their new life as Christians in the Spirit, why they now were trying to be made perfect by the flesh. They would readily admit, he knows, that they had been saved by an operation of the Spirit, through faith on their part. Why, then, should they expect to be brought to spiritual maturity by dependence on the flesh and by performing works of the Law?

Because living the Christian life obviously requires the continued working of the Spirit, Paul centers their attention on how they received the Holy Spirit, not on how they received Christ. That is why he asks in v.2, "Did you receive the Spirit by the works of the Law, or by hearing with faith?" (NASB). Did they receive the Spirit on the grounds of their having kept the Law of Moses, or as a result of their hearing the Gospel accompanied by faith on their part? Obviously, the latter.

Verses 5 and 14 show that the apostle is talking about their receiving the promised gift of the Spirit when they were baptized in the Holy Spirit. The word "miracles" (*dynamis*) in v.5 indicates, even to non-Pentecostal writers, that Paul had in mind "the charismatic manifestations of the Spirit evidenced by some outward sign, such as speaking with tongues or prophesying." This was the observation of Ernest DeWitt Burton, a Baptist professor of Biblical and patristic Greek at the University of Chicago (*The Epistle to the Galatians*, ICC, 1921, p.147). And in v.14 the expression "the promise of the Spirit" is the same as that which Peter used in his Pentecost sermon (Acts 2:33). Peter was referring to the great outpouring of the Holy Spirit when Jesus began to baptize the members of His Church.

According to v.5, the experience which the Galatians had of the Holy Spirit extended beyond the initial reception: "He

therefore that ministereth to you the Spirit." The verb "ministereth" is *epichoregon,* a participle in the present tense that means
"he who is continually supplying in bountiful measure." The
verb "worketh" is similar in construction, and indicates that
God was continuing to perform miracles by His Spirit through
those Galatians who were still walking in faith and had not
reverted to legalistic forms. Therefore it appears that the first
great outpouring of the Spirit among the Galatians was
accompanied with the various spiritual gifts described in I Cor.
12-14. Although it had been checked by the undermining of the
Judaizers, it had not entirely ceased.

From Paul's discussion, then, we learn that the baptism in the
Holy Spirit is received by faith, and that we keep receiving fresh
supplies of the Spirit and His power as we continue to look to
the Lord in faith (see comments on Acts 2:38-40; Eph. 5:15-21).

We also learn that there are many temptations to retreat
from the new freedom which Christ has given to us by His Spirit
(Gal. 5:1,13; John 8:32,36; II Cor. 3:17,18). As Romans 6-8
teaches, the Holy Spirit ministers freedom from the bondage
and oppression of sin and the flesh. But the price we must pay
for this freedom is constant yieldedness to the Spirit's control
and complete dependence on His guidance. Sad to say, many
Spirit-baptized people are not willing to keep on living and
walking in this intimate relationship with the Lord on a
moment-by-moment basis. They do not "take time to be holy,"
as the old hymn puts it. Actually, they find it more convenient
or comfortable to submit to someone else's religious system or to
some outstanding human leader, and to live by adhering to
certain standards or "works of the law."

Christians, as well as the unregenerate, fear the sovereign
unpredictability of the Holy Spirit. The full freedom of the
Spirit, with its consequent necessity for utter obedience and its
responsibility to be available to His prompting at all times, can
be very frightening to some persons. Therefore, even in Full
Gospel churches, the order of worship often becomes an

"elaborately structured non-structure." This is in accord with human nature, for most men seek to escape, not from slavery, but from freedom.

GAL. 5:22,23 — THE FRUIT OF THE SPIRIT.

This lovely passage is itself like a choice fruit. We may not only admire it but we should eat it and benefit from it. It appears in a section of Paul's epistle to the Galatians explaining the right way to use our Christian liberty (Gal. 5:13-26). Galatians 5:13-15 declares that our freedom from bondage to the Law (Gal. 5:1) must not become an excuse for selfishness. We should not abuse our liberty by permitting our old evil nature to have its way. Instead, we should practice liberty in love: "through love serve one another" (Gal 5:13 NASB).

The flesh, or selfishness and self-will, is the capacity to sin that persists in believers. It is the enemy inside us that would destroy our liberty in Christ and bring us into even worse bondage. Therefore, each child of God needs a helping and restraining hand to guard against his own evil nature. He finds this help in the Paraclete dwelling within him. By the Spirit, he can keep walking step by step and day by day and have strength not to fulfill the lust of the flesh. The Holy Spirit can so control us that we will not yield to self-indulgence and gratify the cravings of the old man. By means of the Spirit, we can put to death and rise above the negative attitudes and evil deeds that are the natural activities of our self-nature (Rom. 8:13). If we truly belong to Christ Jesus, we have made the decision to consider the "old man" or flesh, with its passions and desires, as a crucified thing (Gal. 5:24). The "old man" can never be converted. The change takes place only when the "new man" becomes dominant.

The indwelling Holy Spirit and the flesh or godless human nature in a Christian are antagonistic to each other. Each has a strong desire to suppress the other. They are locked in continual combat. They are entrenched in an attitude of mutual opposition to each other so that the Christian is prevented from doing what he wants to do. This fact is developed at greater length by Paul in Rom. 7:14-25, telling of his own Christian experience.

When the Spirit enters a man at the moment of his conversion, it is like the Allied invasion of Normandy in World War II. God has returned to occupy what is rightfully His. The more the new believer, like the local French inhabitants, cooperates with the "invader," the sooner the territory once held by the enemy may be reclaimed and fully liberated.

After listing many of the hideous practices of the flesh (Gal. 5:19-21), Paul paints for us a marvelous contrast. It is like finding a vine laden with luscious grapes or a tree covered with ripe red apples growing in the midst of a thicket of briers and weeds and dense underbrush. "But the fruit of the Spirit is love, joy, peace, patience, kindness, goodness, faithfulness, gentleness, self-control" (v.22,23 NASB).

In v.22 the term "fruit" is singular, which tends to emphasize the unity and coherence of the personality of one who walks in the Spirit. Because the Holy Spirit is guiding and controlling him, his life is an integrated, wholesome, abundant one. In contrast, the term "works" or "deeds" in Gal. 5:19 is plural, stressing the disorganization and instability of a life lived under the dictates of the flesh. The unregenerate life is fragmented and at odds with itself.

Paul always uses the word "fruit" (*karpos*) in the singular, except in II Tim. 2:6 (even in Phil. 1:11 *karpos* is singular). Therefore, we do not have to consider love as the only fruit which is being described in its various aspects by the eight following words. Nevertheless, some may prefer to consider the fruit of the Spirit as one cluster with its individual grapes, or as an orange with its distinct segments.

Love is beautifully described in I Cor. 13 (see comments there). *Agape* is the intelligent and purposeful love which is an act of the will more than of emotion or feeling. It is the inner force which energizes and activates our faith and motivates it to work: "faith working through love" (Gal. 5:6 NASB). It reveals itself in serving others (Gal. 5:13). Such love must be supplied to us from its only source which is God (I John 4:7,8). He has poured out His love within our hearts through the Holy Spirit (Rom. 5:5; II Tim. 1:7).

Joy is the opposite of pessimism. True joy that persists in the midst of sorrow and calamity is bestowed by Christ as He answers our prayers (John 15:11; 16:24), and is mediated by the Holy Spirit (Rom. 14:17; I Thess. 1:6). Our joy in the Lord is our strength (Neh. 8:10).

Peace is shared with us by Christ Himself through His Spirit. It is *His* peace (John 14:27), and we may have it only *in Him* (John 16:33). This peace, which is the opposite of strife (KJV) and disputes and dissensions (NASB) listed among the works of the flesh in Gal. 5:20, consists both of inward repose (Phil. 4:7) and of harmonious relations with others. Christ gives us His peace in order to settle our questionings and to act as arbiter in our hearts (Col. 3:15 NASB margin). It comes to us as we set our thoughts and desires on the things of the Spirit (Rom. 8:5-8).

Long-suffering or patience is manifested when we refuse to retaliate for a wrong done to us. When it is the true fruit of the Spirit, it shows forbearance to others along with joyfulness (Col. 1:11). It is one of the chief attributes of love in I Cor. 13:4.

Gentleness or benevolent kindness is the mark of a sweet spirit, one that is kind and mild and full of graciousness. It is the other positive characteristic of love in I Cor. 13:4. Jesus acted with this type of kindness to the fallen woman-of-the-street who slipped into the banquet hall to wash His feet (Luke 7:37-50). This fruit makes one easy to get along with and thoughtful of the needs and wishes of others.

Goodness is a personal integrity of character and uprightness of soul that abhors evil. A good person is honest in his motives as well as his conduct. Goodness is also generosity; it does good to others.

Faith as a *fruit* of the Spirit means fidelity (as the word *pistis* is translated in Titus 2:10 KJV) and faithfulness to Christ and His cause (Matt. 25:21; Acts 16:15; Col. 1:7; I Tim. 1:12). It shows itself in being a trustworthy steward of God (I Cor. 4:2 NASB) and in being true and obedient to His word (John 14:21,23). Faith as a *gift* of the Spirit enables one to trust God for a miracle (see comments on I Cor. 12:4-11).

Meekness is based on humility and self-denial. It is humble tolerance of others, not pushing oneself forward. It does not press its rights or threaten vengeance; however, it is not cowardly. It is gentle but strong and patiently endures injuries with no spirit of resentment. It is not self-assertive and does not depend on personality or reputation. The man of the world says, "Blessed are the aggressive, for they shall rule the world with their cunning and courage and competitiveness." Jesus said, "Blessed are the meek, for they shall inherit the earth." In His only description of Himself, our Lord said, "I am meek and lowly in heart" (Matt. 11:29). How to achieve meekness? It is a fruit of the Spirit of Jesus!

Temperance is better translated self-control or self-restraint. It enables one to control the self-life, a clear indication that at its deepest level it is a product of the Spirit. It is mastery of one's temper and all carnal appetites, and therefore is opposed to the drunkenness and carousings of Gal. 5:21. Later, Paul would speak to the debauched Roman governor Felix about righteousness, temperance, and the judgment to come (Acts 24:25). No wonder, because for his third marriage Felix had taken Drusilla, another ruler's wife. He was treacherous and cruel, and could commit all kinds of evil with impunity.

The best fruit grows where the soil is fertile and cultivated and when the branches are pruned regularly. Let us break up our fallow ground (Hos. 10:12) and submit to the cleansing and pruning action of the word of Christ (John 15:2,3). The Holy Spirit is the Life-giver who causes the sap of divine life to flow through us from the Vine, its only source. The fruit *will* develop if we do not impede the flow of that sap. And the fruit will bear marked resemblance to those same virtues so perfectly exhibited in the life of our Lord, for they are the result of His life in us.

Let every Spirit-baptized Christian heed the warning of Jesus: "By their fruits ye shall know them" (Matt. 7:20), not by their charismatic gifts and miraculous works (see comments on Matt. 7:21-23). The proofs of being filled with the Holy Spirit are far more convincing in the area of His fruit than of His gifts.

EPHESIANS

Eph. 1:13,14 — SEALED WITH THE HOLY SPIRIT.

The first mention of the Holy Spirit in this magnificent epistle about the doctrine of Christ's Body the Church concerns His work which seals Christians in that Body. The time when this sealing takes place is said to be after we have believed the Gospel. "In Him, you also, after listening to the message of truth, the gospel of your salvation — having also believed, you were sealed in Him with the Holy Spirit of promise" (v.13 NASB). The sealing, then, corresponds to the baptism in the promised Holy Spirit (see comments on Acts 1:4-8; I Cor. 12:13; II Cor. 1:21,22).

In those days an owner often stamped his signet into the still soft clay of a newly made storage jar or of a jar stopper. The impression left by the signet "sealed" the jar, clearly marking it and its future contents as the possession of that man. Similarly, Christ sent His Spirit to come upon His disciples and to endue them with the same supernatural power that characterized His own ministry, thus making them His witnesses (Luke 24:49; Acts 1:8). The Spirit, therefore, in one or more of His various manifestations (as in I Cor. 12-14) is the immediate divine evidence that Christians belong to the Lord. They are marked as His "peculiar people," meaning His very own special possession (Titus 2:14; I Pet. 2:9).

Perhaps the twelve disciples of Acts 19:1-7 were among those who heard this epistle read aloud when it reached the church in Ephesus. The word *pisteusantes,* "after that ye believed" (v.13), would have reminded them of the same word in Paul's initial question to them eight or ten years earlier: "Did you receive the Holy Spirit after you believed (*pisteusantes*)?" (Acts 19:2). They would have remembered how Paul had instructed them to believe in Jesus and had baptized them in the name of the Lord Jesus. When Paul had laid his hands upon them, the Holy Spirit had fallen on them and they had spoken in tongues and prophesied (see comments on Acts 19:1-7). Their fellow-Christians in the church would similarly link being sealed with Christ's Spirit to the time when the Spirit came on *them.*

The Holy Spirit is given to believers as the earnest or pledge or first installment of that full inheritance which will be theirs on the day when God completes their redemption (see comments on II Cor. 1:21,22). He is our seal until that time when even our bodies will be redeemed (Rom. 8:23), transformed to be like Christ's glorious resurrection body (Phil. 3:21). Therefore, during this present life, we should not grieve Him (Eph. 4:30) nor act in any way out of harmony with Christ's mark of ownership upon us.

Eph. 4:3-6 — THE UNITY OF THE SPIRIT.

It is our duty as those who have been called to God in Christ to keep the unity of the Spirit in the bond of peace. The apostle is saying that we must be diligent, we must do our very best, to preserve the oneness which the Spirit produces, by the peace that binds us together. The seven "ones" of vv.4-6 state what the unity of the Spirit consists of, or, to put it another way, what makes this oneness possible. It is based on the fact of one body, one Spirit, one hope, one Lord, one faith, one baptism, and one God and Father.

There is only one true spiritual "body," the Body of Christ, the Church Universal. It is one, even though it has many members. Jew and Gentile are made into a single new people by the reconciling work of Christ, so that all are fellow-members of the one Body (Eph. 2:14-19; 3:6; 4:12,16; Col. 2:19; 3:15; Rom. 12:4,5; I Cor. 10:16,17; 12:12-27). In one sense the spiritual "body" is very physical because it is made up of people. People are visible and tangible. Thus the bodies of true believers are the physical manifestations of Christ in our space and time.

There is only one Spirit, the Holy Spirit. All Christians are regenerated by the same Spirit. He is the Comforter for all believers. Christ baptizes us in only one Spirit (I Cor. 12:13). And the Holy Spirit is the same guarantee for all Christians of their future perfection and inheritance (Eph. 1:13,14).

There is only one hope, the blessed hope of the glorious return of our Lord and Savior, Christ Jesus (Titus 2:13). Every Christian had this hope set before him when God called him by His grace—the hope of sharing the glory of Christ, of relief from this present suffering, and of the final redemption or resurrection of our bodies (Rom. 8:18-25).

There is only one Lord for all Christians, the Lord Jesus Christ (I Cor. 8:5,6). Christ Himself has certainly never been divided (I Cor. 1:13). He is the one Head of the Body (Eph. 1:22,23; 4:15; Col. 1:18; 2:19), the one Commander-in-Chief, who does not issue contradictory commands to His various servants. He is the one way to the Father (John 14:6; Eph. 2:18), and no one can be saved apart from Him (Acts 4:12).

There is only one faith. Subjectively, faith may denote the act and *attitude* of believing coupled with obedience (Rom. 1:5; 16:26; Heb. 5:9; 11:8; I Pet. 1:2); objectively, it may mean *what* one believes, the substance of his belief. In the first sense, to be saved and become a Christian, each one must place his trust in Jesus Christ as Savior and Lord (Acts 16:31). In the second sense, there is only one faith by which God justifies both Jew and Gentile (Rom. 3:30), "the faith which was once for all delivered to the saints" (Jude 3 NASB).

There is one common baptism for all believers. It is true according to Heb. 6:2 that Christians were given instructions regarding various baptisms (or washings, NASB). In Eph. 4:5, however, Paul is obviously referring to Christian baptism. During the apostolic period, the concept of one baptism probably included both water-baptism and Spirit-baptism, for no doubt these often occurred at the same time. One baptism, but with two aspects: baptism in water in the name of Jesus Christ (Acts 10:48), the humanly administered seal with reference to repentance and forgiveness of sins; baptism in the Holy Spirit, the divinely administered seal with reference to Christ's one Body (II Cor. 1:21,22; Eph. 1:13,14; see comments on I Cor. 12:13).

F. F. Bruce, the outstanding British scholar, has written some very helpful notes on this matter: "The baptism of the Spirit which it was our Lord's prerogative to impart took place primarily on the day of Pentecost when He poured forth 'the promise of the Father' on His disciples and thus constituted them the Spirit-baptized fellowship of the people of God. Baptism in water continued to be the outward and visible sign by which individuals who believed the gospel, repented of their sins, and acknowledged Jesus as Lord, were publicly incorporated into this Spirit-baptized fellowship — 'baptized into Christ' (Gal. 3:27). It must be remembered in New Testament times repentance and faith, regeneration and conversion, baptism in water, reception of the Holy Spirit, incorporation into Christ, admission to church fellowship and first communion were all parts of a single complex of events which took place within a very short time, and not always in a uniform order. Logically they were distinguishable, but in practice they were all bound up with the transition from the old life to the new" (*The Epistle to the Ephesians* [London: Pickering & Inglis, 1961], p.79).

There is only one God and Father of all believers. Christian belief in the Trinity — one God eternally existing in three Persons — does not contradict the O.T. doctrine of one God (Deut. 4:35,39; 6:4; Mal. 2:10). Elsewhere, Christians from pagan backgrounds, who had formerly sacrificed to the idols of many gods, are reminded that there is no God but one, and that "for us there is but one God, the Father, from whom are all things, and we exist for Him" (I Cor. 8:4-6 NASB).

Verses 4-6 may very well have been a primitive confession of faith. In it are the basic elements of true Christianity, the common ground of all Christians. In this context of oneness, there exists already a living fellowship in the spirit and by the Holy Spirit. This we are to maintain, even though all Christians have not yet "come in" (attained to, arrived at) the unity of the faith (Eph. 4:13). We are to experience the living, vital unity of the Spirit with all true Christians now, even before we can agree on all points of doctrine.

We preserve the unity of the Spirit by giving careful attention to our own moral and spiritual behavior. We are to walk in a manner worthy of our having been called by God to be Christians. We are to conduct our lives "with all humility and gentleness, with patience, showing forbearance to one another in love" (Eph. 4:2 NASB).

Eph. 4:30 — GRIEVE NOT THE HOLY SPIRIT.

The Bible warns of several ways in which people sin against the Holy Spirit. Some of these sins may be committed by Christians, while others are of such serious nature that they reveal the hopelessly lost condition of the person. They fall into three general categories according to the three areas of ministry of the Spirit of God with human beings — *with, in,* and *upon:*

I. The Holy Spirit is *with* unregenerate men to restrain them and convict them of sin (John 16:8,9) and to draw them to Christ. Those who balk at the tug of God on their hearts, because they love their darkness more than the light (John

3:19,20), try to turn off the convicting influence of the Spirit. They *resist* the Holy Spirit, as the Jewish leaders did who heard Stephen make his magnificent defense of the faith (Acts 7:51). Those men were "cut to the quick" — terribly convicted — and they gnashed their teeth at Stephen (Acts 7:54 NASB). Others may go a step farther and *insult* ("do despite unto," KJV) the Spirit of grace as they make fun of the blood of the covenant and "trample under foot the Son of God" (Heb. 10:29 NASB). Men may even go so far as to *blaspheme* against the Holy Spirit (Mark 3:29) by attributing the miraculous works of the Spirit of God to Satan and thus rejecting the evidence of His power. Such sin is unpardonable (see comments on Matt. 12:22-37).

II. The Holy Spirit is *in* converted men to witness with their spirit that they are sons of God (Rom. 8:14-17) and to develop the new nature of Christ in them. The Spirit of God dwells in the body of the believer just as the Ark of the Covenant which signified God's presence remained in the inner sanctuary of the tabernacle or temple. The work of the Holy Spirit in this respect is one of sanctification (see comments on I Cor. 6:11), for the temple of God must be kept holy, in the N.T. dispensation as well as in the O.T.

The oracle room (I Kings 6:19), also known as the inner sanctuary and as the Holiest of all (KJV) or Holy of Holies (NASB, Heb. 9:3 and Exod. 26:33) was a very quiet, private, holy place. No defiling thing was permitted to mar the beauty and sacredness of God's dwelling on earth. The danger now is that the Christian can *grieve* the Holy Person residing in His newly claimed temple (Eph. 4:30). The Holy Spirit is a Person who is gentle as a dove and has feelings just as you and I do. As the Spirit of Christ in us (Rom. 8:9), He can be grieved, just as Jesus was grieved by the hardness of men's hearts (Mark 3:5).

In Eph. 4 and 5, Paul warns about certain specific forms of sin that disrupt the unity of the Spirit in the one Body of Christ (4:3). Any or all of these sins grieve the Holy Spirit and prevent our being filled and fully controlled by the Spirit (Eph. 5:18).

There are: 1) sins of speech, or what we say; 2) sins of action, or what we do; and 3) sins of attitude, or what we think and feel.

1. Sins of speech. We must put away lying or falsehood (Eph. 4:25) and speak the truth in love (Eph. 4:15), for the Holy Spirit is the Spirit of *truth*. These commands obviously prohibit gossip and the spreading of rumors. No foul talk or rotten, unwholesome words should come out of one's mouth, but only words which will edify (Eph. 4:29). Get rid of all clamor or quarreling, and slander or abusive language (Eph. 4:31). Never be accused of dirty stories, silly or flippant talk, or questionable jokes with a barb in them (5:4).

2. Sins of action. "Do not participate in the unfruitful deeds of darkness, but instead even expose them" (Eph. 5:11 NASB). Stealing can no longer be a part of the Christian's life (Eph. 4:28), and this includes robbing God of His tithe (Mal. 3:8-10) and of His glory (Isa. 42:8; 48:11), as well as stealing from man. Any type of sexual immorality or prostitution has absolutely no place (Eph. 5:3), as Paul makes clear again and again (cf. I Cor. 6:13-20; I Thess. 4:3-8). Drunkenness and dissipation like the loose living of the prodigal son (Luke 15:13) prevent the filling of the Holy Spirit (Eph. 5:18).

3. Sins of attitude. Bitterness and malice (Eph. 4:31) certainly grieve the Spirit, named as they are immediately after Paul's command in Eph. 4:30. Resentment, spite, and grudges come under this category. A Christian husband can become embittered against his wife (Col. 3:19). With or without realizing it, he may project on her his frustrations and hostilities that he feels toward his life situation and "take it out" on the one he married. The Spirit is grieved, and they can no longer pray together effectively (I Pet. 3:7). Paul includes wrath and anger — and hot tempers (Eph. 4:31)! Covetousness or greed (Eph. 5:3) is a distinct problem as we must live in a materialistic society. It is a common manifestation of selfishness which is the essence of sin. And if we grieve our Christian brother in our unconcern about his feelings and scruples, we are

not walking according to love (Rom. 14:15); and therefore we grieve the Spirit and destroy the relationship of unity.

In the O.T., it is said that the children of Israel *vexed* the Holy Spirit (Isa. 63:10). When they rebelled against the Lord's leading them through the hot Sinai desert, they grieved His Spirit. They quickly turned their hearts against the Lord, even though He had so recently saved them from their bondage in Egypt and redeemed them in His love and compassion (Isa. 63:7-9). The lesson is obvious for us, that we can stubbornly refuse to follow His guiding hand even though we are known as God's people today. Furthermore, just as the Israelites often complained and grumbled and lusted after the fleshpots back in Egypt (Exod. 16:2-8; Num. 11:1-6), so the Christian may live after the flesh, under the control of his fleshly old nature, rather than submitting to the control of the Spirit (Rom. 8:5-8).

III. The Holy Spirit is *upon* the Spirit-baptized believer to empower him for witness and ministry. Paul issued another specific command that applies to this aspect of the Spirit's work: "Quench not the Spirit" (I Thess. 5:19; see comments there). To quench means to stifle or suppress, or to put out a fire. We may quench the Spirit in ourselves when we stifle His inner voice prompting us to witness. God has built into us a sensitivity to Him which, however, can be quenched. We put out His fire if we neglect to stir up the charismatic gift He has placed within us (see comments on II Tim. 1:6,7), perhaps through lack of faith to trust the Spirit to use us. Similarly, we quench the Spirit by not employing our charismatic gift to serve one another (see comments on I Peter 4:10,11), or by abusing the gifts in not using them to edify one another (see comments on I Cor. 14:1-33). Another form of this sin is the neglect of praying in the Spirit (see comments on Rom. 8:23-27). Finally, the believer may quench the Holy Spirit moving upon him by not worshiping by the Spirit of God (Phil. 3:3) and serving in His power, but instead worshiping and serving in dead works (Heb. 9:14), works performed in his own strength and ability.

We also quench the Holy Spirit if we hinder someone else who is manifesting Him as He operates charismatically through that individual. Many have sinned against God's Spirit by teaching that spiritual gifts such as speaking in tongues and healing are not meant for this period of Church history. Certainly the Spirit is quenched when His good gifts are called psychological aberrations or Satanic counterfeits.

EPH. 5:15-21 — BE FILLED WITH THE SPIRIT.

This command is one of the key principles for victorious Christian living. It is not merely a teaching or an exhortation, but a precept for the believer's daily conduct. We find it embedded among other precepts and rules laying down the great laws directing our walk in love and self-control. Therefore these five words should never be construed as an excuse for loosing the Christian life from the moorings of all holy restraints and disciplined order under the guise of "being free in the Spirit."

The command to be filled with the Spirit comes after the seventh occurrence of the verb "walk" in this epistle. Paul has written that his readers should walk in a manner worthy of their Christian calling (Eph. 4:1), not walk as the Gentiles walk with darkened minds (Eph. 4:17,18), walk in love (Eph. 5:2), and walk as children of light (Eph. 5:8; see also 2:10). Now he has just penned the command to be careful how they walk, not as unwise men, but as wise (v.15). They are to redeem the time, or as the NEB renders it, "use the present opportunity to the full" (v.16). They should understand, or gain insight into, what the will of the Lord is (v.17). Certainly His will includes being filled with the Spirit!

In v.18 Paul intentionally contrasts the artificial and de-grading stimulation of drunkenness with the divine enthusiasm of the Spirit. Perhaps he had in mind that on the Day of Pentecost, the disciples, who were newly baptized in the Holy Spirit, were scoffingly accused of being drunk (Acts 2:13).

Intoxication was common in Greek and Roman society, and these pagans sometimes went to the extreme of confusing its accompanying excitement of emotion and wit with divine inspiration, as in the frenzied worship of Dionysius or Bacchus. But the believer is to seek a loftier inspiration!

Recklessness and self-abandonment accompany intoxication, and this leads to the involuntary stimulation of the sensual and passionate elements of the old nature. But the Holy Spirit produces self-control in the life and appeals to the new nature without forcing a man against his own will. Wine in excess debases and destroys; the Spirit of God ennobles and edifies. Instead of dissipation (see also Titus 1:6; I Pet. 4:3,4) as in the case of the Prodigal Son (Luke 15:13), there is holiness and Godlikeness. The word for "excess" or "dissipation" is *asotia*, the character of one who is un-savable (from an old form of the verb *sozo*, to save, deliver). In his despair, the alcoholic seems unable to be saved or delivered; he is incorrigible. But the Holy Spirit effects deliverance of all areas of one's life to make him a whole man. As Jonathan Edwards said in a sermon in this verse, there may be excess in wine, but one cannot be too filled with the Spirit. Likewise, there may be undue emotionalism in some charismatic meetings. But this is a human reaction, not the direct working of the Holy Spirit, for He produces self-control in all things, including worship and praise.

In discussing the exact meaning of the words "be filled with the Spirit" (*plerousthe en pneumati*), some scholars believe Paul meant, "to be filled in one's human spirit" in contrast to being intoxicated in mind and body. But Paul uses the phrase *en pneumati* ("in the Spirit," without the definite article in Greek) four times in all in this letter (Eph. 2:22; 3:5; 5:18; 6:18) and once in Colossians (1:8). These verses show the phrase means that the personal working of the Holy Spirit is in view, i.e., what the Spirit produces. Therefore it means "by the Spirit" — not *with* the Spirit, for the Holy Spirit is a Person, not a substance like a liquid beverage.

People are said to be filled with wine when they are completely under its influence. Similarly, the Bible says they are filled with or by the Spirit when He controls all their thoughts, feelings, words, and actions. Therefore v.18 commands the believer to be controlled by the Spirit, to live and walk always under His influence. Handley C. G. Moule, the warm-hearted Anglican Bishop of Durham until his death in 1920, explained that the fullness of the Spirit is a supernatural thing: "It is a state of man wholly unattainable by training, by reasoning, by human wish and will. It is nothing less than — God in command and control of man's whole life, flowing everywhere into it, that He may flow fully and freely out of it" (*Ephesian Studies* [London: Hodder & Stoughton, 1900], pp.275f.). For further discussion of the meaning of "filled," see comments on Acts 4:8.

Several things may be noted about the verb *plerousthe,* "be filled." (1) It is an imperative, a command, not an optional matter. (2) It is plural, indicating that the command is meant for all, universal in application. It is not a privilege to be enjoyed by a few elite Christians, but is the duty of every believer. (3) It is passive, showing that we cannot fill ourselves with the Spirit — we must let Him fill us. Yet we are not purely inactive in receiving the Spirit's fullness, any more than in getting drunk. A man gets drunk by drinking; even so, we receive the Spirit by drinking (see comments on John 7:37-39). (4) The verb is in the present tense, teaching that being filled with the Spirit is a continuous process. We were baptized and sealed in the Spirit once; we are to be continually controlled by the Spirit at all times. This means that we must continually yield to His direction and control, and continually appropriate His supplies of grace and power.

It is very instructive to compare v.18 with the parallel passage in Col. 3:16. Paul wrote both these epistles while he was under guard in his rented quarters in Rome (Acts 28:30 NASB), and there are interesting similarities and differences of expressions. In Colossians, instead of commanding, "Be filled with the Spirit," he wrote, "Let the word of Christ richly dwell within you" (NASB). The remainder of Col. 3:16 is very similar to v.19,20. Therefore one may conclude that an integral part of being filled with the Spirit is to know the N.T. thoroughly and to memorize as much as possible of it so that the Holy Spirit can use the Word He inspired to guide him.

In v.19-21, four clauses follow the command about the Holy Spirit. In each, the verb or verbs appear as a participle: speaking, singing and making melody, giving thanks, and submitting yourselves. These are evidences or results of the fullness of the Spirit. The *continual* evidence of His filling is moral, seen in the fruit of the Spirit (see comments on Gal. 5:22,23). The *occasional* evidence is miraculous, seen in the gifts of the Spirit which He distributes only when a need arises (see comments on I Cor. 12-14 and I Cor. 12:4-11). One of the best discussions of vv.19-21 is to be found in the booklet by John R. W. Stott entitled *The Baptism and Fullness of the Holy Spirit*, pp.26-33; many of the following thoughts are from his writing.

The consequences of being filled with the Spirit are to be found in intelligent, controlled, healthy relationships with God and with other Christians. The Spirit's control results in genuine worship of God and in spiritual fellowship with our brethren.

The first of the four evidences stated in this passage is "speaking to yourselves in psalms and hymns and spiritual songs." Not talking to oneself, but conversing with one another. This basically is fellowship. As Dr. Stott reminds us, however deep and intimate our communion with God may seem, we cannot claim to be filled with the Spirit if we are not on speaking terms with our Christian acquaintances. But this fellowship centers around the Lord. *The Living Bible* paraphrases the clause, "Talk with each other much about the Lord, quoting psalms and hymns and singing sacred songs." Note how God takes delight in our having such fellowship together

according to Malachi 3:16: "Then those who feared the Lord
spoke to one another, and the Lord gave attention and heard
it" (NASB).

In the centuries prior to the printing press and to the mass
distribution of inexpensive Scriptures in the language of the
people, often the only portions of God's Word which Christians
of even average means knew were those they had learned in the
music of the church. It would be words and phrases from their
psalms and hymns and spiritual songs that would season their
speech like salt (cf. Col. 4:6). Thus even in their everyday
conversation with other Spirit-filled believers, as well as in times
of actual worship, their talk would be that of spiritual devotion
and thankfulness. The parallel part of Col. 3:16 is enlightening:
"With all wisdom teaching and admonishing one another with
psalms and hymns and spiritual songs" (NASB), revealing that
the speech of the early Christians — and ours today was to
be good for edification according to the need of the moment,
that it might impart grace to those who hear (Eph. 4:29
NASB).

The "psalms" were almost certainly the canonical O.T.
psalms sung to instrumental accompaniment. The "hymns"
may denote Christian compositions sung with or without music.
"Spiritual songs" (*odais pneumatikais*) were those inspired on the
spot by the Holy Spirit, unpremeditated words with unrehearsed melodies sung "in the Spirit," whether in tongues or in
the language of the congregation. Writing before the twentieth
century, when the Lord has been restoring charismatic singing
in churches of the West, the Scottish theologian S.D.F. Salmond
concluded that there were *Christian* psalms, "psalms which the
Holy Spirit moved the primitive Christians to utter when they
came together in worship (I Cor. 14:15,26), as He moved them
to speak with tongues (Acts 2:4; 10:46; 19:6). It is probable,
therefore, that these are intended here; especially in view of
what has been said of being 'filled by the Spirit' " ("Epistle to
the Ephesians," EGT, III, 363). It is very possible that the

origin of chants in the Church before the time of Constantine lies in this type of "singing in the Spirit."

The second evidence of the Spirit's fullness is "singing and making melody in your heart to the Lord." The rendition of the RSV, "with all your heart," brings out the proper idea here. The Holy Spirit came to glorify the Lord Jesus, and so manifests Him to His people that they delight to sing His praises (Stott, *The Baptism and Fullness of the Holy Spirit*, pp.28f.). The early Christians knew what it was like to worship under persecution. The younger Pliny as the Roman governor of Bithynia was ordered by Emperor Trajan to stamp out the Christians there. In a letter (A.D. 112) he reported that they were in the habit of assembling on an appointed day (Sunday) before sunrise and singing responsively "a song to Christ as to God." Writing in North Africa around A.D. 200, Tertullian described the Christian love feast as a time when "each is invited to sing to God in the presence of others from what he knows of the holy scripture or from his own heart" (see F. F. Bruce, *Ephesians*, p.111).

Thirdly, Spirit-filled believers are "giving thanks always for all things unto God and [or, "even" (NASB)] the Father in the name of our Lord Jesus Christ." Paul himself is an outstanding example of one who thanked God for *all* things, manifesting joy as he did in prison and in all his afflictions. His exhortations to rejoice in the Lord (Phil. 4:4), rejoice always, and in everything give thanks (I Thess. 5:16,18) cannot be dismissed, therefore, as beautiful but impossible idealism. It *is* possible when the Spirit fills us. Whenever we start grumbling and complaining, however, it is proof positive that we are *not* filled with the Spirit (Stott, *The Baptism and Fullness of the Holy Spirit*, p.29).

The fourth mark of the Spirit's fullness refers again to our relationship with one another. The first was speaking to one another; now it is being "subject to one another in the fear of Christ" (v.21 NASB). In the following verses, the apostle goes on to describe in detail the submission of a wife to her husband, children to their parents, and slaves to their masters (5:22-6:9). But here he lists the attitude of sweet yieldedness to others in the church as the hallmark of a Christian filled with the Spirit.

Paul has listed some of the wholesome results of the fullness of the Spirit in everyday living. If we are filled with the Spirit, we shall be praising and worshiping the Lord Jesus and thanking the Father for everything, and speaking helpfully and submitting to one another. These right relationships with God and man are lasting evidences of the Spirit's control.

Do you ask how to be filled with the Spirit? or How can I maintain this fullness? or, How does one receive a fresh empowering by the Spirit? The answer must be, as for every aspect of the Christian life and walk, *by faith*. Paul made it clear to the Galatian believers that just as they had received the promised Spirit by faith (Gal. 3:2,14), so they were continually supplied with the Spirit by faith, even for the working of miracles in their midst (Gal. 3:5; see comments on Gal. 3:2-5,14). The continual filling of the Holy Spirit, as well as our initial reception of Him, is based on our *believing* God that He *does* fill and control us by His Spirit.

At the same time, we must recognize that the Holy Spirit is a Person. This means that we must consciously yield to His control, just as we deliberately submit to one another. Again, we need to realize that all the fullness is to be found in Christ (Col. 1:19; 2:9,10; John 1:16). It is Jesus our Lord who fills His Body with His fullness (Eph. 1:23). Therefore our attention must remain centered on Him, and should not be diverted by an overbalanced interest in the Holy Spirit. The Spirit of truth, said Jesus, would not come to speak of Himself or of His own authority, but to glorify the Son (John 16:13,14). The more we are in love with our precious Lord, the more filled we are with His Spirit.

EPH. 6:17 — THE SWORD OF THE SPIRIT.

The only weapon listed in the description of the Christian's armor in Eph. 6:10-20 is a sword. All the other pieces are for his protection against the powers of darkness. "The word of the Spirit," which is explained as being the word of God, is the only combat equipment included for striking a blow to defeat the devil.

This sword is one which the Spirit of God supplies. Therefore, it is not "carnal" or physical, not a material weapon. Since He is the One who provides it and enables us to wield it, this sword is invincible. It is one of our divinely powerful weapons for the destruction of Satan's fortresses (II Cor. 10:4 NASB). Yet we must look to the Lord to train our hands how to use it and to teach our fingers how to fight (Ps. 144:1; 18:34). We need to become proficient in spiritual warfare, even as David's mighty men (I Chron. 12) and Solomon's royal bodyguard were experts in military warfare (Song of Sol. 3:7,8).

But what is the meaning of the figurative expression "the sword of the Spirit"? It is "the word of God" (*rhema theou*). The wording is different in Greek from that in a somewhat parallel verse, Heb. 4:12: "For the word of God (*ho logos tou theou*) is living and active and sharper than any two-edged sword . . ." (NASB). Here the reference is both to Christ as the living Word (the Logos, as in John 1:1,14) and to God's revelation, the *written* word considered as a whole. But in v.17 the term *rhema* designates particularly a *spoken* word. It is "an utterance of God" because it leaves God's mouth (cf. Isa. 49:2). It is the Greek word found in Matt. 4:4 in Jesus' quotation of the O.T. Scripture, "Man shall not live on bread alone, but on every word (*rhemati*) that proceeds out of the mouth of God" (NASB). True, many of God's words spoken first through the prophets were later recorded and became part of the written word or holy Scriptures. But here the emphasis is on a specific word from God as spoken by the Spirit through the mouth of a believer.

In Hos. 6:5 God makes two figurative statements regarding those who transgress the covenant and deal treacherously against Him: "Therefore I have hewn them in pieces by the prophets; I have slain them by the words of My mouth" (NASB). The Greek translation (the Septuagint) employs *rhema* in the singular where we have "words" (plural) in English. Combining the two statements enables us to realize that words of prophecy are involved.

An utterance of God supplied directly and immediately by the Spirit becomes the sword which can rout demons. This is one of the surprising facts taught in the Bible. The gift of prophecy, manifested in the power of the Holy Spirit, can reveal the secrets of a man's heart and humble him before God (I Cor. 14:24,25). A word of wisdom or of knowledge spoken with charismatic force can pierce the resistance of the most hardened sinner and bring deliverance to his captive soul. Even the written word or Bible only becomes effective against the devil when we speak a portion of it against him in the authority of Christ and in the power of the Spirit (see comments on Rev. 12:9-11).

Martin Luther stated this fact in his hymn "A Mighty Fortress is Our God" (excerpts from verses 3 and 4):

> *The prince of darkness grim—*
> *We tremble not for him;*
> *His rage we can endure,*
> *For lo! his doom is sure,*
> *One little word shall fell him.*
>
> *That word above all earthly powers—*
> *No thanks to them—abideth;*
> *The Spirit and the gifts are ours*
> *Through Him who with us sideth.*

I THESSALONIANS

I THESS. 5:19 — QUENCH NOT THE SPIRIT.

This command is given in the midst of a number of brief directives which every Spirit-filled Christian should follow. He should continually manifest joy (I Thess. 5:16), which is a fruit of the Spirit (Gal. 5:22). He can pray without letup (I Thess. 5:17), both in his native language and in tongues (I Cor. 14:14,15). Also the Spirit enables him to pray when he does not know how to pray as he should (Rom. 8:26,27). Another mark of being filled with the Spirit is to give thanks in everything (I Thess. 5:18; Eph. 5:18,20).

I Thessalonians 5:19,20 are especially pertinent for the charismatic believer. It is possible for him to quench the Holy Spirit in himself or in another Christian. That is, he may extinguish the flame or put out the fire of the Spirit (see how the verb for "quench" is used in Matt. 12:20; Mark 9:48; Eph. 6:16; Heb. 11:34). Through harsh criticism, he may pour cold water on the Spirit as He is manifested through a charismatic gift in someone else. Or, he may stifle or suppress the prompting of the Spirit to manifest any gift. I Thessalonians 5:20 indicates that at Thessalonica there were some who quenched the Spirit by despising prophetic utterances. In Matt. 25:8 the Greek verb for "quench" appears in the words of the foolish virgins who said, "Our lamps are going out" (NASB). Thus by neglecting to "stir up" his gift, one may simply let the fire of the Spirit die down, which had formerly been burning brightly in his heart (see comments on Matt. 25:1-13; Eph. 4:30; II Tim. 1:6,7).

I Thessalonians 5:20,21 have a general application in all areas of the Christian walk. But they are particularly relevant to the meetings of believers when the gifts of the Spirit are manifested. We have clear-cut responsibility to "prove" or examine every manifestation of the Spirit. Paul teaches in I Cor. 14:29 that when a prophet speaks, the others are to "judge" or discern whether it is a genuine prophecy by manifesting the gift of the discerning of spirits (see comments on I John 4:1-6). If the message is in agreement with the written word of God, it is a good prophecy and we should hold fast to it and not quench the Spirit by ignoring it. As the NEB translates I Thess. 5:19-22, "Do not stifle inspiration, and do not despise prophetic utterances, but bring them all to the test and then keep what is good in them and avoid the bad of whatever kind."

For other sins against the Spirit, see comments on Eph. 4:30.

II THESSALONIANS

II THESS. 2:2 — DISTURBED BY A SPIRIT.

Paul begs the saints at Thessalonica not to be troubled or disturbed by a spirit (NASB). He implies that a demon may have incited someone to give a false prophecy regarding the second coming of our Lord Jesus Christ and the time of the rapture of the Church. To avoid being deceived, Christians should adhere to the apostolic teaching regarding future events — the teaching which we have in the N.T. Concerning false prophets and teachers, see comments on II Pet. 2:1-22.

II THESS. 2:6,7 — THE RESTRAINER OF THE MAN OF LAWLESSNESS.

The Thessalonian Christians were wrongly being led to believe that the eschatological period known as the Day of the Lord was already present. This would mean that Jesus Christ had arrived in the first stage of His coming (*parousia*) to gather His saints unto Himself (I Thess. 4:15-17). Because the Thessalonians had not been taken into His physical presence, they were alarmed to think that they had been left behind to undergo the fearful sufferings of the great tribulation.

Paul corrects this error by reminding them of certain key events that must take place in relationship to Christ's second coming. The Day of the Lord is not a single event, but rather a period when God in His wrath will judge sin far more directly than through present natural calamities, and when He will wonderfully deliver and bless His people by the return of Christ.

That "day" cannot be in progress unless the "falling away" (Greek *apostasia*) as its first event and the revealing of the man of lawlessness as the next distinct event have come to pass.

While many have fallen away from the faith ever since apostolic times (Heb. 3:12; I Tim. 4:1; II Tim. 3:1-9; 4:3,4), the particular event Paul refers to here is the final and complete apostasy. This will be the deliberate and official denial of the doctrine of Christ and the worldwide suppression of all organized Christianity. As long as there are true believers on earth openly and publicly worshiping the Lord Jesus Christ together, the great apostasy has not begun.

The man of lawlessness ("man of sin," KJV) is further described as the son of perdition. So complete is his revolt against God that by nature he is doomed to eternal loss and ruin. "He sets himself in opposition to anyone bearing the name of god, or anything that people worship; indeed, he exalts himself above all such, going so far as to enthrone himself in the temple of God and proclaim that he himself is God" (II Thess. 2:4, Bruce, *The Letters of Paul*, p.59). He is Satan's man (II Thess. 2:8-10), known also as the Antichrist (I John 2:18) and the Beast (Rev. 13:1-10).

At present, however, Satan is being restrained from bringing his man on the stage of history. Paul says that the Thessalonian believers know the force that "withholds" the Antichrist so that he will be revealed in his own time, the time appointed by God, and not prematurely. In v.6, "what withholdeth" (*to katechon*) is a neuter participle; in v.7, "he who now letteth" (*ho katechon*) is a masculine participle of the same verb meaning to restrain or hold back. Both participles are in the present tense, indicating that the restraining force is already active. It is keeping under control the "mystery of iniquity" that is also already at work. The latter expression denotes the spirit of lawlessness which Satan is currently promoting and which will dominate the career of the man of lawlessness.

The big question that Bible commentators have about this

passage is the identification of the power who exercises the restraint at present. According to Paul's words, the Restrainer is both a principle and a person; he is well known to the readers; and he is more powerful than Satan, since he is able to hold back the efforts of the devil. Many commentators have explained the Restrainer as the principle of human government — manifest in Paul's day as the Roman state and its head, the emperor. Such government maintains law and order so that the Church may fulfill its great commission to evangelize the world (Rom. 13:1-7). No human government, however, is stronger than Satan himself. Furthermore, human government will not be removed during the tribulation period, for when the Antichrist gains worldwide control he will establish a super-government, not anarchy.

Only a supernatural person can effectively thwart the supernatural operations of the devil. Therefore, the Restrainer must be God Himself. In particular, the Holy Spirit is in view. The use of the neuter participle in v.6 may be accounted for by the fact that the Greek word *pneuma* for "spirit" is neuter. Yet the masculine gender in v.7 would point either to the Spirit Himself as a person, or to the individual Spirit-filled believer in this age, acting as the salt of the earth to preserve human society from the full effects of lawlessness (Matt. 5:13).

The Restrainer will continue His work "until he is taken out of the way," literally, "until he is out of the midst." The fact that the Restrainer will be "out of the midst" points to one who is now "in the midst." This also suggests the Holy Spirit who is now resident in the saints on earth. The Spirit who indwells every believer will be "out of the way" — no longer "in the way" of Antichrist — after Christ returns to take His Church to Himself. Being God and therefore omnipresent, however, the Holy Spirit will not be taken *away*, but will continue to be present in the world during the tribulation (see comments on John 14:15-18). Many will be convicted of sin by the Spirit and led to Christ at that time, and He will enable believers to give answer when on trial for their faith (Mark 13:11). But the universal and continual abiding of God's Spirit upon His people which began at Pentecost will be terminated at the Rapture, and the Spirit will resume the relation to mankind that He had before Pentecost (D. Edmond Hiebert, *The Thessalonian Epistles* [Chicago: Moody Press, 1971], pp.310-14). Since the removal of the Restrainer must occur before the Antichrist is revealed, the Rapture seems to take place before the Tribulation.

I TIMOTHY

I TIM. 4:14 — NEGLECT NOT THE GIFT THAT IS IN THEE.

This is an important command to every Spirit-baptized Christian, for the word "gift" is the Greek word *charisma*. Every Spirit-baptized believer is assigned at least one charismatic gift as the manifestation of the Holy Spirit in his life, and he is to use it as a good steward (see I Pet. 4:10,11 and comments there).

Paul reminds Timothy how he had received his spiritual ministry. It was given to him through prophetic utterance with the laying on of hands of the presbytery. The occasion may have been Timothy's ordination to the special ministry to which Paul assigned him at Ephesus (I Tim. 1:3). His task, like that of Titus on Crete, was to help organize and supervise the work of the churches in the province of Asia, to teach sound doctrine, and to refute certain heretical teachers whose errors were threatening to corrupt the churches.

At that time, various prophecies were made concerning Timothy, which would encourage him to fight well in the war against wickedness and to hold firmly to the faith (I Tim. 1:18,19). One of the prophecies to Timothy revealed the nature of the charismatic ministry being bestowed upon him and perhaps how he should exercise it.

The gift was imparted in connection with the laying on of hands by the presbytery, the local body of elders. Perhaps these were the elders of the church at Ephesus whom Paul had so lovingly addressed on his third missionary journey (Acts 20:17-38). Their hands placed on Timothy's head symbolized the fact that a spiritual ministry was being communicated to Timothy; but they did not actually confer the gift, for it was given merely "with" (*meta*), not "by," the laying on of their hands. Paul was also present at the ceremony, because he says in II Tim. 1:6 that Timothy had received the gift of God (the Holy Spirit) "by" or "through" (*dia*) "the laying on of my hands" (NASB), indicating that Paul was the intermediate agent. Evidently then Paul, as the first among equals (*primus inter pares*), exercised the decisive role as the channel of God's power in the consecration service, but Timothy was installed with the full sanction of the local church leaders at Ephesus. See comments on II Tim. 1:6,7; for the laying on of hands, see comments on Acts 6:6.

We are not told what Timothy's charismatic gift was. Presumably he had much earlier spoken in tongues following his baptism in the Spirit. Here the *charisma* was probably a spiritual endowment to enable him to perform his special work as an evangelist (II Tim. 4:5) and to oversee the churches. It has also been suggested that it was a gift of teaching (I Cor. 12:28; Rom. 12:7), or of "government" or administration (I Cor. 12:28; Rom. 12:8; I Tim. 5:17) to guide the churches in Asia, or a special ability to discern the spirits of error that were motivating the false teachers (I Tim. 4:1-3; I Cor. 12:10; I John 4:1-6).

Paul urged Timothy not to forget and leave unused this special ministry he had within him for his public ministry of reading Scripture, of exhortation, and of teaching (I Tim. 4:13 NASB). Such God-given enablement is not a charm that works automatically. It requires human cooperation for its full exercise (cf. Phil. 2:12,13; II Tim. 1:6). To neglect such a gift of God is a sin. *The Living Bible* paraphrase of I Tim. 4:15 lets us feel Paul's concern for his son in the Lord: "Put these abilities to work; throw yourself into your tasks so that everyone may notice your improvement and progress."

II TIMOTHY

II TIM. 1:6,7 — STIR UP THE GIFT OF GOD.

In the last letter we have from Paul, the apostle, now awaiting execution in a dungeon in Rome, writes once again to his beloved son Timothy. The old veteran of the Gospel is familiar with Timothy's cautious and somewhat timid temperament. He realizes what a blow the news of his impending death will be to his affectionate disciple. Therefore he exhorts Timothy not to lose heart, but to be zealous and unashamed and loyal to the Gospel as persecutions grow hotter.

Paul's very first concern is to remind Timothy to stir up the gift of God, the *charisma* which he received at the time he was set apart for his special mission at Ephesus. For the nature of Timothy's charismatic gift and its bestowal, see comments on I Tim. 4:14. The verb "stir up" occurs only here in the N.T. It means to rekindle or fan into flame. The present tense of the infinitive indicates that Paul is telling him to keep the gift blazing. By resisting the promptings of the Holy Spirit within us, we can quench the Spirit and His charismatic manifestation (I Thess. 5:19). Paul does not necessarily imply that Timothy had altogether stopped ministering the gift, but as a father he is appealing to his son to be constantly at work manifesting it in the face of suffering and serious difficulty.

Our incentive to use our charismatic gifts with burning zeal is the Holy Spirit Himself, whom God has given us. He is not a spirit of fear, cowardice, or timidity so that we shrink back and let our fire go out. "For you have not received a spirit of slavery leading to fear again" (Rom. 8:15 NASB). Instead, it is His Spirit who "fills us with power and love and self control" (II Tim. 1:7 TEV). The Holy Spirit supplies power (*dynamis*) to overcome the Wicked One, to witness concerning our risen Lord to all men, and to minister to the needs of other Christians as well as of those who are not yet saved. This aspect of the Spirit's work in us may be compared with the dynamic functioning of the Body of Christ by means of the spiritual gifts of I Cor. 12.

The Holy Spirit also supplies love, the *agape* love which Paul so beautifully describes in I Cor. 13. It is a self-forgetting love for Christ, for fellow believers, and for all men. The third quality the Spirit produces is "a sound mind." The Greek word implies self-control, self-discipline, a responsibleness under pressure and opposition that enables one to keep a clear head. It is the quality which is needed to maintain balance and order, not only in one's personal life, but also in the local congregation and in its meetings when each believer may share something to edify the others (I Cor. 14).

By aggressive energy in the face of difficulty, by self-denying love and thoughtfulness, and by self-discipline, the Spirit of God enables each Christian to overcome his tendency to cowardice. He strengthens the child of God to work, to endure, and even to die for Christ's sake if need be. This was the supply that Paul counted on when he testified, "I can do all things through Him who strengthens me" (Phil. 4:13 NASB). "For the Holy Spirit, God's gift, does not want you to be afraid of people, but to be wise and strong, and to love them and enjoy being with them" (II Tim. 1:7 TLB).

TITUS

Titus 3:4-7 — THE RENEWING OF THE HOLY GHOST.

Paul's epistle to Titus contains two beautiful descriptions of salvation as the foundation for all Christian conduct. In Titus 2:11-14 he states that salvation is made available to every human being. It is freely provided on the basis of God's grace as shown in Jesus Christ, "who gave Himself for us that He might redeem us from every lawless deed and purify for Himself a people for His own possession, zealous for good deeds" (NASB). We are to deny worldly desires while we wait expectantly for "the blessed hope and the appearing of the glory of our great God and Savior, Christ Jesus" (NASB).

Paul next describes how Christians ought to act toward all men (Titus 3:1-3). Godly conduct should be inspired as we recollect how we ourselves were once as bad as anyone else (Titus 3:3), and how God in His kindness and mercy saved us (vv.4,5). God actively intervened in our lives. The cause for the moral and spiritual transformation in us believers is not to be found in ourselves. It is not on the basis of any deeds which we performed in the realm of righteousness. Rather, salvation reaches us through the initial washing of regeneration and the continuing process of renewing by the Holy Spirit (v.5).

The term "washing" (*loutron*) does not refer to a laver or place of washing, as some writers have suggested, but to the moral and spiritual bath at the time of conversion. It is the divine work of cleansing that accompanies regeneration. Our Lord explained this to Nicodemus as being "born of water and Spirit" (John 3:5). The sinner is forgiven and cleansed by the blood of Christ as he responds to the convicting message and the promise of salvation in the word of God. At the same time, he is regenerated or made spiritually alive by the Spirit of God (see comments on John 3:1-8).

In writing to the Ephesians, Paul views the initial cleansing from another aspect. There he states that Christ gave Himself up for the Church in order that He might ultimately and completely sanctify her, "having cleansed her with the washing of the water (of baptism) in connection with a spoken word (of confession and testimony)" (Eph. 5:26, original translation). Paul is briefly referring to the proper human response to the justifying work of Christ: having repented, the new believer through water baptism washes away the stain on his character left by his sins, and on that same occasion he orally confesses his newfound faith in Christ (see comments on Acts 22:16).

In other passages, the renewing which the Holy Spirit accomplishes in the believer seems to be a phase of His progressive work of sanctification. Paul teaches that the new "man" or new nature "is constantly being renewed until it attains fulness of knowledge after the image of its Creator" (Col. 3:10, Bruce, *The Letters of Paul*), and that "our inner man is being renewed day by day" (II Cor. 4:16 NASB). The present tense of the command. "Be ye transformed by the renewing of your mind" (Rom. 12:2), also suggests that the work of renewal is still going on in order to complete the good work of Christ already begun in us (Phil. 1:6). II Cor. 3:18 likewise states that we are being transformed into the very image or likeness of our dear Lord, from one degree of glory to another, "even as by the Spirit of the Lord." On sanctification, see comments on I Cor. 6:11.

Returning to v.6, we are reminded of the Pentecostal outpouring of the Spirit, for the word "shed" is the same verb translated "pour out" or "shed" in Acts 2:17,18,33; 10:45. Here the abundance or richness of God's precious gift sent to us through Jesus Christ our Savior is brought out. The baptism in the Spirit is an integral part of our full salvation. All three Persons of the Trinity are active to make that wonderful salvation ours!

HEBREWS

HEB. 2:1-4 — GOD'S JOINT WITNESS.

The first of the warning passages in the Epistle to the Hebrews forewarns professing Christians of the danger of drifting away and neglecting our great salvation. Our message is far greater than the word received by Moses, and every transgression and disobedience of the Law received a just retribution. Whereas God gave the Sinaitic law through angels to Moses for the nation of Israel (Acts 7:53; Gal. 3:19), the Gospel of salvation was spoken to men directly by the Lord Jesus, God Himself manifested in human flesh.

The message of salvation is also extremely important because of the unusual nature of its confirmation. At the first, it was confirmed by the evidence of eye-witnesses, by those who actually heard Christ. But God Himself joins in the witness "by signs and wonders and various miracles and by gifts of the Holy Spirit distributed according to his own will" (v.4 RSV). The Greek participle *sunepimarturountos* is in the present tense and literally means "jointly bearing witness," not merely with the apostles but with Christians in all centuries of Church history. *The Living Bible* brings out this truth in paraphrase: "God always has shown us that these messages are true by signs and wonders and various miracles and by giving certain special abilities from the Holy Spirit to those who believe; yes, God has assigned such gifts to each of us."

While the word for "gifts" of the Holy Spirit is not *charismata* but *merismoi*, this latter term (literally meaning "distributions") emphasizes the fact that the gifts are not of man's appointing but are wholly according to God's pleasure (cf. I Cor. 12:11). In Rom. 12:3, where Paul writes that God has "dealt" or allotted to each Christian a measure of faith, the verb is from the same root as the noun *merismos*. When properly translated and understood, Heb. 2:4 gives strong testimony to the fact that miracles and gifts of the Spirit had not ceased in the latter part of the apostolic age. For other passages pertaining to spiritual gifts, see Mark 16:9-20; Rom. 12:3-8; I Cor. 12-14; I Pet. 4:10,11.

HEB. 6:4-6 — PARTAKERS OF THE HOLY GHOST.

Theologians have argued throughout the history of the Church whether the persons described in vv.4,5 are truly regenerate, and whether a born-again individual can lose his salvation.

The writer is urging his readers, who are Jewish Christians, to go on from the doctrines and rituals of the O.T. and of Judaism to maturity in Christ. But some have fallen away (v.6), i.e., they have committed apostasy. They have become enemies of Christ; they are crucifying the Son of God again, as far as they are concerned, and are putting Him to open shame (Greek present-tense participles). As long as they persist in their active hostility to Christ, it is morally and spiritually impossible to renew them again to repentance by any human agency (see B. F. Westcott, *The Epistle to the Hebrews* [Grand Rapids: Eerdmans, reprinted 1950], pp.150f.).

The author uses strong terms to describe the former spiritual condition of the apostates: they "have once been enlightened and have tasted of the heavenly gift and have been made partakers of the Holy Spirit, and have tasted the good word of God and the powers of the age to come, and then have fallen away" (vv.4-6 NASB). They have been illuminated (same Greek word as in Heb. 10:32) by the light of the Gospel of Christ shining in their hearts (II Cor. 4:4,6). They have had a taste of the supernatural gift (*dorea*) of salvation and life in Christ (John 7:10; Rom. 5:17). They have even been made sharers or partners of the Holy Spirit. The Greek word *metochous* means real sharers, those who participate in the object. The same word is used in Heb. 3:1, where the recipients of the epistle are said to be "partakers of the heavenly calling"; in Heb. 3:14, "For we have become partakers of Christ" (NASB); and in Heb. 12:8, which says that all true children of God are partakers of His chastening. The word is also used in the sense of associate or partner in Heb. 1:9 ("fellows") and Luke 5:7. In every case, personal involvement is indicated. Before falling by the wayside, the apostates had also "tasted the good word of God and the powers of the age to come" (v.5 NASB). They had experienced how good God's spoken "word" (*rhema*) is in prophecy and as the sword of the Spirit in overcoming the devil (Eph. 6:17). They had even received or performed miracles, the powers that even now are a foretaste of the coming age of Christ's kingdom on earth (see comments on Matt. 7:21-23).

Hebrews 6:6 may be taken in conjunction with the warning in Heb. 10:29 ("How much severer punishment do you think he will deserve who has trampled under foot the Son of God . . . and has insulted the Spirit of grace?" — [NASB]). Together, the verses suggest that those men were as guilty of blaspheming the Holy Spirit as were the Pharisees who ridiculed Jesus' ministry of exorcism (see comments on Matt. 12:22-37). Theirs was a deliberate and persistent rejection of Christ's witness, not the isolated act of a moment without premeditation.

Those who fell away seemed to be Christians. Whether they were actually born again or whether they had a superficial experience of Christianity like the "stony ground" believers of Matt. 13:5,6, 20,21, God alone knows. The remarks of Harold Lindsell in the *Harper Study Bible* (Grand Rapids: Zondervan, 1965, [p.1810]) are pertinent: "Whichever view we adopt of the apostate man prior to his apostasy, the outcome is virtually the same. That is to say, if a man openly rejects Jesus Christ, he is, in either view, to be regarded as an unregenerate, unsaved man, even though he had formerly appeared to human observers to be converted. The Arminian would say that he had lost his salvation; the Calvinist that he had never had it, but the result is identical."

On the basis of their experience, the writer of the Epistle to the Hebrews is warning his readers of the real danger of not holding fast their confession (Heb. 4:14; 10:23) and of throwing away their confidence and shrinking back (Heb. 10:35-39). He seeks to awaken them to the peril of sloth and urges them to be diligent "so as to realize the full assurance of hope until the end" (Heb. 6:11,12 NASB). Andrew Murray has given some priceless remarks on the matter of our assurance in commenting on Heb. 6:4-8: "The only sure sign that the perseverance of the saints will be ours is — perseverance in sainthood, in sanctification and obedience. 'We are His house[-hold], we are become partakers of Christ, if we hold fast, firm unto the end.' My assurance of salvation is not something I can carry with me as a railroad ticket or a bank note, to be used as occasion calls. No, God's seal to my soul is the Holy Spirit; it is in a life in the Spirit that my safety lies; it is when I am led by the Spirit that the Spirit bears witness with my spirit, and that I can cry Abba, Father (Rom. 8:14-16). Jesus not only gives [life], but is Himself our life. *My assurance of salvation is alone to be found in the living fellowship with the living Jesus in love and obedience*" (*The Holiest of All* [London: Nisbet, n.d.], p.209).

JAMES

JAMES 3:1-12 — TAMING THE TONGUE.

In this classic discourse on the control of the tongue, James declares that while men have been able to tame every species of beasts and birds, no one can tame the tongue (vv.7,8). He compares the tongue to the bit in the mouth of a horse, a small object that directs the whole animal, or to the rudder of a big ship, able to control the entire vessel with very little movement. But, he says, the tongue is "a restless evil, full of deadly poison"

(v.8 RSV). The uncontrolled tongue is set on fire by hell (i.e.,
by Satan). As in a forest ignited by a spark, the blaze spreads to
all the baser passions in the human nature (vv.5,6). Nothing but
the grace of God can bring it under subjection.

The tongue is the chief means of expressing what is in the
heart (Mark 7:20-23). As such, it is a focus of our intellectual
pride. Therefore, the faculty of speech, which plays such a great
part in influencing the entire personality, is the main obstruc-
tion to the freedom of the Holy Spirit in the believer's life. In
connection with the natural human unwillingness to yield
control to the Spirit, a neurosurgeon has explained God's
purpose in having Christians speak in tongues. He points out
that the speech centers dominate the brain. God's Spirit,
therefore, must regulate the faculty of speech in order to have
full control of the mind and emotions and will.

Who can tame the tongue? The answer is: "The Holy
Spirit!" Speaking in tongues is a key step in the process. The
Spirit says in effect, "I want to inspire and rule the most
important means of expression you have — the ability to speak.
I also want to tame and purify that with which you *sin* the most,
your tongue!" (Dennis and Rita Bennett, *The Holy Spirit and You*,
pp.61-2).

JAMES 4:5 — GOD'S JEALOUS YEARNING OVER HIS
SPIRIT.

This is a difficult verse to translate. The KJV gives a
misleading rendering in the second half of the verse. The RSV,
however, brings out the meaning quite well: "Or do you
suppose it is in vain that the scripture says, 'He yearns jealously
over the Spirit which He has made to dwell in us'?"

While James quotes no one verse of the O.T., a number of
passages speak of the Lord as a jealous God who will not permit
His people to worship any other god (Exod. 20:5; 34:14; Deut.
4:24; 32:16), and of His jealousy for Zion (Zech. 8:2). By
participating in any idolatrous practices, Christians also may

provoke the Lord to jealousy (I Cor. 10:22). He has bethrothed us to Himself (Hos. 2:19) and will tolerate no rival for our affections. "The Lord your God is in your midst, a victorious warrior. He will exult over you with joy, He will be quiet in His love, He will rejoice over you with shouts of joy (KJV, singing)" (Zeph. 3:17 NASB). His love for us is everlasting (Jer. 31:3), and nothing can make Him forget us (Isa. 49:15,16).

The Holy Spirit dwelling in Christians is grieved when we prove unfaithful to Christ our Bridegroom and Lord (see comments on Eph. 4:30). When we love the world and have friendship for it (James 4:4; I John 2:15-17), we show a divided allegiance and thereby offend God. He yearns over us with a deep godly jealousy to have us completely for Himself, for our Creator-Redeemer-King cannot be content with a love triangle.

JAMES 5:7 — THE EARLY AND THE LATTER RAIN.

"Be patient, therefore, brethren, until the coming of the Lord. Behold, the farmer waits for the precious fruit of the earth, being patient over it until it receives the early and the late rain" (RSV).

In 5:1-11, James is seeking to prepare his readers for the second coming of Christ. First (vv.1-6), he warns those nominal Christians who have become wealthy by cheating their employees. He mocks their accumulation of riches and says, "It is in the Last Days that you have stored up your treasure!" (v.3 NASB). Then he urges the godly believers to exercise patience as a farmer does while they wait for the coming (Greek *parousia*) of the Lord, and to establish their hearts — to strengthen and confirm them in the final certainty — for His return is "at hand," imminent (vv.7,8). They should not complain about each other, for the great Judge Himself is standing at the very door of heaven, waiting to come and do whatever criticizing must be done (v.9 TLB). Instead, they should endure suffering just as Job and the prophets did (vv.10,11).

The illustration of the farmer waiting patiently for the early and latter rain is drawn from the Palestinian agricultural scene. In that region, the early or autumn rain (mid-October — mid-December) softens the ground for plowing and waters the freshly seeded fields. The latter or spring rain (late February — early April) brings the grain to full growth. Barley is harvested in April and May, and wheat in May and June. God had promised the Israelites before they crossed into Canaan that if they would obey His commands, "I will give the rain for your land in its season, the early and late rain, that you may gather in your grain and your new wine and your (olive) oil" (Deut. 11:14 NASB; cf. Jer. 5:24; Prov. 16:15; Zech. 10:1). A few verses before his prophecy of the outpouring of the Spirit, Joel tells that God will pour down the early and the latter rain as before (Joel 2:23). In a beautiful prophecy of the coming of the Lord, Hosea exhorts God's people, "So let us know, let us press on to know the Lord. His going forth is as certain as the dawn; and He will come to us like the rain, like the spring rain watering the earth" (Hos. 6:3 NASB).

In describing the history of the Church, many Bible teachers have compared the outpouring of the Spirit at Pentecost and in the succeeding years to the early rain. Likewise, a commentary published a century ago states, "The latter rain that shall precede the coming spiritual harvest, will probably be another Pentecost-like effusion of the Holy Ghost" (JFB, p.1459). The twentieth century seems to be the time of the latter rain. The return of the Lord Jesus therefore must be very near, and as we wait for His coming, we are privileged to engage actively in the great end-time harvest that will complete the Church. In this way, we may actually hasten the coming of the day of God (II Pet. 3:12 NASB).

Especially since the end of World War II, the Church has witnessed mighty downpours of the Holy Spirit all over the earth. The phenomenal growth of the Pentecostal churches in Latin America, the charismatic movement in nearly all churches in the English-speaking world, and the great Indonesian revival are some of the evidences of the latter rain. Along with the rebirth of Israel as a nation in 1948, this modern-day outpouring of the Spirit is one of the key signs of the soon coming of Christ.

JAMES 5:13-20 — THE PRAYER OF FAITH.

When the Lord Jesus Christ returned to heaven, He sent the Holy Spirit to continue His work of saving the lost and healing the sick. In James 5:13-20, specific provision is made for His ministry of divine healing to be conducted in each local church. Employing this scriptural order of prayer for the sick would eliminate the opportunity for cultists and charlatan faith healers to make merchandise of God's people.

The primary intention of this passage is to provide physical healing and spiritual restoration for "any among you," for everyone who has professed faith in the Lord Jesus Christ. Other passages such as Mark 16:17,18 extend the healing ministry to people who have not yet believed.

The two Greek words for "sick" in vv.14 and 15 indicate a serious affliction. In v.14 the word is *asthenei,* from the word root most frequently used in the New Testament. It denotes bodily weakness as a result of the infirmity, and is the term used of the "impotent" man in John 5:7. He had been an invalid for thirty-eight years. Such a person has no power within himself for recovery. The word in v.15 is *kamnonta,* suggesting a person who is worn out, wasting away, and hopelessly sick. The Christian who is sick, however, is to ask for prayer that he might be *healed,* not that he might receive the last rite of Extreme Unction, which is administered only when a person is dying.

James very clearly places the responsibility upon the sick person. He is to call for the elders of his local church to perform the service of anointing and prayer. It is a definite command, as the imperative mood of the verb in v.14 indicates. It is not the duty of the elders to go scouting for the sick. Such a call gives evidence that the afflicted one has faith that the Lord will heal him.

If the sick person is bedfast, he is to call the elders to come to his side. If they do not bear the title of "elder," they should be men of leadership and prominence in the local congregation. Personal uprightness and special ability will characterize these men, since these are among the qualifications of an elder. Being members of the same church, they have opportunity to know the sick person, his testimony, the nature of his illness, and whether personal sin is a factor in the case. Likewise, the sick one will know the elders to be ordinary men. When healing comes, he will give *God* the glory. Because two or more are involved in praying, no one may claim he has supernatural power in himself and thereby enhance his own reputation.

First of all, the sick person should be given opportunity to confess any known sins ("sins," v.15, and "faults," v.16, are the same Greek word, *hamartias*). It is no mercy to the sufferer to omit this step in hoping to avoid embarrassment to him, for guilt troubling his conscience may have triggered the sickness. It is always God's will to forgive confessed sins (I John 1:9) and to grant spiritual healing. The practice of confessing and forsaking sins that are already known in the church and of praying for one another, will go far to clear away hostilities and resentments and to allow healing to begin in sick bodies and souls. This will also promote the spiritual health of the whole Christian community.

It is important to take time to inspire expectancy and trust in the Lord on the part of the patient before the anointing and prayer. Scripture passages about healing and personal testimonies may be shared with him. Encourage him to stand upon the promises of God's Word. Instruct him to release his faith and receive his healing when he is touched with the oil and the elders pray for him.

After his confession, and after instructing him in the Word, the elders are to anoint the sick person with oil. This follows a practice which Jesus' own disciples used (Mark 6:13). Because olive oil is a symbol of the Holy Spirit in the Bible, the oil is used as an aid to faith, not for any possible therapeutic value. Today, the usual custom is to touch the forehead of the sick person with the oil. For the value of touching the patient, see comments on Mark 5:25-34. The name of the Lord is the authority by which the elders are to perform this rite. Thus the healing of the believer is placed into the all-powerful hands of God. Yet the purpose of the service should not be construed to rule out medical help as the means which God will use. Paul did not forbid the services of a doctor, for he spoke of Luke as "the beloved physician" in one of his later epistles (Col. 4:14).

Having anointed the person, all the elders present are to pray, "and the prayer of faith shall save the sick, and the Lord shall raise him up" (v.15). The Greek reads literally, "the prayer of the faith." The definite article used with the word "faith" may imply that their prayers are inspired by a manifestation of the charismatic gift of faith (see I Cor. 12:9 and comments on I Cor. 12:4-11). James elaborates on the prayer of faith by adding, "The effectual fervent prayer of a righteous man availeth much" (v.16). The word for "effectual fervent" (Greek *energoumene*) signifies that the prayer is "energized" or wrought within each elder by the Holy Spirit. This is "praying in the Spirit" (Eph. 6:18). Such a prayer accomplishes much, because God is the energizer (cf. Phil. 2:13). Elijah prayed this kind of prayer, and James reminds us that he was "a man with a nature like ours" (NASB). His prayers were remarkably answered, not because he was a supersaint, but because God working in him produced powerful prayer. The elders, therefore, should wait on the Lord until He enables them to pray the prayer of faith with utmost boldness and assurance.

Along with the gift of faith, other charismatic gifts may come into operation to strengthen the prayer of faith. A word of knowledge (I Cor. 12:8) may have revealed to one of the elders the nature of the illness or its underlying cause, even before the sick person calls for him to come. This will give the sufferer great assurance and faith to reach out and receive his healing. Even at the bedside, one of the elders may receive a word of knowledge or of wisdom to detect some forgotten sin or subconscious harmful attitude that is blocking the healing and restoration. Of course, one of the gifts of healing may be manifested along with the anointing with oil.

When the scriptural order has been followed, the promise of healing is unconditional: "The Lord shall raise him up." All healing comes from God, no matter what aids to faith may be used, or who offers the prayers, or what spiritual gifts may be exercised. The Lord may heal with or without medical attention. He may do so instantly or over a period of time. The words "shall raise up" do not indicate how soon the healing will take place, but they do guarantee God will act. We have no scriptural warrant to end a healing prayer with the faith-destroying phrase, "if it be Thy will." Where healing does not come, it is evidence that those involved did not follow the divinely ordained procedure, or did not pray a Spirit-given prayer of faith, or that some hidden sin has not yet been truly confessed.

The ultimate purpose in this service of anointing and prayer is suggested in vv.19,20. It is to reach the hearts of professing believers and deal with sins in their lives. If a Christian has erred or wandered from the truth, such a service of confession and prayer may be the means of "converting" or turning him back from the error of his way and saving his soul from eternal death. Those ministering to him will invoke the blood of Christ, and the sins of the restored brother will be "covered" and forgiven.

I PETER

I Peter 2:5,9 — A HOLY PRIESTHOOD OFFERING UP SPIRITUAL SACRIFICES.

In this passage, the apostle Peter beautifully portrays the responsibilities and privileges of all Christians as priests of the living God. He explains that in our continual coming or drawing near (same Greek as Heb. 10:22) to Christ, the living, life-giving Stone, we also as living stones "are being built up as a spiritual house for a holy priesthood, to offer up spiritual sacrifices acceptable to God through Jesus Christ" (v.5 NASB).

Peter may well have had in mind the Lord's words to him, "Thou art Peter (Petros, a stone), and upon this rock (petra, a rock formation, bedrock) I will build my church" (Matt. 16:18). Note that Peter makes Christ, not himself, preeminent in the constructing of the spiritual house which is the Church Universal. The apostle emphasizes the corporate aspect of our Christian worship, for the house or temple is the community of believers as in Eph. 2:20-22, not the individual as in I Cor. 6:19.

God's dwelling on earth in this dispensation is not a single physical structure but a worldwide spiritual habitation in the combined body of all believers. Furthermore, there is not a select priesthood from the members of one tribe, but the entire "nation" of Christians is chosen and holy, and all believers constitute a holy, royal priesthood, "the King's priests" (v.9 TEV). Jesus Christ has made us to be priests to His God and Father (Rev. 1:6), prophesied long before by Isaiah (61:6; 66:21). During this age, the Church is replacing Israel as God's kingdom of priests and holy nation (cf. Exod. 19:6). It is our duty to announce His salvation to all peoples and to "proclaim the excellencies of Him who has called you out of darkness into His marvelous light" (I Pet. 2:9 NASB).

Part of our priestly function is to offer up spiritual sacrifices to God. Imperfect as our worship and service may be, they are made acceptable and well-pleasing to Him because they are offered through Jesus Christ. They derive all their worth from our High Priest who presents them to God, and with whose one perfect sacrifice they are combined. According to Phil. 3:3, we worship, we render sacred service (Greek *latreuontes*), by the Spirit of God. We may sing and pray and bless God in the spirit as well as with the mind (I Cor. 14:14-16).

Through the Lord Jesus, we are to offer up a "sacrifice of praise to God continually, that is, the fruit of our lips giving thanks to his name" (Heb. 13:15; cf. Isa. 57:19; Hos. 14:2). In the Psalms we often read about the sacrifice of thanksgiving (Ps. 50:14; 107:22; 116:17). We may sing with all our heart to the Lord in psalms and hymns and spiritual or charismatic songs (see comments on Eph. 5:15-21). Acts of self-dedication and faith are also spoken of as sacrifices (Rom. 12:1; II Cor. 8:5; Phil. 2:17). In fact, no sacrifice can be considered spiritual without self-surrender and obedience (I Sam. 15:22). In addition to praise and prayer, material gifts may be sacrifices that are pleasing to God (Heb. 13:16; Phil. 4:18). Paul even includes the people that he has won to Christ as an acceptable offering to the Lord. He says that God's grace "has made me a minister of Christ Jesus to the Gentiles; my priestly service is the preaching of the gospel of God, and it falls to me to offer the Gentiles to Him as an acceptable sacrifice, consecrated by the Holy Spirit" (Rom. 15:16 NEB). May we as priests bring similar offerings to our precious Lord and Savior.

I Peter 3:18-20 — PREACHING TO THE SPIRITS IN PRISON.

According to the NASB translation of v.18, Christ "died for sins once for all . . . having been put to death in the flesh, but made alive in the spirit." The next verse should be translated as follows: "at which time also He went and made proclamation to the spirits in prison" (original translation). Who were the spirits?

Verse 20 states that they were disobedient during the days when Noah was constructing the ark. Therefore, many have taught that they are the departed souls of the humans who drowned in the worldwide flood. But there is no trace in the New Testament that the simple term "spirits" is ever used to connote departed human spirits. In Heb. 12:23 the term is qualified: "the spirits of righteous men made perfect" (NASB). On the other hand, there is ample evidence, both in Jewish theology of that period and in the New Testament itself (Matt. 8:16; 12:45; Luke 10:20; I John 4:1; plus the many verses mentioning evil spirits, seducing spirits, etc.), that Peter could be referring to evil spirits. The "prison" he mentions must be the realm known as Hades, the underworld (Phil. 2:10), or "the abyss" where Christ commanded the evil spirits to go (Luke 8:31 NASB, where KJV has "the deep"; in Rev. 9:1,2,11; 20:1,3 the "abyss" is called the "bottomless pit"). Elsewhere, Peter writes about angels that sinned, whom God cast down to hell and committed to pits of darkness, reserved for judgment (II Pet. 2:4; cf. Jude 6).

Why did Christ preach to those particular evil spirits? First of all, He did not preach the Gospel to them, for the verb "made proclamation" has other meanings than to evangelize. After He finished His twofold work on the cross of dying to save mankind from their sins and of defeating Satan (John 12:31; Heb. 2:14), Christ the Victor descended to hell (Hades) to proclaim His universal triumph. As Paul described it, by His cross Christ "despoiled the cosmic powers and authorities, and boldly made a spectacle of them, leading them as captives in his triumphal procession" (Col. 2:15 NEB margin).

According to this interpretation, the victorious Christ singled out the evil spirits who were disobedient in Noah's time, probably because they were the ones who masterminded the corruption and wickedness of practically the whole human race before the flood. That was the worst period of violence and opposition to God's rule that the world has ever seen, even up to our time. Therefore, the spirits responsible for it were brought under condemnation along with all humanity except for Noah and his household.

Peter's statement, then, does not seem to teach that unrepentant souls will have a chance to hear the gospel of salvation preached to them after death. Hebrews 9:27 clearly says that it is appointed or destined for men to die once, and after death comes judgment. What Peter writes in the next chapter (I Pet. 4:6) does not contradict this. He is saying that the lascivious, idolatrous heathen will have to give an account to God who is ready to judge the living and the dead (I Pet. 4:3-5). "But for this reason the gospel was preached (during their lifetime) to those (past members of the church) who are (now) dead, that though they were judged as (all) men are in the flesh (by physical death), they may keep on living eternally, as God does, in the spirit" (I Pet. 4:6; see the NEB and TAB for this interpretation). They heard the Gospel and accepted Christ as their Sinbearer while alive, so that after death they would not have to suffer eternal punishment.

I PETER 3:21 — HOW DOES BAPTISM SAVE US?

Peter gives here an illustration of our salvation which is suggested by his reference to Noah's ark. In it, "a few, that is, eight persons, were brought safely through the water" (I Pet. 3:20 NASB), the water of destruction and judgment on the rest of mankind. Referring to water, he continues, "Which now saves also you, the antitype, namely (the water of) baptism" (v.21, original translation). Noah and his family act as a type of true believers in Christ; we members of the true Christian community are the antitype.

In what sense does baptism save us? John the Baptist had

demanded repentance and evidence of their having repented before he would baptize his converts (Luke 3:8-14; see comments on Matt. 3:11-17). It is clear that baptism did not produce the required repentance, but was a seal or proof of it. In like manner, Christian baptism does not produce repentance, belief, and conversion nor cause regeneration and salvation to take place. Rather, baptism is the confession and demonstration of one's death, burial, and resurrection with Christ that have already occurred. Baptism saves us in the same sense that confession of Christ with the mouth saves a believer (Rom. 10:9,10) — it clinches or seals the act.

Peter goes on to explain in v.21 how baptism saves: "not (by) the removal of filth from the body but (by) the pledge of a good conscience to God" (original translation). It is far more than the mere washing of a dirty body, as the mockers were probably saying. No, the desire for baptism when it proceeds from a clear or good conscience, when one is truly sincere, is a desire for the opportunity to make a pledge of commitment unto God.

The KJV word "answer" does not bring out the full sense of the Greek *eperotema*. It meant the consenting answer to the formal question that preceded the sealing of a contract or covenant. Thus the candidate for baptism would be questioned regarding his faith and repentance. As he gave his answer, he was pledging himself to God. The baptismal act was the seal of his New Covenant relationship with God. Water baptism is the humanly administered aspect of this seal, while baptism in the Spirit is the divinely administered counterpart, the two aspects — water and Spirit baptism — together making the "one baptism" of Eph. 4:5.

Peter concludes v.21 by stating that we are saved through the resurrection of Jesus Christ. This is fully in agreement with his note of praise in I Pet. 1:3: "Blessed be the God and Father of our Lord Jesus Christ, who according to His great mercy has caused us to be born again to a living hope through the resurrection of Jesus Christ from the dead" (NASB). See also comments on Acts 22:16.

I PETER 4:10,11 — MINISTERING YOUR CHARISMATIC GIFT.

I Peter 4:7-11 is similar in many respects to Romans 12. Both passages talk about a sober, serious-minded attitude, about prayer, about genuine, fervent love (charity), and about uncomplaining hospitality. Also both Peter and Paul urge every Christian to exercise his charismatic gifts, for the word "gifts" in Rom. 12:6 and "gift" in v.10 is Greek *charisma*. Peter writes: "As each one has received a special gift, employ it in serving one another, as good stewards of the manifold grace of God. Whoever speaks, let him speak, as it were, the utterances of God; whoever serves, let him do so as by the strength which God supplies; so that in all things God may be glorified through Jesus Christ" (vv.10,11 NASB).

In the early church, every Christian was assumed to have been baptized in the Holy Spirit concurrent with (e.g., Cornelius, Acts 10:43-48) or soon after his conversion (see comments on Acts 19:1-7; I Cor. 12:13) and therefore to have been given "the manifestation of the Spirit for the common good" (I Cor. 12:7 NASB). "The Spirit's *gifts* . . . are the common property of the Christian community, each Christian being but a steward for the edifying of the whole, not manifesting the gift merely for his own use" (JFB, p.1480). As fellow members of a local church, we are to minister our measure of God's grace to one another, so that the body may be built up in love and be knit together "by that which every joint supplies" (Eph. 4:16 NASB). We must not bury our talent or gift, as the slothful servant did in Jesus' parable (Matt. 25:24-30).

Peter classifies the charismatic gifts in two main categories, gifts of speaking and gifts of ministering or serving. He instructs the man who speaks in the Spirit, such as a prophet or someone interpreting a message in tongues or a teacher manifesting a word of knowledge in the church assembly, to speak with sincerity and dignity. Let what he says be as words spoken by God Himself, "as the oracles of God" (KJV). In the only other passages where this term occurs (Acts 7:38; Rom. 3:2; Heb. 5:12), it refers to the O.T. inspired writings, the written word of God. Those in the congregation who hear the divinely inspired spoken message should treat it with similar seriousness. "Do not despise prophetic utterances," wrote Paul (I Thess. 5:20 NASB).

Whoever ministers to other members of the Body through miracles or gifts of healings, helps, ruling or administrating, giving, or showing mercy (I Cor. 12:28,29; Rom. 12:7,8), let him do so as out of the large supply of strength which God furnishes abundantly (TAB). May every precious saint who feels called by God to such a ministry, but who is hindered by bodily weakness or illness, claim this provision. God's supplies are unlimited! But all is to be done to the glory of God, the true motive for all Spirit-filled service.

II PETER

II PETER 1:19-21 — A MORE SURE WORD OF PROPHECY.

As he nears the end of his life, Peter is deeply concerned about the growing spirit of lawlessness and skepticism toward Christ's second coming (II Pet. 3:2-4). He and the other apostles had been making known "the power and coming of our Lord Jesus Christ" (II Pet. 1:16; cf. Matt. 24:30). He denies the charge that the apostles followed cleverly devised stories — the false teachers were maintaining that the Gospel miracles were only allegories or fictional tales with a spiritual truth. No, Peter,

James, and John had actually been eyewitnesses at the preview of Jesus' coming majesty and glory, for they were present at His transfiguration. At that time, they heard God's voice from heaven, "This is my beloved Son, in whom I am well pleased" (II Pet. 1:16-18).

Moreover, writes Peter, there is something even more certain and valid to counteract false teaching than the voice of God heard with the natural ear, and that is the word of prophecy in the Scripture. "And we possess the prophetic word as something altogether reliable" (v.19, Arndt-Gingrich, *Lexicon*, p.137). The apostles uniformly agree in holding the O.T. prophets to be most trustworthy. Peter earlier had recognized that the Spirit of Christ within them predicted the sufferings of Christ and the glories to follow (I Pet. 1:10,11).

Then Peter advises his readers to pay attention in their hearts to prophecy, as one depends on a lamp shining in a dark, murky place. The prophetic word will continue to guide God's people to the end of the age, until the day of Christ's return dawns and the morning star arises (Rev. 2:28; 22:16; cf. Mal. 4:2; Luke 1:78). "For the day has already dawned in the heart of believers; what they wait for is its visible manifestation at Christ's coming" (JFB, p.1489).

Why are the prophecies in the Bible the most dependable revelation from God that we have available today? The answer is given in vv.20,21: "Because you recognize this truth above all else, that no prophecy . . . has ever yet originated in man's will, but men who were led by the Holy Spirit spoke from God" (Williams).

The phrase "of any private interpretation" (v.20) means that the interpretation of the Word of God is not a matter of one's own personal explanation. The Greek noun for "interpretation" is from the same word root as the verb "expound" or "explain" in Mark 4:34. In studying the writings of the O.T. prophets and the N.T. apostles, first of all we need to understand that we must not interpret them according to our whim. The false teachers were already twisting the epistles of Paul and the rest of the Scriptures to their own destruction (II Pet. 3:16; cf. II Cor. 2:17). We need a reliable teacher to explain God's Word correctly.

This teacher, ultimately, is the Holy Spirit, who has been sent to guide us into all the truth (John 16:13; see comments on John 14:15-18,26). As Johann Gerhard (1582–1637) once said, "He who is the author of Scripture is its supreme interpreter." The Spirit may give direct understanding of a passage by the anointing which enables all believers to know the truth (see comments on I John 2:20,27). Or He may use a Spirit-filled teacher to "open" the Scripture (Luke 24:27,32,45), as Philip guided the Ethiopian eunuch (Acts 8:30-35), as Priscilla and Aquila explained the Way of God more accurately to Apollos (Acts 18:26), and as Paul expounded the kingdom of God to the Jews in Rome (Acts 28:23).

The Bible is to be understood in its natural or literal sense and in its proper context. One should not allegorize and transform events and doctrines into myths and symbols, so that he evades the plain sense of the passage. Because the divine revelation in the Scriptures is cumulative and never contradictory, one passage illumines the meaning of another. The Bible is "a single book with a single Author, a perfect unity growing out of its integrating theme, Jesus Christ" (Clark H. Pinnock, *Biblical Revelation* [Chicago: Moody, 1971], pp.212f.).

II Peter 1:21 is a forthright statement regarding the origin and authorship of the prophetic Word. *The Amplified Bible* helps to bring out the meaning of this verse: "For no prophecy ever originated because some man willed it . . . it never came by human impulse — but as men spoke from God who were borne along (moved and impelled) by the Holy Spirit." The word "moved" means carried along as a ship by the wind (Acts 27:15,17). Here the Spirit is the wind (cf. John 3:8; Acts 2:2). The prophets spoke from God, as spokesmen of God, not by their own will. The initiative lay with God.

Verse 21 reveals that Scripture is simultaneously the product of both divine and human authorship. Peter was already recognizing Paul's letters as being part of the "Scriptures" (II Pet. 3:15,16), so that both O.T. and N.T. are included in this term (also cf. I Tim. 5:18b with Luke 10:7). Paul declares that all Scripture is inspired by God (II Tim. 3:16), thus asserting the plenary or complete inspiration of the writings. Here Peter asserts the inspiration of the writers. But what does divine inspiration imply in the twin processes of revealing and recording God's Word? In what manner and to what extent did the Holy Spirit stimulate and control the human authors?

The charismatic gift of prophecy in its manifestation is illustrative in a lesser degree of the *complete* inspiration and supervision that the writing prophets experienced. Prophesying is a matter of yielding to the Spirit's guiding control, while at the same time it is a harmonious cooperation as one uses his own vocabulary, grammatical style, inflection, gestures, etc. The writers of Scripture may be compared with the first violinist or concertmaster, playing with his own style and skill, in a symphony orchestra which is conducted in person by the composer of the music. A Paul retained his individuality and made use of his literary capabilities, as distinct from those of a John or a Peter.

The work of inspiration guarded the writers from any and every error in recording the direct revelation of God to them, and in employing eyewitness reports (Luke 1:1-4) and historical sources such as genealogical records and court archives (e.g., I Kings 4; 14:19,29). The very words which communicate to us the thoughts of God were "taught" by the Holy Spirit (I Cor. 2:13). Nevertheless, as explained above, by plenary inspiration of the Scriptures we do not mean mechanical dictation. But the divine superintendence guarantees that the sacred writings are God's Word to man, without error in the original manuscripts before copying began. "Divine authorship implies complete reliability and assures us the Bible will not ultimately contradict itself" (Pinnock, *Biblical Revelation*, p.210).

II PETER 2:1-22 — FALSE PROPHETS AND TEACHERS.

The Lord Jesus warned His disciples in the Sermon on the Mount, "Beware of the false prophets, who come to you in sheep's clothing, but inwardly are ravenous wolves. You will know them by their fruits" (Matt. 7:15,16 NASB). They may produce mighty works and a display of charismatic gifts, but what is their conduct? (See comments on Matt. 7:21-23.) Again, in His Olivet discourse on future events, Jesus flatly stated concerning the days as the end of this age approaches: "And many false prophets shall rise, and shall deceive many" (Matt. 24:11). During the great tribulation, false Christs and false prophets will appear who will be able to perform such amazing signs and wonders that even God's own people could be fooled (Matt. 24:24).

Therefore, the child of God needs to be alert and instructed in the Word so that the Holy Spirit will enable him to detect false teaching (Acts 20:28-31; see comments on I John 2:20,27). Each congregation has a duty to pass judgment on the messages that the prophets and teachers who are present may bring forth (I Cor. 14:29). At the same time, the Bible teacher must recognize his great responsibility, and that as a teacher he will incur a stricter judgment (James 3:1 NASB). Like the elders, among whose qualifications is the ability to teach (I Tim. 3:2), the teacher needs to demonstrate a godly character in his own home as well as in the church. He should not be self-willed, but be above reproach as a steward of God's Word (I Cor. 4:1). "He must hold fast to the sure and trustworthy Word of God as he was taught it, so that he may be able both to give stimulating instruction and encouragement in sound . . . doctrine, and to refute and convict those who . . . . oppose it" (Titus 1:9 TAB).

The Bible gives some definite clues regarding the general

character and actions of false prophets and apostate teachers.
Usually several of the following categories mark any particular
heretical teacher and his followers:

1. Doctrinal error. Peter writes that they "secretly bring in
destructive heresies, even denying the Master who bought
them" (v.1 RSV). Such men deliberately oppose God's revealed
truth and are rejected by Him as regards the faith (II Tim. 3:8).
Usually their wrong teaching eventuates in a denial of the
Trinity, or of the deity of Christ and the full efficacy of His
blood by God's grace (Jude 4; Phil. 3:18; Heb. 10:29). The
distinctive doctrine to which the teacher gives special emphasis,
however, may veil the seriousness of his error. He tends to
accept other wrong interpretation or heresies in order to
support his main teaching. Finally, his pet doctrine becomes an
obsession with him, being driven by a spirit of error to promote
it. That is why Paul spoke of such teachings as doctrines of
demons (I Tim. 4:1 NASB). Religiously minded people who do
not want sound doctrine but who want "to have their ears
tickled" will gather to themselves one teacher after another to
satisfy their own likings (II Tim. 4:3 NASB).

2. Arrogant pride. The false teacher gains a following because
he is forceful and dogmatic. At the same time, he lacks humility
and love. He is self-willed and speaks arrogantly (Jude 16; II
Pet. 2:10,12), belittling other Christians. He claims his special
doctrine makes his group superior and "more spiritual" than
other churches. He demands total loyalty to his leadership and
permits no difference of opinion. He is intent on building his
own kingdom. Like Diotrephes, he tries to get rid of those who
oppose him (III John 9,10), or he withdraws from contact with
all other groups. Thus he causes divisions in the Body of Christ
(Jude 19 NASB). Paul commands us to avoid such men (Rom.
16:17). In some cases, the seclusive nature of the false teaching
hinders all activity in evangelism and detracts from an interest
in missions. While the teacher may make an undue stress on

love for God and man, it is a hypocritical love for others outside his group of disciples.

3. Rebellion against authority. According to Peter and Jude, false teachers despise and reject authority (II Pet. 2:10; Jude 8 NASB). They speak evil of and scoff at dignitaries (literally, "glorious ones," whether human rulers of the Church and of government, or glorious angelic beings). They are unruly or rebellious men (Titus 1:10), not allowing themselves to be placed under the authority of any other Christians. Along with their rebellious and strongly independent spirit goes their tendency to grumbling and faultfinding (Jude 16 NASB).

4. Deceit. The Lord Jesus warned of coming deceivers (see above), and Paul also alerted his readers to "false apostles, deceitful workers, disguising themselves as apostles of Christ" (II Cor. 11:13 NASB). Paul himself had renounced the hidden things of dishonesty, refusing to walk in craftiness, and not handling the word of God deceitfully (II Cor. 4:2). He was not like many who were corrupting the word of God by watering down the message in order to make money from it (II Cor. 2:17 TLB). Peter said that the false teachers would exploit his readers with feigned (false or fabricated) words, enticing unstable souls, and alluring people with fleshly desires by their great swelling words of vanity (vv.3,14,18). They often employ flattery (Jude 16 RSV) and lies (Titus 1:12; Jer. 23:25-32; 27:9-16; Zech. 13:3). Instead of rightly dividing the word of truth, of handling it accurately and presenting it in a straightforward way (II Tim. 2:15), the false teacher presses his favorite passages to an extreme without discussing the balancing passages of the Bible. One needs to weigh all the Scriptures that pertain to a certain doctrine in order to keep it in balance or proper perspective with the rest of God's word.

5. Monetary greed. Very often, false teachers are marked by covetousness (vv.3,14). Like Balaam, the false prophet who was hired to pronounce a curse on Israel, he is desirous of making

money by means of his spiritual gift (II Pet. 2:15; Jude 11). He is in the ministry for the sake of filthy lucre or sordid gain (Titus 1:11). He supposes that a showing of godliness or piety can be a moneymaking business (I Tim. 6:5). See comments on III John 5-8.

6. Fleshly indulgence. While some false teachers are overscrupulous and legalistic regarding morals and ethics, others turn the grace of God into lasciviousness (Jude 4). Many people follow their teaching that there is nothing wrong with sexual sin (v.2 TLB). Their eyes are full of adultery and never cease from lusting (v.14). In his day, Jeremiah cried out against the sins of the prophets of Jerusalem, which included adultery with their neighbors' wives (Jer. 23:14; 29:23). Their appetite ("belly") is the god of such teachers (Phil. 3:18,19). They indulge the flesh in its corrupt desires and count it a pleasure to revel, even in the daytime (v.10,13). "Always eager for a good dinner, they make of such occasions an opportunity for raucous mirth and continued false teaching" (WBC, p.1460). By satisfying the desire for some sort of religion without demanding abandonment of sin, they worm their way (Phillips) or "insinuate themselves into private houses and there get miserable women into their clutches, women burdened with a sinful past, and led on by all kinds of desires, who are always wanting to be taught, but are incapable of reaching a knowledge of the truth" (II Tim. 3:6,7 NEB). The New Morality or Situation Ethics is a modern-day example of such teaching on a large scale within the ranks of Christianity. Very often the false teacher begins his apostasy by covering up a sin of the flesh. When he is not truthful about an ethical matter in his own life, he seeks to justify it by twisting the Scriptures — to his own destruction (II Pet. 3:16). He deceived himself, which in turn opens him up to further lies and deception.

How can one be sure a certain man is a false teacher or false prophet? God in His Word lays down some definite tests in the Book of Deuteronomy that are applicable today. First, does the

man profess to be a believer in the Lord? Before the coming of
Christ, a prophet in O.T. times had to be an Israelite, like unto
Moses as the representative or spokesman of the one true, living
God (Deut. 18:15). Today, a true prophet or teacher must at
least profess to belong to the Israel of God (Gal. 6:16), to be a
born-again Christian.

Second, does he claim that his teaching is from God, that it is
the Gospel of Christ? Moses said that any prophet who claims
to give a message from other gods must die (Deut. 18:20). Is the
man "a dreamer of dreams" (Deut. 13:1), telling his own
dreams (Jer. 23:25,28,32; 29:8), or do his words have the
authoritative ring of "Thus saith the Lord," because God has
put the words of prophecy in his mouth by the Spirit? (Deut.
18:18).

Third, does his message agree with Scripture? The Spirit will
never contradict Himself. Any new revelation must be in accord
with the written word of God. Even if he should perform a sign
or wonder (a Satanic miracle), yet if the prophet encourages
people to follow other gods, his message is wrong (Deut. 13:2).
Today, prominent churchmen are leading people into the
mysteries of the occult. But all practices of witchcraft and magic
— incantations, divination, the horoscope, the Ouija board, the
spiritist seance — all are expressly forbidden in the Word of
God and will only turn the child of God away from the Lord
who has redeemed him (Deut. 13:5; 18:9-14; Isa. 8:19,20). God
permits false prophets and heresies to come among His people
in order to prove whether the believers really love Him
wholeheartedly and will remain loyal to His Word (Deut. 13:3;
cf. I Cor. 11:18,19).

Fourth, do his predictions come true? If the thing which the
prophet foretells does not happen or come true, "it is not the
Lord who has given him the message; he has made it up
himself" (Deut. 18:22 TLB). A Christian should never be in
bondage to such prophecies that often evoke fear or anxiety:
"thou shalt not be afraid of him" (Deut. 18:22).

The uniform instruction of God's word is to steer clear of all false teachers, of those who have the outward form of godliness but who deny the power of the Spirit who energizes the Christian life (II Tim. 3:5).

I JOHN

I JOHN 2:20,27 — AN ANOINTING FROM THE HOLY ONE.

The words "unction" (v.20) and "anointing" (v.27) translate the same Greek word, *chrisma*. It refers to anything smeared on, such as the ointment prepared by the Israelites from olive oil and aromatic herbs. Anointing oil was applied as an outward symbol of the Spirit of God in the inaugural ceremony for priests (Exod. 29:7,21; 30:23-33; 40:15; Ps. 133:2), for kings (I Sam. 9:16; 10:1; 16:3,13), and sometimes for prophets (I Kings 19:16).

In I John 2:20,27, the "anointing" refers to the abiding gift of the Holy Spirit from the Holy One, i.e., from Christ Himself (Mark 1:24; John 6:69; Acts 3:14; Rev. 3:7; 6:10). It is the fulfillment of the promise written in the O.T. prophets, "And they shall all be taught by God" (John 6:45 NEB; cf. Isa. 54:14). The "anointing" provides each believer with the capacity to know the truth about the person of Jesus Christ (I John 2:21-23). In many Christian circles, people use the word "anointing" in the sense of filling, when they pray that they or their minister may receive a "fresh anointing of the Holy Ghost." They are really asking to be filled anew with the Spirit (see comments on Luke 11:5-13; Eph. 5:15-21).

The words "Christ" (*christos*, anointed one) and "anointing" (*chrisma*) are from the same Greek root. As Christ was anointed with the Spirit for His ministry and office of Messiah (Hebrew, *mashiah*, anointed one — Ps. 2:2; Dan. 9:25,26; cf. Isa. 61:1; Ps. 45:7; Acts 10:38), so too are "Christians" little anointed ones (II Cor. 1:21,22). Therefore John seems to be drawing a deliberate contrast in his epistle (I John 2:18-27) between Antichrist and his many antichrists on the one hand and Christ and His Christ-ians (anointed ones) on the other.

Toward the end of the first century, when John wrote his epistles, a heresy was developing known as Gnosticism (from Greek *gnosis*, knowledge). The Gnostics boasted that they had superior knowledge and insight into spiritual truths and claimed that the divine Christ came down upon Jesus at His baptism and left Him before the crucifixion. Thus, they denied that Jesus Himself *is* the Christ, one person, the unique Son of God (I John 2:22). This lie continues to be propagated in such erroneous religious systems as Christian Science, which teaches that Christ is a divine idea while Jesus was only a human.

The two oldest Greek manuscripts containing I John indicate that the second half of v.20 should be translated, "and you all know" (RSV), or, "you all have knowledge" (NEB). The baptism in the Holy Spirit was available to *all* Christians, so that all of them might have the Spirit promised by Jesus to teach them the truth and guard them from error (John 14:26; 16:7,13; see comments on John 14:15-18,26). In genuine Christianity, no select group such as the Gnostics may claim secret knowledge. The Spirit of truth teaches each one who has received the anointing to be able to discern the truth from error in all its varied forms. "To the true believer and faithful seeker after the knowledge of God He gives an instinct for truth, a sense for the Divine in knowledge and in doctrine, which works through the reason and yet above the reason, and which works collectively in the communion of saints" (George G. Findlay, *Fellowship in the Life Eternal* [London: Hodder & Stoughton, 1909], p.222). Out of the collective faith of a body of believers emerges a spiritual common sense, a Christian group opinion produced by the inner witness of the Spirit.

In v.27, John writes, "And you have no need for any one to teach you" (NASB). Because the Holy Spirit is an *abiding* anointing ("the anointing which ye have received of him abideth in you"), He is in a position to teach believers continually. His teaching is true and is not a lie, but it does not guarantee a precise agreement in every point of doctrine and practice. It covers essential truth, such as the deity of Jesus Christ, here in question. To edify the church as a whole and individual believers in particular, Christ has given teachers to explain His Word and apply it in given situations (Gal. 6:6; Eph. 4:11-13; Col. 1:28; 2:7; 3:16; Heb. 13:7,17). Mutual teaching or sharing is not set aside by the Spirit's teaching, but is highly valued among those who are fellow-partakers of the anointing.

As the Head of His Body, the Lord Jesus has provided three safeguards against error: (1) the anointing, (2) the apostolic word, "that which ye have heard from the beginning" (I John 2:24), now recorded for us by their pen, and (3) His own promise of eternal life (I John 2:25). In receiving these, we need not fear or be deceived by the spirit of antichrist. See comments on I John 4:1-6.

I JOHN 4:1-6 — TESTING THE SPIRITS.

John's warning not to believe every spirit but to keep testing the spirits to see whether they are from God, is intensely practical. He is not writing about some eerie situation such as a seance — although these verses apply equally well to spiritist mediums. Rather, he is teaching Christians how to detect false prophets and teachers in their own ranks.

The spirits under discussion here are those which motivate and guide teachers of religion and in that sense speak through such men. There is one "spirit of truth," the Holy Spirit; there are many spirits of error, sent forth by Satan (v.6). The latter are the seducing spirits that Paul wrote about to Timothy: "But the Spirit explicitly says that in later times some will fall away from the faith, paying attention to deceitful spirits and doctrines of demons, by means of the hypocrisy of liars seared in their own conscience as with a branding iron, *men* who forbid marriage *and advocate* abstaining from foods which God has created to be gratefully shared in by those who believe and know the truth" (I Tim. 4:1-3 NASB). The O.T. also taught that a deceiving spirit speaking through the mouth of a false prophet could entice a man such as King Ahab to his doom (I Kings 22:19-23).

To protect a local church from false prophets, the Holy Spirit may manifest Himself through a certain member of that body with the gift of the discerning of spirits (I Cor. 12:10). In Philippi, a young woman kept following Paul and his friends to the prayer meeting day after day. She would interrupt with a message which sounded like a prophecy: "These men are the servants of the most high God, which shew unto us the way of salvation" (Acts 16:17). What she was saying was true enough, but she was speaking under the influence of Satan. When Paul discerned that it was a spirit of divination, he was grieved within. He then commanded the evil spirit in the name of Jesus Christ to come out of her, and she was set free.

Even when the charismatic gift of discerning of spirits is not manifested, Christians are responsible to examine carefully every seeming work of the Spirit. We must not quench the Spirit or despise prophetic utterances; but we are to "prove all things" — test all messages and signs — and hold fast to the genuine manifestations of the Spirit and abstain from everything which appears to be evil (I Thess. 5:19-22; I Cor. 14:29). In vv.1-6 and II John 5-7 the Lord has given us certain tests to use in "trying" the spirits. Employing standards such as these, the church at Ephesus put certain self-styled apostles to the test and found them to be false (Rev. 2:2).

First and most important, what is the spirit prompting the person in question to teach about Jesus? "Every spirit" — i.e., the Holy Spirit — "that confesses that Jesus Christ has come in the flesh is from God" (v.2 NASB). The person's confession of faith is that Jesus as the Christ has arrived from a spiritual sphere outside of "flesh" in order to participate in human, physical existence, and that He still remains incarnate. Thus he acknowledges the divine origin and rights of Jesus and His coming in this capacity into human bodily life. Anyone who does not so confess Jesus is not of God, but is under the influence of the antichrist spirit, i.e., of Satan. Paul's watchword to test whether one is speaking by the Spirit of God is similar; only by the Holy Spirit can one genuinely say, "Jesus is Lord" (I Cor. 12:3), for Christ exercises total lordship over one's life only when he is baptized in the Spirit. John has already written that it is the anointing of the Holy Spirit which enables all the believers to know the truth about Christ (see comments on I John 2:20,27).

Second, what is their relationship to the world? "They proceed from the world *and* are of the world, therefore it is out of the world [its whole economy morally considered] that they speak, and the world . . . (pays attention) to them" (v.5 TAB). The true children of God do not love the world (Greek *kosmos*, the prevailing order of human affairs that is hostile to God), nor the things in the world (I John 2:15-17). Therefore, through Christ, they have overcome the world (I John 5:4,5; John 16:33) and the evil one and his spirits (I John 2:13,14; 4:4). Christians rest upon the absolute assurance that greater is the Holy Spirit in them than Satan who is in the world as its ruling spirit (I John 4:4; John 12:31).

Third, what is their attitude to the apostolic testimony? Do they listen and pay attention "to us," to John and the other apostles (cf. I John 1:1-5)? The young Christian who is getting to know God has a hunger for the words the apostles have spoken and written, but he who is not from God does not care to read the N.T. (v.4). We must abide in the doctrine or teaching of Christ in order to be assured that we have both the Father and the Son (II John 9; John 8:31).

Fourth, what is their attitude toward true Christians? In his second epistle (II John 5-7) John contrasts the Lord's commandment that we love one another (John 13:34) with the many deceivers who have gone out into the world, "those who do not acknowledge Jesus Christ *as* coming in the flesh" (II John 7 NASB). John says in effect that this is clearly the work of the arch-deceiver and the antichrist spirit, namely, the devil. If anyone comes to a local church or to a believer's home and does not bring the correct teaching of Christ and about Him, that person must not be welcomed and admitted or encouraged in any way (II John 10,11). For further discussion of false teachers, see comments on II Pet. 2:1-22.

I JOHN 5:6-12 — THE THREEFOLD WITNESS TO THE SON OF GOD.

How can we know with certainty that Jesus Christ is the Son of God? And how can we be sure that having believed that Jesus is the Son of God we actually possess eternal life? The answer lies in the witness that God has borne concerning His Son, as John sets it forth in this section of his epistle. One should study these verses in a modern version such as the RSV or NASB, because v.7 of the KJV was not in John's original letter.

The witness is both historical and inward or personal. The two parts of the historical witness are summed up under the terms "water" and "blood." These are evidently sacred and well known symbols, since John again refers to them with the definite article, "the water" and "the blood." The most satisfactory explanation is that "the water" signifies Jesus' baptism when His ministry was inaugurated in the waters of the Jordan and He received the Father's testimony to His divine Sonship; and that "the blood" signifies His crucifixion, the consummation of His ministry. The Greek preposition *dia* in the phrase "by water and blood" here suggests both that Jesus passed *through* actual water and blood and that *by means of* baptism and death He came to fulfill His role as Messiah.

While the Gnostics who were followers of the heretic Cerinthus were willing to accept Christ's coming "by water" when the divine Christ emanation supposedly came on Jesus, they insisted the Christ left the purely human Jesus before Calvary and therefore did not "come by blood." But after His resurrection, Jesus proved from the O.T. prophecies that the Messiah had to suffer death in order to enter into His glory (Luke 24:25-27, 44-46).

According to v.8, the third witness is the Spirit. All three are in agreement, and together form the united testimony or witness that God has given concerning His Son (v.9). Whereas the first two are objective events, the two supreme manifestations of Jesus' Messiahship, the Holy Spirit is a continuing subjective, inner witness. Verse 10 says that the one who believes in the Son of God has the witness *in himself*. A literal translation of the last part of v.6 in the KJV (v.7 in modern versions) states that the Spirit is "the continual Witnesser." He is the one who is ever illuminating and persuading men in their innermost being. He convinces them that the objective historic facts regarding Jesus Christ are true and that they ought to believe and keep trusting in the Son of God. The Holy Spirit is the effective witness or persuader, "because the Spirit is the truth" and therefore can be absolutely trusted. Regarding the Spirit of truth, see comments on John 14:15-18; *re* the inner witness of the Spirit to one's sonship, see comments on Rom. 8:14-17.

III JOHN

III JOHN 5-8 — SUPPORTING TRAVELING MINISTERS.

In areas where inns and hotels were either nonexistent or dens of iniquity, traveling evangelists and teachers were largely dependent on the hospitality of local Christians. John wrote to commend Gaius for the faithful service he was rendering to Christian brethren, especially when they were strangers. These itinerant missionaries had gone forth in obedience to Christ's Great Commission (see comments on Matt. 28:18-20) and for the sake of His Name, and they were accepting nothing from the Gentiles, i.e., the unbelieving pagans. So John urged Christians to support such men by receiving them as guests, in order that "we may be fellow workers in the truth" (v.8 RSV). Paul taught that it is God's will for those who proclaim the Gospel to get their living from the Gospel (I Cor. 9:7-14; cf. Luke 10:7; I Tim. 5:17,18).

Other passages of Scripture, however, warn us not to receive any false teacher into our house (II John 7-11; see comments on I John 4:1-6), and to avoid every brother who leads an unruly life or who refuses to work (II Thess. 3:6-15). Even in the early years of the Church, some men evidently were in the ministry for the sake of money (I Pet. 5:2; I Tim. 3:3,8; 6:9,10). The Didache (Teaching of the Twelve Apostles, one of the earliest writings of the Church Fathers and thought to date about A.D. 100) tells how Christians were to prevent visiting ministers from living off the generosity of others: "Let every apostle who comes to you be received as the Lord. But he shall stay only one day; and a second day, in case of special need. If he stays for three days he is a false prophet. When the apostle goes away let him receive only bread, to suffice until he finds his next lodging: if he asks for money he is a false prophet. . . . Not everyone who speaks in the spirit is a prophet; he is only a prophet if he has the ways of the Lord. The false and the genuine prophet will be known therefore by their ways. Every prophet who orders a table [i.e., a meal, to satisfy the needs of others] in the spirit does not eat of it: if he does, he is a false prophet. If a prophet teaches the truth but does not practice what he teaches, he is a false prophet" (*The Early Christian Fathers*, ed. and trans. by Henry Bettenson [London: Oxford Univ. Press, 1956], p.71).

REVELATION

REV. 1:4 — THE SEVEN SPIRITS BEFORE GOD'S THRONE.

In his salutation to the seven churches in the Roman province of Asia, John the Apostle extends grace and peace from the eternal God, from "the seven spirits which are before His throne," and from Jesus Christ. What is the correct interpretation of the seven spirits?

Some have explained the seven spirits to be the same as the seven angels of the seven churches (Rev. 1:20). It is true that angels are ministering spirits who render service for the sake of redeemed human beings (Heb. 1:14). But Rev. 1:4,5 apparently is a greeting from the triune God; and in Rev. 3:1; 4:5, and 5:6, it seems more in keeping with the contexts to understand "the seven Spirits of God" as a symbolic reference to the Holy Spirit. In Isa. 11:2 the manifold energies of the Spirit of God are described as follows:

> And the Spirit of the Lord will rest on Him,
> The spirit of wisdom and understanding,
> The spirit of counsel and strength,
> The spirit of knowledge and the fear of the Lord.
>   (NASB)

This is one of the prophecies of the Holy Spirit upon Messiah, the Servant of the Lord (see comments on Matt. 12:15-21; Luke 4:14-21).

In Rev. 3:1, "He who has the seven Spirits of God" (NASB) speaks to the church in Sardis. Because the number seven often suggests completeness or perfection, the quoted expression is an Oriental way of saying, He who has all the fullness of the Spirit, He who has the Spirit without measure (see John 3:34 and

comments there). Thus Christ is perfectly prepared to know our
deeds and to convict of sin.

The sevenfold Spirit of God is represented in Rev. 4:5 as
seven lamps of fire burning before the throne. Like a fire, He
purifies the godly and consumes the wicked (see Matt. 3:11 and
comments on Matt. 3:11-17). The symbolism is most apparent
in Rev. 5:6, which describes "a Lamb standing, as if slain,
having seven horns and seven eyes, which are the seven Spirits
of God, sent out into all the earth" (NASB). The seven horns
symbolize fullness of power, and the seven eyes, perfect insight.
In conjunction with Zech. 3:9 and 4:10 where the seven eyes
are said to belong to the Lord, John's strange vision represents
our Savior as being omnipotent and omniscient. The seven
Spirits have been sent forth into all the world, suggesting the
extension of Christ's ministry by His Spirit on His disciples.

REV. 1:10 — IN THE SPIRIT ON THE LORD'S DAY.

One way of outlining the last book of the N.T. is to note that
the expression "I was in the Spirit" or "He carried me away in
the Spirit" occurs four times (Rev. 1:10; 4:2; 17:3; 21:10). This
suggests four separate visions that John had. Apparently the
Holy Spirit took full possession of him, so that his spirit had
immediate contact with the invisible world. His experiences
were very similar to those of the prophet Ezekiel. For instance,
both saw four living creatures which acted as guardians of God's
throne (Ezek. 1:5-26; Rev. 4:6-9; 5:6; 6:1, etc.). Both were
carried by the Spirit (Ezek. 3:12,14; 8:3; Rev. 17:3; 21:10).
Both books, along with the Book of Daniel, are apocalyptic in
nature; i.e., they contain detailed prophecies of the end time
and are full of figurative language and symbols with their
background in the ancient Near East.

John's first vision came to him "on the Lord's day." It is
certain that he means Sunday, and not that he was projected in
this instance into the time of Christ's second coming. The Greek

wording here is different from that in the expression "the day of the Lord." Furthermore, in his first vision he saw Christ as He is now in heaven, and received messages for churches already in existence in the first century.

It is the earliest mention of the term "the Lord's day." But the observation by Christians of the first day of the week for worship, the Lord's Supper, and giving of offerings is implied in Acts 20:7 and I Cor. 16:2. The Christians very early changed from meeting on Saturday (the Jewish sabbath) to Sunday, apparently in commemoration of Jesus' resurrection. Before his martyrdom about A.D. 107 (or 116), Ignatius, a bishop of Antioch, wrote: "Let every friend of Christ keep the Lord's day as a festival, the resurrection day, the queen and chief of all days of the week."

Rev. 2:20-24 — THE SELF-STYLED PROPHETESS JEZEBEL.

This passage is a warning to all of God's children of the dangers of witchcraft. A woman in the neighborhood of Thyatira was strongly influencing that church for evil, just as the wicked Jezebel corrupted her husband King Ahab (see II Kings 9:22, "the whoredoms . . . of Jezebel and her witchcrafts"). Jezebel's spiritual counterpart at Thyatira was luring Christ's "servants" astray by her system of teaching and utterance under demonic inspiration. By a false spiritualism, she may have been persuading them that sexual vice and foods offered to idols could not affect the inner man, and therefore could be indulged in with immunity. More likely, sexual acts were part of her idolatrous system that led them to know "the deep things of Satan" (Rev. 2:24 NASB; cf. I Cor. 2:10, "the deep things of God," which only the Spirit of God can explore and make known). In modern witchcraft, the rituals are often conducted in the nude. "Naked women are occasionally used as altars, and phallic symbols are shaken toward each point of the compass for benediction" (Brian Vachon, "Witches Are Rising," *Look*, Aug. 24, 1971, p.40).

Because many false cults have been started or led by a woman, and because so many spiritist mediums and fortune-tellers are women, Paul's prohibition is exceedingly worthy of note: "I do not allow a woman to teach or exercise authority over a man" (I Tim. 2:12 NASB).

REV. 9:21 — SORCERIES.

The Greek word for "sorcery" and "sorcerer" here and in Rev. 18:23; 21:8; 22:15; and Gal. 5:20 comes from *pharmakon*, "poison," "magic potion," or "drugs." It is the word root from which we get the English word "pharmacy." The magician or sorcerer was one who mixed drugs or poisons.

Revelation 9:20,21 indicates that during the tribulation, along with the use of drugs goes the worship of demons. Drugs are often employed to achieve the desired state of trance in Satan worship. Losing all sense of moral righteousness, the devotees resort to theft to sustain their habit and engage in wanton immorality. They murder with no qualms of conscience, a fact made clear in the trials of members of drug communes convicted of grisly killings. The tremendous increase of interest in the occult and in drug use in recent years is a clear sign of the approaching end of this age.

REV. 12:9-11 — OVERCOMING THE ACCUSER OF THE BRETHREN.

The fullest description in the Bible of Satan is found in v.9. He is the great dragon of Rev. 12-13, out of whose mouth come forth demonic spirits (Rev. 16:13,14). The concept of the seven-headed dragon (Rev. 12:3) originated in the Semitic world, and is found in the O.T. where he is called Leviathan (Ps. 74:13,14; Isa. 27:1). He is identified with the serpent of old, who tempted and deceived Eve in the Garden of Eden (Gen.

3:1; II Cor. 11:3). He is called the devil (Greek *diabolos*) and Satan (from Hebrew *satan*), both meaning "adversary" or "slanderer." He is the one who opposed Job before God had accused him of unworthy motives (Job 1:6-12; 2:1-7). Later, Satan tried to accuse Joshua the high priest, but the Lord rebuked Satan (Zech. 3:1,2). Therefore, he is called the accuser of the brethren (Christians as brothers in the Lord), because he accuses them before God day and night (v.10). His strategy is to deceive the whole world, and he has a great army of wicked angels to aid him in the spiritual warfare that he wages incessantly against God and His people (Rev. 12:7-9).

Victory, however, is assured to the saints of God. "They overcame him by the blood of the Lamb, and by the word of their testimony" (v.11). The ones who overcome the devil are those who place implicit trust in the redemptive work of Christ on the cross, signified by His blood which He shed as He died in their stead. Because Christ the Redeemer paid the debt in full for every sin of the believer, His blood answers every charge and accusation of Satan. Christ is the only one who would have a right to condemn us, but He is our Intercessor and Advocate (Rom. 8:33,34; I John 2:1). He came to destroy the works of the devil and to render him powerless (I John 3:8; Heb. 2:14).

The testimony of Christian believers confirms the efficacy of Jesus' death in their lives. The "word of their testimony" has a twofold significance: (1) the word of God to which they bear witness, corresponding to the figure in Eph. 6:17 of the sword of the Spirit, which is the Word of God; and (2) their faithful testimony to Jesus (Rev. 1:9; 6:9; 12:17; 20:4), even unto death, by which they confess themselves to be followers of the slain Lamb and not worshipers of the beast, Satan's representative (Rev. 13:15; 15:2). Even before times of persecution and martyrdom, the Christian achieves spiritual victory over sin and Satan by the application of the cross in his life in the crucifixion of self (see comments on Luke 9:23-26).

Rev. 19:10 — THE SPIRIT OF PROPHECY.

"The testimony of Jesus is the spirit of prophecy." These are the words of explanation to John from the angel who instructed him regarding the marriage supper of the Lamb, and whom John wanted to worship. He restrained John and said, "You must not do that! I am [only] another servant with you and your brethren who have [accepted and hold] the testimony borne by Jesus. Worship God! For the substance (essence) of the truth revealed by Jesus is the spirit of all prophecy — the vital breath, the inspiration of all inspired preaching and interpretation of the divine will and purpose" (TAB).

The "testimony of Jesus" includes both the historic witness which Jesus Himself gave on earth, preserved in the Gospels (cf. I Tim. 6:13), and the witness which the ascended Christ continues to impart by His Spirit, such as the revelations of this last book of the Bible. Thus every true testimony to the Lord Jesus and His saving work and coming kingdom is the result of the operation of the same Spirit of prophecy that inspired the apostles and prophets of the N.T. No prophecy recorded in Scripture was ever thought up by the prophet himself, but came from men who spoke from God as they were moved by the Holy Spirit (II Pet. 1:20,21; see comments at II Pet. 1:19-21).

A proper test, then, for a prophetic message in an assembly of believers is to ascertain whether its testimony about Jesus corresponds to that of the holy Scriptures. The Holy Spirit, "the Spirit of prophecy," will never contradict Himself.

Rev. 22:17 — THE SPIRIT AND THE BRIDE SAY, COME.

This is the last mention of the Holy Spirit in the Bible. The Spirit, perhaps through prophetic messages (cf. Rev. 19:10 and comments there), inspires the Church, the Bride of Christ, to pray for the Lord Jesus to come back. Christ has promised in vv.7,12,13,16 that He is coming quickly (cf. also v.20).

Prompted by the love for Christ which the Spirit has poured into their hearts, and filled with that same Spirit of Jesus, they love His appearing (II Tim. 4:8) and respond to His dear voice by saying, "Come!"

The hearer of the prophecy of this book is invited to join the Bride as a true believer and to take part in the call for the Lord to return. And as the members of the Bride pray to Jesus, "Come," so they urge everyone who is spiritually thirsty to come to Christ and drink of the living waters of salvation without cost to himself. This becomes his first taste of the water of life.

In the regenerated heaven and earth, every child of God will enjoy in full measure the life-giving waters from the river that flows clear as crystal out from the throne of God and of the Lamb (Rev. 22:1).

APPENDIX

BIBLIOGRAPHY

Henry Alford. *The Greek Testament*. 4th ed. 1861.

W. F. Arndt and F. W. Gingrich, eds. *A Greek-English Lexicon of the New Testament and Other Early Christian Literature*. Chicago: Univ. of Chicago Press, 1957.

John P. Baker. *Baptized in One Spirit*. London: Fountain Trust, 1967.

Baker's Dictionary of Theology. Grand Rapids: Baker Book House, 1960.

Dennis and Rita Bennett. *The Holy Spirit and You*. Plainfield: Logos, 1971.

Arnold Bittlinger. *Gifts and Graces: A Commentary on I Corinthians 12-14*. London: Hodder and Stoughton, 1967.

F. F. Bruce. *The Book of the Acts*. Grand Rapids: Eerdmans, 1959

F. F. Bruce. *The Letters of Paul: An Expanded Paraphrase*. Grand Rapids: Eerdmans, 1965.

F. F. Bruce. *The Epistle to the Ephesians*. London: Pickering & Inglis, 1961.

Frederick D. Bruner. *A Theology of the Holy Spirit*. Grand Rapids: Eerdmans, 1970.

Ernest DeWitt Burton. *The Epistle to the Galatians*. ICC, 1921.

Samuel Chadwick. *The Way to Pentecost*. New York: Revell, n.d.

Laurence Christenson. *Speaking in Tongues*. Minneapolis: Bethany Fellowship, 1968.

Finis J. Dake. *Dake's Annotated Reference Bible*. Grand Rapids: Zondervan, 1961.

The Early Christian Fathers, ed. and trans. by Henry Bettenson. London: Oxford Univ. Press, 1956.

C. J. Ellicott. *A Bible Commentary for English Readers*. London: Cassell, n.d.

Epistles of Pliny, x 96 and 97.

Howard Ervin. *These Are Not Drunken As Ye Suppose*. Plainfield: Logos, 1968.

George G. Findlay. "I Corinthians" *EGT*, II.

George G. Findlay. *Fellowship in the Life Eternal*. London: Hodder & Stoughton, 1909.

Donald Gee. *Concerning Spiritual Gifts*. Springfield, Mo.: Gospel Publishing House, n.d.

Donald Gee. *Spiritual Gifts in the Work of the Ministry Today*. Springfield, Mo.: Gospel Publishing House, 1963.

Frederic Godet. *Commentary on St. Paul's Epistle to the Romans*, trans. by A. Cusin. Edinburgh: T. & T. Clark, 1881.

Frederic Godet. *Commentary on St. Paul's First Epistle to the Corinthians*, trans. by A. Cusin. Edinburgh: T. & T. Clark, 1889.

A. J. Gordon. *The Ministry of the Spirit*. Philadelphia: American Baptist Publ. Soc., 1896.

Adolf Harnack. *The Mission and Expansion of Christianity*. New York: Harper Torchbooks, 1962.

Michael Harper. *Power for the Body of Christ*. London: Fountain Trust, 1964.

Michael Harper. *Walk in the Spirit*. Plainfield: Logos, 1968.

D. Edmond Hiebert. *The Thessalonian Epistles*. Chicago: Moody Press, 1971.

James B. Hurley, "Did Paul Require Veils or the Silence of Women? A Consideration of I Cor. 11:2–16 and I Cor. 14:33b–36." *Westminster Theological Journal*, xxxv, 1973.

Maynard James. *I Believe in the Holy Ghost*. Minneapolis: Bethany, 1963.

Joachim Jeremias. *Jerusalem in the Time of Jesus*. Philadelphia: Fortress Press, 1969.

Morton T. Kelsey. *Tongue Speaking*. Garden City: Doubleday, 1964.

R. C. H. Lenski. *The Interpretation of St. Paul's Epistle to the Romans*. Columbus: Wartburg Press, 1945.

R. C. H. Lenski. *The Interpretation of St. Paul's First and Second Epistle to the Corinthians*. Columbus: Wartburg Press, 1946.

Gordon Lindsay. *All About the Gifts of the Spirit*. Dallas: Christ for the Nations, 1962.

Harold Lindsell. *Harper Study Bible*. Grand Rapids: Zondervan, 1965.

Handley C. G. Moule. *Ephesian Studies*. London: Hodder & Stoughton, 1900.

Terence Y. Mullins. "Paul's Thorn in the Flesh," *JBL*, LXXVI, 1957.

Johannes Munck. *The Acts of the Apostles*. Garden City: Doubleday, 1967.

Andrew Murray. *The Holiest of All.* London: Nisbet, n.d.

Andrew Murray. *The Spirit of Christ*. London: Nisbet, 1888.

T. L. Osborn. *Three Keys to the Book of Acts*. Tulsa: Osborn Evangelistic Association, 1960.

Clark H. Pinnock. *Biblical Revelation*. Chicago: Moody, 1971.

K. F. W. Prior. *The Way of Holiness*. Chicago: Inter-Varsity Press, 1967.

Bernard Ramm. *The Witness of the Spirit*. Grand Rapids: Eerdmans, 1960.

A. T. Robertson. *A Grammar of the Greek New Testament in the Light of Historical Research*. Nashville: Broadman, 1947.

C. C. Ryrie. *The Acts of the Apostles*. Chicago: Moody Press, 1961.

S. D. F. Salmond. "Epistle to the Ephesians," *EGT*, III.

John R. W. Stott. *The Baptism and Fullness of the Holy Spirit*. Chicago: Inter-Varsity Press, 1964.

Mel Tari. *Like a Mighty Wind*. Carol Stream: Creation House, 1972.

Joseph H. Thayer. *Greek-English Lexicon of the New Testament*. Grand Rapids: Zondervan, 1956.

Brian Vachon. "Witches Are Rising," *Look*, Aug. 24, 1971.

B. F. Westcott. *Gospel of St. John*. London: John Murray, 1898.

B. F. Westcott. *The Epistle to the Hebrews*. Grand Rapids: Eerdmans, reprinted 1950.

A. Skevington Wood. *Life by the Spirit*. Grand Rapids: Zondervan, 1963.

Wycliffe Bible Commentary. Chicago: Moody Press, 1962.

VARIOUS USES OF
THE GREEK VERB *BAPTIZO*
IN THE NEW TESTAMENT

KIND OF BAPTISM references	SUBJECT The Baptizer	OBJECT The Baptized	THE ELEMENT (with Greek *en*)	THE PURPOSE (with Greek *eis*)
FIGURATIVE I Cor. 10:1-2	GOD (understood)	THE ISRAELITES (God's people, already redeemed by the Passover blood)	IN THE RED SEA (typical of burial and resurrection) and IN THE CLOUD (typical of the Holy Spirit) cf. Exod. 13:21,22; Num. 10:34	unto, with ref. to Moses their leader; to identify them with Moses and seal them unto him. In I Cor. 10:2 Moses is a type of Christ our Deliverer and Mediator.
SUFFERING Mark 10:38-39 Luke 12:49-50	GOD? (implied)	JESUS CHRIST and HIS FOLLOWERS	immersed in pain, suffering, and the agony of death (implied). No prepositions are used with *baptizo* in this metaphorical sense.	to purify and refine Christ's faithful disciples (implied). See comments on Luke 12:49-53.
JOHN'S Matt. 3:5-11 Luke 3:1-16 Acts 19:3	JOHN THE BAPTIST	PEOPLE OF JUDEA (those who had already repented)	IN THE JORDAN RIVER IN WATER Mark 1:5; John 1:26,31	unto, with ref. to the repentance and the remission of sins which they had already been granted.
CHRISTIAN a) Matt. 28:19 Acts 2:38 Gal. 3:27 Rom. 6:3,4	CHRISTIAN MINISTER acting upon (*epi*) the name or authority of Jesus Christ (Acts 2:38)	THE PROFESSING BELIEVER	IN WATER (implied on basis of Acts 8:36-39)	unto, with ref. to the name of the Trinity or to the name of the Lord Jesus (Matt. 28:19; Acts 8:16; 19:5; cf. I Cor. 1:13-15). unto, with ref. to the forgiveness of sins (Acts 2:38). unto, with ref. to Christ (Gal. 3:27). unto, with ref. to His death (Rom. 6:3,4), as the outward sign or seal that positional death has taken place — like burial in physical death.
b) Matt. 3:11 Mark 1:8 Luke 3:16 John 1:33 Acts 1:5; 11:16 I Cor. 12:13	CHRIST THE BAPTIZER (implied in Acts 1:5; 11:16; and I Cor. 12:13)	THE REGENERATED BELIEVER	IN THE HOLY SPIRIT IN ONE SPIRIT	unto, with ref. to the one Body, to identify those who belong to the Body of Christ with a continuing seal.

(for extended explanation
see pp. 146-51)

CHRONOLOGY OF THE WORK OF THE
HOLY SPIRIT IN NEW TESTAMENT TIMES

The following chronology is by Ray Corvin. The dates are based on the work of James L. Boyer, *New Testament Chronological Chart*, revised, Winona Lake, Ind.: Grace Theological Seminary, 1962.

DATE	SCRIPTURE	ANNOUNCEMENTS OF BIRTH AND INFANCY OF JESUS
10 B.C.?	Luke 2:26	Revelation to Simeon "by the Holy Ghost, that he should not see death before he had seen the Lord's Christ."
5/4 B.C.	Luke 1:35	Gabriel announced to Mary, "The Holy Ghost shall come upon thee, and the power of the Highest shall overshadow thee: therefore also that Holy thing which shall be born of thee shall be called the Son of God "
	Matthew 1:18	The child Jesus was conceived by the Holy Spirit.
	Luke 1:41	Elizabeth was filled with the Holy Spirit, and her unborn baby, John, leaped in her womb.
	Matthew 1:20	Angel informed Joseph that Mary's baby was conceived by the Holy Ghost.
	Luke 1:67	At the birth of John, Zacharias was filled with the Holy Spirit and prophesied.
4 B.C.	Luke 2:27	Simeon came into the temple, led by the Spirit to see Jesus, and prayed the "Nunc Dimittis."

OPENING EVENTS IN CHRIST'S MINISTRY
(From the coming of John the Baptist until the public appearance of Jesus.)

DATE	SCRIPTURE	
A.D. 26/27	John 1:33	God bore witness to John that he would know Jesus the Son of God by seeing the Spirit descending and abiding upon Him.
	Matthew 3:11 Mark 1:8 Luke 3:18	Prophecy of John that Jesus would come and baptize in the Holy Spirit.

	Matthew 3:16 Mark 1:8 Luke 3:16	At the baptism of Jesus, the Spirit descended in the form of a dove.
	Matthew 4:1 Mark 1:12 Luke 4:1	Jesus, full of the Spirit, was led or driven by the Spirit into the wilderness where He was tempted by Satan during and after a 40-day fast.
	John 1:32	John bore witness saying, "I have beheld the Spirit descending as a dove out of heaven; and He remained upon Him" (NASB).

EARLY JUDEAN MINISTRY

A.D. 27	John 3:1-8	Jesus taught Nicodemus that to see the kingdom of God he must be born of the Spirit.
A.D. 27	John 3:34	John the Baptist at Aenon bore witness of the superiority of Christ, "for God giveth not the Spirit by measure unto him."
	John 4:24	To the woman of Samaria, Jesus said, "God is Spirit: and those who worship Him must worship in spirit and truth" (NASB).

FIRST PERIOD OF THE GALILEAN MINISTRY
(From the Return to Galilee until the Call of the Twelve.)

A.D. 27/28	Luke 4:14	Jesus returned in the power of the Spirit into Galilee.
	Luke 4:16-20	In the Nazareth Synagogue, Jesus took the book of Isaiah and read "The Spirit of the Lord God is upon me . . ."

SECOND PERIOD OF THE GALILEAN MINISTRY
(From the choosing of the Twelve until the withdrawal into Northern Galilee.)

	Matt. 10:1-20	Jesus called and commissioned His disciples. He advised them not to be anxious under persecution, imprisonment, and court trials, "for it shall be given you in that same hour what ye

shall speak. For it is not ye that speak, but the Spirit of your Father which speaketh in you."

Matt. 12:15-21   God fulfilled Isaiah's prophecy (42:1-4) about Christ, which includes: "I will put my Spirit upon Him."

Matt. 12:22-45   Jesus warned the Pharisees and the
Mark 3:20-30   scribes of the danger of their sinning
Luke 11:14-23   against the Holy Spirit, for they accused him of casting out devils by Beelzebub, the prince of devils.

THIRD PERIOD OF THE GALILEAN MINISTRY
(From the withdrawal into Northern Galilee until the final departure unto Jerusalem.)

A.D. 29   John 7:37-39   Jesus at the Feast of Tabernacles in Jerusalem stood in the temple and cried out, "If any man thirst, let him come unto me and drink. He that believeth on me, as the scripture hath said, out of his belly shall flow rivers of living water." He was speaking of the Spirit.

THE PEREAN MINISTRY
(Final departure from Galilee until final arrival at Jerusalem.)

A.D. 29/30   Luke 10:1-24   Jesus had called and commissioned the 70 disciples. They had obeyed and returned victorious over demons. Then Jesus rejoiced in the Holy Spirit (10:21) and gave praise and thanks to the Father.

Luke 12:10   Jesus warned about blaspheming against the Holy Ghost.

THE PASSION WEEK
(From final arrival in Jerusalem until the Resurrection.)

A.D. 30   John 14:16-17,26   On the night of our Lord's betrayal, He was with His disciples in the upper room when He said, "I will pray the Father, and He shall give you another Comforter, that He may abide with you forever;

even the Spirit of truth; whom the world cannot receive."

John 16:7-11   Again that night, just before going into the Garden of Gethsemane, Jesus explained further to His disciples about the work of the Comforter.

THE FORTY DAYS
(From the Resurrection unto the Ascension.)

A.D. 30   Matt. 28:16-20   On a mountain in Galilee, by appointment, Jesus met with His disciples in His resurrected body, and they worshiped Him. Jesus gave them one of His farewell orders:

"Go ye therefore and make disciples of all nations, baptizing them in the name of the Father and of the Son and of the Holy Spirit: teaching them to observe all things whatsoever I commanded you: and lo, I am with you always, even unto the end of the world" (ASV).

Luke 24:44-49   One of the last appearances that Jesus made to His disciples before ascending was in Jerusalem. Jesus gave them careful instructions and then said, "Behold, I send the promise of my Father upon you: but tarry ye in the city of Jerusalem until ye be endued with power from on high."

Acts 1:4-8   On the fortieth day after the resurrection, Jesus gave His last commandments, led the disciples to the Mount of Olives near Bethany and discussed with them the coming baptism in the Holy Spirit and the difference between the kingdom of Israel and His kingdom. Then He said, "But ye shall receive power, after that the Holy Ghost is come upon you, and ye shall be witnesses unto me both in Jerusalem, and in all Judea, and in Samaria, and unto the uttermost part of the earth."

HISTORY OF THE WORK OF THE HOLY SPIRIT
IN THE EARLY CHURCH

DATE	SCRIPTURE	FROM THE ASCENSION UNTO THE DEATH OF STEPHEN
A.D. 30	Acts 1:13,14 Luke 24:52-53	The apostles, Jesus' relatives, and certain women went to the upper room to await the coming of the Holy Spirit. Others of the 120 disciples were continually in the temple, praising God, until Pentecost.
	Acts 2:1-4	Descent of the Holy Spirit on the Day of Pentecost. All 120 were filled with the Holy Spirit and began to speak with other tongues as the Spirit gave them utterance.
	Acts 2:5-13	Representatives from many nations came together to witness the Spirit-filled Christians.
	Acts 2:14-40	Peter's sermon about Christ and the Holy Spirit.
	Acts 2:41	Three thousand were converted in one day, were baptized, and received the gift of the Holy Ghost.
	Acts 3:1-26	After healing a beggar at the temple gate in the name of Jesus, Peter preached to the people in the power of the Holy Spirit.
	Acts 4:8-12	Peter, full of the Holy Spirit, witnessed to the rulers of the people and the elders of Israel, explaining how a 40-year-old cripple was made whole.
	Acts 4:23-37	Following prayer, the apostles and Christians were filled with the Holy Spirit, and the disciples became bold in declaring the resurrection, and liberal in giving of their possessions.
A.D. 31	Acts 5:12-42	It was after many signs, wonders, and miracles where multitudes were made

believers and the sick were healed that the apostles were imprisoned and delivered. Then Peter again witnessed boldly to the rulers, informing them that the Holy Ghost was given to them who obey.

A.D. 31/32   Acts 6:1-8

To settle a church problem concerning the fair distribution of food to widows, seven men of honest report, full of the Holy Spirit and wisdom, were appointed to take charge of the task.

Acts 6:8-15

Stephen, a man full of faith and the Holy Spirit, did wonders and miracles among the people.

Acts 7

Stephen delivered his defense to the Jewish court and condemned the members of the Sanhedrin as resisters of the Holy Spirit. He became the first Christian martyr after the resurrection.

FROM THE DEATH OF STEPHEN UNTO THE FIRST MISSIONARY TOUR OF PAUL

A.D. 32   Acts 8:14-18

Peter and John ministered concerning the Holy Spirit in Philip's Samaritan revival, and many received Him when the apostles' hands were laid upon them.

Acts 8:26-40

The Spirit directed Philip to go toward Gaza, and then to ride in the chariot of an official of Ethiopia. After the conversion and baptism of the Ethiopian, the Spirit of the Lord caught away Philip.

A.D. 32   Acts 9:1-17

Three days after Saul of Tarsus was converted after being blinded by the Lord while on the way to Damascus, Ananias prayed for Saul to receive his sight and to be filled with the Holy Spirit.

A.D. 32-40   Acts 10

The Spirit directed Peter to go with three men who were to invite him to the house of Cornelius. There he spoke to the household of Cornelius, and all who heard the word received the Holy Ghost and spoke with tongues as they did on the Day of Pentecost.

Acts 11:1-18   Peter went to the Christian leaders in Jerusalem to defend his actions and the right of Gentiles to salvation by claiming that "the Spirit bade me go with them, nothing doubting." He also said, "And as I began to speak, the Holy Ghost fell on them, as on us at the beginning. Then remembered I the word of the Lord, how that he said, John indeed baptized with water, but ye shall be baptized with the Holy Ghost. Forasmuch then as God gave them the like gift as he *did* unto us, who believed on the Lord Jesus Christ; what was I, that I could withstand God?"

about A.D. 40   Acts 11:23,24   Barnabas was sent from Jerusalem to Antioch, "for he was a good man, and full of the Holy Ghost and of faith."

A.D. 45/46   Acts 11:27,28   Agabas the prophet went from Jerusalem to Antioch and signified by the Spirit that there would be a great famine throughout the known world.

DURING PAUL'S THREE MISSIONARY JOURNEYS

A.D. 45-50   James, being inspired by the Holy Spirit, wrote his epistle.

A.D. 47   Acts 13:1-4   After various prophets and teachers had been ministering and fasting in the church at Antioch, the Holy Spirit said, "Separate me Barnabas and Saul for the work whereunto I have called them." And when they had fasted and prayed, the others laid their hands on them and sent them forth. Thus the Holy Spirit launched the first missionary program.

Acts 13:6-12   Paul, being full of the Holy Ghost, encountered and defeated Elymas in the palace of Sergius Paulus.

A.D. 48   Paul wrote his epistle to the Galatians from Antioch after returning from his

		first missionary journey. He reminded them that they had received the Spirit by faith.
A.D. 49	Acts 15:5-9,28	In the great Jerusalem council where major decisions were to be made as to whether Gentile Christianity would observe circumcision and the Mosaic law, Simon Peter stood and rehearsed his experience among Gentiles saying, "And God, which knoweth the hearts, bare them witness, giving them the Holy Ghost, even as he did unto us."
A.D. 50-65		The Gospel of Mark was written, containing John's prophecy that Jesus would baptize with the Holy Spirit.
A.D. 50-80		The Gospel of Matthew was written, recording Jesus' conception by the Holy Spirit.
A.D. 50	Acts 16:6-10	On his second journey, Paul, accompanied by Silas and Timothy, was forbidden by the Spirit to preach the Gospel in Asia, and the Spirit did not permit them to go into Bithynia. Guidance was given to Paul by night in a vision. A man from Macedonia was saying, "Come over into Macedonia, and help us."
A.D. 51-52		Paul wrote I and II Thessalonians, admonishing the Thessalonians not to quench the Spirit, and reminding them of their sanctification by the Spirit.
A.D. 52-53	Acts 19:1-7	On Paul's third missionary journey, he came to Ephesus, and found certain disciples of John the Baptist who did not know the Holy Spirit had been given. Instructing them, Paul baptized them in the name of the Lord Jesus and laid hands on them. The Spirit came on them, and they spoke with tongues and prophesied.
A.D. 54/55		Paul wrote I Corinthians from Ephesus, explaining in detail about the gifts of the Spirit and how they are to be used.

A.D. 55

Paul wrote II Corinthians from Macedonia, then to the Romans from Corinth. Both letters contain teachings about the Holy Spirit. He reminded the Corinthians that where the Spirit of the Lord is, there is liberty. And in the letter to the Romans, Paul explained how the Spirit makes us free from the law of sin and death — and even intercedes for us.

A.D. 54-56   Acts 20:1-3, 17-28

Paul left Ephesus, journeyed into Greece, and came back to Asia. At Miletus he spoke to the Ephesian elders. "Behold, I go bound in the spirit unto Jerusalem, not knowing the things that shall befall me there: save that the Holy Ghost witnesseth in every city, saying that bonds and afflictions abide me [await me (RSV)]." He also advised them, "Take heed therefore unto yourselves, and to all the flock, over which the Holy Ghost hath made you overseers, to feed the church of God, which he hath purchased with his own blood."

Acts 21:4

As Paul journeyed on to Jerusalem, the ship stopped in the seacoast town of Tyre to unload her burden. They remained there seven days and had fellowship with certain disciples who informed Paul through the Spirit that he should not go to Jerusalem.

Acts 21:10-14

While Paul was in Philip's home in Caesarea, there came down from Jerusalem a certain prophet named Agabus. He took Paul's girdle and bound his own hands and feet, and said, "Thus saith the Holy Ghost, so shall the Jews at Jerusalem bind the man that owneth this girdle and shall deliver him into the hands of the Gentiles."

FROM PAUL'S ARRIVAL IN JERUSALEM UNTO THE END OF THE BOOK OF ACTS

A.D. 56-58

Luke came with Paul to Palestine and was free to talk to those who knew Christ and to write his Gospel, with considerable emphasis on the work of the Holy Spirit.

A.D. 59-61   Acts 28:25-26   After the imprisonments in Jerusalem and Caesarea, and after the long voyage to Rome, Paul was a prisoner in his own rented quarters. He was guarded by a soldier, and visitors were permitted to see him. The Jewish leaders in Rome came; however, they believed not, and Paul said, "Well spake the Holy Ghost by Isaiah the prophet unto our fathers, saying, Go unto this people, and say, Hearing ye shall hear, and shall not understand; and seeing ye shall see and not perceive."

Paul wrote his epistles to Philemon and to the churches at Ephesus, Colosse, and Philippi. Luke wrote Acts. All were written under the anointing of the Holy Spirit, to glorify Jesus.

FROM PAUL'S FIRST ROMAN IMPRISONMENT TO THE END OF THE FIRST CENTURY

A.D. 61-62   Paul was released from imprisonment in Rome and traveled throughout the Mediterranean area. He wrote to Titus and his first letter to Timothy. Peter wrote his first epistle. These were years of the rapid spread of Christianity, by the power of the Holy Spirit, and Christians — and their pastors — needed such instruction in right conduct as the letters provided.

A.D. 64/65   Paul was arrested and placed in a dungeon in Rome awaiting execution. He wrote his last letter, II Timothy. In it, by the prophetic gift of the Holy Spirit, he foretold the wickedness of the last days. Peter wrote his second epistle, prophesying other things about the last days. Peter and Paul were executed.

A.D. 65-70   The Epistle of Jude.   ⎫ "Holy men of
                      The Epistle to the   ⎪ God spake as
                        Hebrews.   ⎬ they were
A.D. 85-95   The Gospel of John.   ⎪ moved by the
                      The Epistles of John.   ⎪ Holy Ghost"
                      The Book of Revelation.   ⎭ (II Pet. 1:21).

SCRIPTURE INDEX

(Entries in **boldface** are section headings in the text.)

For a free copy of
LOGOS JOURNAL
send your name and address to
Logos Journal
Box 191
Plainfield, New Jersey 07060
and say, "one free Journal, please."